THE VOLUNTARY SECTOR IN RURAL DEVELOPMENT

THE VOLUNTARY SECTOR IN RURAL DEVELOPMENT

LESSONS FROM SOCIAL MARKETING BASED ON STUDY OF NGOs IN SOUTH INDIA

VIMALA PARTHASARATHY

Editors: Michael Wales and Astrid Bressler

PARTRIDGE

A Penguin Random House Company

To order additional copies of this book, contact
Partridge India
000 800 10062 62
orders.india@partridgepublishing.com

www.partridgepublishing.com/india

Contents

About the Author

 Vimala Parthasarathy, graduated in Economics from Madras University with an all India gold medal and scholarship which she utilized for acquiring a master's degree in French Literature from the same University. After working with reputed advertising organizations for a few years she pursued her studies in French from McMaster University in Ontario writing her thesis in that language on *Bilingual Advertising.* She followed it up with a Masters in Communications from the University of Texas at Austin. She taught Communications and Marketing Management in several business schools in Bangalore and last held position as Head of Department of Marketing Management in Sikkim-Manipal University and as consultant on distance education. For her thesis on the role of NGO sector in socio-economic development she was awarded the degree of Doctor of Philosophy by Manipal University, India.

Vimala Parthasarathy worked in industry and academia for several years, contributed several papers on advertising and communication issues. This book is compiled from notes and papers, some completed and some others in process, she had left when she died of bronchitis in 2012. She lived in Bangalore, India.

FOREWORD

I have a special reason to write the foreword of this book. When Manipal University received a request from the parents of the late Vimala Parthasarathy for her thesis to be submitted for evaluation, the matter was referred to me, as Vice Chancellor. I looked into all the aspects of the research work carried out by the candidate. I was immensely impressed by the work that was done. Completing a PhD is no easy task, but to complete it after surmounting the formidable difficulties she had to face was true grit and determination. The external referees who evaluated the thesis commended the research and recommended the award of the degree.

The university had, since inception, not awarded a PhD degree posthumously. I now had a challenge as there was no provision in the university for the award of a PhD posthumously. This challenge was also an opportunity to test the basic tenet of my belief regarding the role of a university. It is my firm conviction that a university should be responsive to a genuine need and that the spirit of the law is more important than the letter of the law. In the words of Jawaharlal Nehru, "A university stands for humanism; for tolerance, for reason, for the adventure of ideas and for the search of truth. It stands for the onward march of the human race towards even higher objectives." I am a strong advocate of this. I wanted Manipal University to take the path not trodden, and reward the industrious work of the candidate, even though she was not destined to receive the degree when she was alive. In a momentous decision, the Senate of Manipal University, chaired by me in my capacity as the Vice Chancellor, approved to award the degree posthumously to Vimala Parthasarathy. The degree was received on her behalf by her parents at the Seventeenth Convocation of Manipal University in November 2013. Vimala

Parthasarathy is no more, but her doctoral research work captured in this book will be etched in our memory for all time to come.

Professor K Ramnarayan, MBBS, MD, PG Dip. Higher Education
Vice Chancellor
Manipal University
Manipal 576104, Karnataka, India

EDITORS' NOTE

In editing the book by Vimala Parthasarathy we have taken a 'light touch' approach in order to retain the author's authentic voice and the basic structure of the compilation. We have added as annexes a summary of good practices and a guide for NGO evaluation derived from the author's papers and research questionnaires. In our view these are tools of practical significance for small and medium sized NGOs. We believe these supplements enhance the value of this publication.

Whilst reading the book, we were both struck by the topicality of the theme and relevance for our own work. The US$ 200 million Myanmar Livelihoods and Food Security Trust Fund (LIFT) operates almost exclusively through international and local NGOs. As an external adviser to the Board of LIFT, I find that the constant challenge is how to select, monitor and incentivize the NGOs that are the implementing partners of the program. Vimala's research provides invaluable insights and imparts a structure to these issues. Astrid's studies and research for an MBA are focused on corporate social responsibility and the book's exploration of social marketing illustrates how responsibility and accountability are increasingly demanded of the voluntary sector.

Michael Wales
Astrid Bessler
Windsor, United Kingdom
June 2014

ACKNOWLEDGMENT

This book is brought out by the family of the author with invaluable assistance and encouragement from several sources.

First and foremost, the family owes its gratitude to Manipal University for not only giving permission to the use of the thesis material in the compilation of the articles but also for encouraging the family to bring about this publication in memory of the author.

Our grateful thanks, at the very outset, are due to Dr. N. S. Viswanath and Dr. P. V. Raju, eminent management educationists, based in Bangalore, who appreciated the author's doctoral thesis and goaded us with every possible help to bring her work to the public domain.

The family selected such material from the author's collection as would be useful for publication as also articles in stages of completion. We approached Michael Wales to help us in editing them. We would like to express our deepest gratitude for the efforts put in by Michael Wales and Astrid Bressler for making the book readable and for important suggestions and supplements to enhance its practical value.

Mike is a senior economist with vast experience on issues of rural development, food security and poverty alleviation in the countries of Asia and Africa. He was earlier Principal Advisor in the Investment Centre of the Food & Agriculture Organization of the United Nations in Rome. Astrid, who specializes in corporate social responsibility issues, gives him valuable research and back office support.

Dr. K. Ramnarayan, Vice Chancellor of Manipal University, most kindly acceded to our request to write the Foreword which he did in the midst of work pressures that inevitably go with the high office he occupies in India's premier educational complex.

The acknowledgments will be incomplete without the mention of the CEOs of the NGOs in the states of Karnataka and Tamil Nadu, India, who generously gave the author, during her research, their time and benefit of experience. For want of space here, their names are listed in the Profiles in Annex 1. To them individually we wish to convey our expressions of gratitude.

The publishers, Partridge Penguin, extended much needed technical help in finalizing the copy, design and format of the book, and made it available extensively. We are happy to record our appreciation of their contribution.

The book is dedicated to the vast number of frontline NGO workers and volunteers who, by maintaining close touch with distant communities, contribute their mite to bring better and healthier living conditions to people in rural areas.

We request readers to send their suggestions and observations addressed to the author at pacha1931@gmail.com

July 2014
Chennai, India

PREFACE

Limited resources are a major constraint on the ability of governments, especially of developing countries, to fulfil the needs of community development. The tax base is too narrow to generate adequate funds to cope with a bewilderingly long list of competing needs. Nor do Governments have sufficient number of trained staff with a focused approach to implement social marketing programs effectively at the grass roots level. Often, frontline staff qualified for a specialty, say, agronomy or primary health, are saddled with additional duties unrelated to the main responsibility. Inadequate support facilities like transport, vehicle spares, fuel supply and reasonable living allowances are other handicaps. Bureaucracy is not familiar with the value of applying marketing practices to enhance the effectiveness of extension services to promote socio-economic welfare in rural areas. To fill this space and make up for the deficiencies, the voluntary sector is in a position to play an important role in rural areas. While the sector has the opportunity and ability to play a complementary role, in some situations, governments tend to view NGOs with suspicion and look upon them as usurpers. This book comprises select articles highlighting the challenges and issues faced by the voluntary sector in contributing to rural development.

The articles are based on the data and information researched and gathered by the author for her doctoral thesis. Unfortunately, the author died of acute bronchial infection after submitting her dissertation, leaving behind some articles fully written and some incomplete, but with notes, perhaps aimed at publishing a book of this format. She was awarded the title of Doctor of Philosophy posthumously in November 2013 by Manipal University, a premier educational institution in India. Her research material and written papers have been retrieved and completed in fulfilment of her objective. In doing so it is possible that, despite the best effort, shortcomings have crept in. For these the family that provided the material accepts responsibility.

As her research has been liberally drawn upon for these articles, readers may kindly note that mentions of *the Research* or *the Study* in the articles refer to her Thesis - *Social Marketing Strategies & Traits of Successful NGOs in India - A Strategic Perspective with Reference to Select NGOs in the States of Karnataka & Tamil Nadu, India,* Manipal University, Manipal, India, 2013.

The author's research was based on a "holistic probability sampling" selecting ten non-governmental organizations (NGOs) engaged in different aspects of development in the two states of South India. The area chosen for study was based on available statistical information from the website of the Planning Commission, Government of India indicating a total strength of 16,976 NGOs in the country, 1209 functioning NGOs in the state of Tamil Nadu which ranks among the first four states and 727 NGOs in the state of Karnataka, ranking eighth. The two states are positioned neither among the intensive NGO active states nor among the low activity ones. They can be considered to be in the upper middle segment of the national spectrum representing a typical profile of the active and potentially active areas of the country.

A multi-faceted profile consisting of factors like fund size, continuity, number of years' experience, clarity of objectives and geographical coverage was applied to each of the 67 NGOs examined. This was the final sampling frame selected from a total universe of 365 NGOs in the two southern states engaged in social development. These criteria were assigned relative weights which then formed the basis for profiling the NGOs. The NGOs were ranked to select the first ten for the study. A summary profile of the ten NGOs is in Annex 1.

The research involved in-depth study of the sample organizations guided by a questionnaire covering a wide range of functions and responsibilities of NGOs. The authenticity of the study was considerably enhanced by the willing participation of the CEO or equivalent authority of each NGO. The primary research included both quantitative research in the form of a survey and structured questionnaire for NGOs and donors/experts and qualitative research in the form of observation and in-depth interviews. The data gathered from quantitative and qualitative research were integrated. A benchmark matrix was designed for fifteen organizational and marketing traits and over ninety sub-traits. The traits and sub-traits were identified and selected by secondary research of scholarly articles, published works of eminent authors, case studies, website publications, NGO models and experiences of leading funding agencies.

The second step in developing the benchmark traits was to connect each of the sub-traits to the responses from the questionnaire for NGOs and the post interview notes. This way, the quantitative data and the qualitative data were integrated. Next, a scoring method was devised for the answers to the different types of questions – dichotomous (yes/no) questions, questions that involved checking multiple options, and open-ended questions. Dichotomous/yes-no questions carried one mark for positive answers and zero marks for negative answers. Multiple option questions carried as many marks as options chosen and open-ended questions were assigned marks according to the category of the responses as high, moderate or low compliance, carrying three, two and one marks respectively. In this manner, all responses were converted to numerical values. The scores for the ten NGOs in the sample were calculated for the different traits, through a build-up of values for each sub-trait and finally converted to percentages for each NGO for all traits and for each trait for all NGOs. In order to judge the values and interpret them, a grading scale, based on a popularly accepted model, was adopted as follows – 35% or less is poor, 36-50% is moderate (combined as below satisfactory), 51-60% is satisfactory, 61-75% is good and above 75% is very good. The references to scores in the analysis of findings in some of the articles that follow this chapter are to be interpreted by this grading scale.

The purpose of the study was not to compare different NGOs, but to see how strong or weak the NGOs were on different criteria. The scores thus make it possible to identify not only the weak aspects, but also the weak areas within each aspect or trait, by identifying low sub-trait values.

The primary objective of the research, which forms the basis of this book, was to analyze the traits and marketing strategies of NGOs and to assess their relative impact upon the organization's resource utilization efficiency and capacity to achieve its goals. It was the aim of the study to derive, from the findings, success factors, benchmarks and a social marketing model.

This study placed emphasis on the relevance and application of marketing principles in the transfer of products, ideas and concepts towards social development which often called for extensive behavior transformation. If this can be categorized as social marketing it is necessary to explain the special features of social marketing, spell out how it differs from commercial marketing for profit and separate the types of NGOs that could and should use marketing principles in the pursuit of their vision. These are dealt with in the first two articles followed by others covering some of the issues and challenges hindering the emergence of a strong voluntary sector. The articles on *Donor Expectations* and *Program Effectiveness* are reproductions of her papers published in research journals.

Institutions complementing with government programs of social development have been referred to by various names in different countries and contexts, none of them fully capturing their distinguishing characteristics. They are not government institutions and so they are referred to, rather loosely, as non-government organizations (NGOs). But then even the private sector is non-governmental but dedicated to profit making and enhancement of share value whereas institutions with social development as their objective do not aim at making profit. For this reason the same NGOs are called "Non-Profits". There is no ownership of the "Non-Profits" / NGOs and so they can be distinguished by referring to them as voluntary organizations with the implication that voluntary activity for a social purpose is not impelled by profit as a motive. Various voluntary private initiatives in clubs for sports or social activities or groups of apartment owners do not aim at profits could also be called as "Non-Profits" or voluntary organizations thereby blurring the terminology that we seek for social development organizations. How do we distinguish non-profits engaged in community development from convenience-driven group activities like sports bodies, clubs and libraries? Sometimes private enterprise may deliberately sell its products or services at cost or marginal cost as part of its predatory strategy to capture market share for subsequent exploitation. It is difficult to argue that they qualify to be categorized as "Non-Profits". Besides, government agencies are also non-profits by this definition whereas what we want is a defining term for the non-government, non-private owned, non-profit making organizations that exclude convenience groups like clubs and apartment owners! Another term often used is "civil society organizations" implicit in which is the assumption that civil society is not profit-motivated and is engaged in matters of community concern. The word "voluntary" imparts a sense of spontaneity and the word "civil society" is indicative of concern of a whole group. Both seem equally preferable to "non-government" and "non-profit" which are negative definitions saying what is not rather than what is. The foregoing discussion is to highlight the difficulties in arriving at a name with an ideal fit to describe intermediating institutions that play a role in wide ranging community development activities. Perhaps the least mismatching among various terms is *voluntary organizations* and collectively as the *voluntary sector*. The term *NGO* is not accurate but being widely familiar in many countries outside the USA its use serves the purpose of ready recognition and may be taken as being equivalent to and substitute for the term *voluntary organization*. Accordingly, these two terms have been used in the book inter-changeably.

Within the voluntary sector, as delineated above, there is a vast variety of activities all of which did not concern the author's study but only those engaged in community development. The Figure at the end of the first article identifies the categories of non-government organizations, and indicates categories among them that fall within the scope of the author's study.

Voluntary sector organizations operate at different levels ranging from those with an international coverage to those operating at district or village levels. The latter dominate the scene and operate at the frontline staying in day-to-day touch with communities. This category and the issues and challenges that face it are the focus of articles in the following pages.

The author's review of literature comprising scholarly articles, research papers and books shows that the subject of social marketing has not been adequately researched in developing countries and that there is a dearth of published material on critical parameters influencing the effectiveness of social organizations in the fulfilment of their mission. Paucity of published material on NGO sector in developing countries is indicative of the large scope for research in the area of social marketing and the functioning of social organizations in the context of the special sensitivities and needs of developing and under-developed economies. It is also indicative of the insufficient appreciation of the immense potential of the voluntary sector to function as an accelerator of community development.

At the end of this book two tools are presented in the hope that they would be of some practical use as check-list or training material. A summary of good practices under different aspects of NGO management is presented in Annex 2. This does not claim to be exhaustive or as a 'one-size-fits-all' model. It is at best an indicative list derived from literature survey reflecting experiences and scholarly opinions as well as the specific findings of the author's study of the ten sample NGOs. Annex 3 is a comprehensive and in-depth list of check points on most aspects of NGO management designed such that it can be evaluated quantitatively. The list of check-points can be used either for independent management audit or for periodic honest self-evaluation by the NGO management itself. The aim in presenting these tools is to bring the contents of the articles to convergence for practical application.

It is hoped that the experiences and observations in these articles will be of interest to those engaged in strengthening rural institutions in developing countries of Asia and Africa with a view to improving the living conditions of the poor.

CAN THE VOLUNTARY SECTOR ACCELERATE COMMUNITY DEVELOPMENT?

Abstract

Available resources with developing countries are already strained under pressure of competing demands of equal criticality. Consequently, efforts towards improving living conditions of the poor through increased productivity are incommensurate with needs. NGOs can fill the gaps to a significant extent since they have the potential to attract funds from donors and ability to offer the services of trained professionals. Funding agencies are quicker to react to mal-practices and inefficiencies of NGOs and are able to turn off fund flow whenever warranted. This keeps the NGOs on their toes and under pressure to deliver results. The article traces the growth of the voluntary sector in India and draws upon some of the experiences of other countries – Tanzania, Ethiopia and Bangladesh. It also cites examples of areas in which NGOs have indeed made valuable contributions such as water management, micro-finance, creating off-farm productive activity and poverty alleviation, besides taking up programs for empowerment of women, and tribal communities. NGOs do have an important contribution to make toward development but the country's context, political sensitivities and the status and strengths of locally bred institutions would determine the kind of structure which NGOs could fit into to enhance the total effect.

BACKGROUND

Developing economies are characterized by heavy dependence of a large part of population on low productivity agriculture, leading in turn to, poor living conditions, heavy indebtedness and low health standards in rural areas. Unlocking the productivity potential and improving overall health and well-being of the rural people calls for not only enormous funds but also expertise in technology transfer and institution building. These efforts require commitment and tenacity over an extended time span. Paucity of resources implies not the mere need to establish funding links but, importantly, the exercise of maximum efficiency in use of available resources already under pressure of competing demands of equal urgency. Inherent in the nature of developing agrarian economies is the confinement of the revenue base to a very small percentage of the population that creates wealth; the base is so narrow and susceptible that any attempt to raise more revenue dis-incentivizes productive activity and becomes self-defeating. Compounding the problem of too many needs and too little money to meet them with, there is, in countries yet to develop strong democratic practices and public accountability, the prevalence of large scale corruption. It diminishes net effective availability of resources such that it does not make significant impact on people's welfare. NGOs can fill some of these gaps to a significant extent since they have the potential to attract funds from donors and are able to offer the services of trained professionals. Funding agencies are quicker to react to mal-practices and inefficiencies of NGOs which keeps them under pressure to use available resources effectively.

WHAT ARE NGOs?

Non-governmental organizations (NGOs) are assuming an increasingly important role in the rural areas of developing and under-developed countries of Asia and Africa. As explained elsewhere in the introductory chapter the term NGO denotes a vast category of groups and organizations and does not specifically apply only to organizations devoted to rural development issues.

The World Bank defines NGOs as "private organizations that pursue activities to relieve suffering, promote the interests of the poor, protect the environment, provide basic social services, or undertake community development." A World Bank document, *Working with NGOs*, adds: "In wider usage, the term NGO can be applied to any non-profit organization which is independent from government. NGOs are typically value-based organizations which depend, in whole or in part, on charitable donations and voluntary service. Although the NGO sector has become increasingly professionalized over the last two decades, principles of altruism and voluntarism remain key defining characteristics."

Different terminologies are used to refer to organizations dedicated to promote social projects - NGOs, Civil Society Organizations (CSOs), Voluntary Organizations (PVOs), Non-Profits, Third Sector and so on. This study, however, is focused on NGOs working in the area of rural development either through direct contact with communities or working as apex bodies engaging the services of community-based NGOs for implementation of specific projects.

Since the 1970s, there has been a rapid growth in the number of NGOs, in their size and in territorial coverage. Simultaneously, there has been a diversification of program content to cover a wide range of issues affecting the economic status, health and empowerment aspects of the rural poor.

GROWTH OF NGO SECTOR

The above-mentioned World Bank document points out that "Since the mid-1970s, the NGO sector in both developed and developing countries has experienced exponential growth.... It is now estimated that over 15 percent of total overseas development aid is channeled through NGOs." That is, roughly $8 billion dollars. The World Bank adds that the number of community-based organizations in the developing world number in the hundreds of thousands.

While NGOs are meant to be politically independent, in reality it is difficult because they receive funds from governments. All or many of these do exert some degree of pressure on program selection and implementation.

The growth of this sector has been rapid in recent years because of several factors - increase in fund availability for social causes, capacity of the voluntary sector to address social issues and the limitations of state agencies to reach out effectively to affected communities needing support.

Government agencies are not only constrained by resource availability, but face a number of procedural and operational hurdles to the smooth execution of development programs. Enlightened governments in developing countries began to collaborate with NGOs with experience in areas such as poverty alleviation and environmental protection and with closer understanding of local communities' needs. Many governments began to appreciate the value of the voluntary sector as a partner, shedding their perception of them as competitors and intruders. However, it cannot be said that these misconceptions have been totally eradicated.

Taking India as an example, the growth of voluntary organizations had roots in the pre-independence period in the social reform movements of the late 19th century. During this period, a number of individuals and associations were involved in social service, such as helping the poor and the destitute, as well as social reform against practices such as bride burning and widow re-marriages. Christian missionary groups contributed to the growth by setting up a network of hospitals, schools and welfare services for the poor. Gandhi's approach, clubbing village development programs with social reform, contributed largely to the growth of the voluntary sector.

Social historians (Misra 2008)[7] have divided the history of voluntary organizations in India since the 19th century into eight phases. Hereunder is a summary of the various stages of progress. A reading of it shows how growth of the sector has been the outcome of the unfolding political and social progress of the country.

> **First phase: 1800-1850** – Social reform movements and social uplift activities of Christian missionaries encouraged growth of voluntary organizations.

> **Second phase: 1850–1900** –English education and setting up of communication links influenced growth of the sector.

Third phase: 1900–1947 – Mass mobilization and Gandhi's initiation of constructive work in rural areas for improvement of education, health and employment, set a new operating model for NGOs.

Fourth phase: 1948-1965 – Central and State governments started community development in rural areas. NGOs were approached by the government to implement these programs. The Fifth Five Year Plan document stated that social welfare services should be provided by voluntary agencies, with government co-operation.

Fifth phase: Mid-sixties to early seventies –A section of people rejected the development model followed by the government, since they felt that it did not address the root cause of poverty. This led to the increasing role of NGOs.

Sixth phase: Early seventies–1979 –A number of social action groups supported by foreign funding began to mushroom during this phase.

Seventh phase: The eighties – Two different types of grassroots NGOs emerged – (a) development NGOs involved in agriculture, environment, health and literacy and used participatory and innovative approaches and (b) empowerment NGOs for the poor in rural areas helping them to articulate their concerns. Issues such as women's development, environment and water pollution emerged on the NGO agenda.

Eighth phase: The nineties –The Planning Commission also emphasized the role of NGOs in the Seventh Five Year Plan document (1985–1990). A total Plan expenditure of ₹ 1.5 billion ($ 30 million) was set aside for collaboration between government and NGOs. The Council for Advancement of People's Action and Rural Technology (CAPART) was established in 1986, to provide support to NGOs involved in rural development.

NGOs COMPLEMENT GOVERNMENT'S ROLE

Governments in developing countries by virtue of state control over the economy tend to be large and "multi-layered" lengthening decision-making and reducing effectiveness of programs. In contrast the voluntary sector is not only quicker but also has the advantage of being close to the ultimate beneficiaries.

NGOs have the potential to become highly specialized by repetitive experience and be able to focus on problems that are unique to each community. They can help to make the development process more transparent and accountable. The better equipped ones among them, having had the benefit of training in marketing methods, are able to function to a higher level of their potential.

According to Fowler (1991), quoted by Zaidi (1999)[19], NGOs are perceived to be more cost effective than the government in delivery of services, more participatory in their approach and better equipped to target vulnerable sections of society. He says that NGOs contribute to "greater democratization and institutional accountability" in comparison with the public sector.

Many governments that focus on women's issues, reduction of poverty, awareness and prevention of AIDS, have not been able to reach these groups as effectively as NGOs. NGOs, thanks to their experience, are also better equipped to deal with environmental issues than the government or the private sector.

Thus, while NGOs have inherent advantages, how far they have used these strengths to good effect is altogether another issue requiring study. In some developing countries, NGOs have been surrounded by controversy, since some of them are reported to be corrupt, guilty of diverting funds and engaged in using foreign funds for political and religion related activities. The extent to which commitment to development is diluted by diversion or through inefficiency is difficult to assess as systematic data on impact is rarely available impeding a comparison of what it costs with what was achieved. In many countries, NGOs have also become contractors in delivering services operating, in effect, as tax-exempt consulting firms.

DURING CIVIL STRIFE

Omana (2005)[8] has emphasized the importance of the role played by NGOs in an environment of conflict where traditional systems such as the government break down. He cites the case of civil society organizations in war-ravaged Gulu District of Northern Uganda. He argues that the situation in Northern Uganda is representative of war-torn environments in other developing countries, notably Afghanistan, Sudan, Somalia and Congo. He points to the failure of the government as well as the private sector in such environments in providing services to people whereas the "third sector" (NGO sector) is able to fill the breach. Omana visualizes a role for civil society organizations, including NGOs in such environments, in three major areas – (a) in providing essential goods and services (b) in restoring peace and advocating human rights and (c) in developing infrastructure. Civil society organizations, according to him, are more visible than the government, due to their "participatory" methods of intervention. This approach implies working closely with beneficiaries, building trust, creating transparency and making NGOs more recipient-friendly. Omana calls upon governments in such conflict environments to support the efforts of NGOs and to create a favorable policy environment to facilitate their growth. At the same time, civil society organizations need to strengthen themselves by building co-operation and partnerships among themselves and with the government.

ON WATER ISSUES

Water related issues plague many communities at the local level in most parts of the developing world. There is enough experience to show that NGOs have the potential to play an important part in promoting water harvesting techniques, water conservation habits and building local institutions for self-management of the community's water resources.

IN MICRO-FINANCE

Micro finance operations of NGOs began in a small way in Bangladesh and India and later grew into large-scale operations. Initially, only the savings of members of Self Help Groups (SHGs) were used to meet the credit requirements of other members. Since this was sufficient only to meet consumption credit needs, the NGOs gradually began to raise funds from outside donors through agencies such as NABARD (National Bank for Agricultural and Rural Development in India). SHGs not only helped to expand credit availability in rural areas but also set new norms for recoveries through novel disciplines like collective surety or joint liability and peer social pressure.

Loan applications are submitted by members to the leader of the SHG. The decision to sanction the loan is made by the entire group, based on factors such as ability to repay the loan, attendance at group meetings and contribution to savings. All loans have to be guaranteed by two other members. In most cases, members can apply for a second loan only after the first loan was repaid. However, in emergency situations, such as health reasons, a second loan could be granted. The loan amounts generally varied from as low as ₹ 50 ($ 1) to a maximum of ₹ 10,000 ($ 200). The average loan amount for most of the NGOs was ₹ 1500 ($ 30). The annual interest rates were fixed by the NGOs, based on market rates and varied from 12% to 24% per annum.

Some banks do not support the idea of NGOs playing the role of financial intermediaries. During a workshop organized by the Small Industries Development Bank of India (2002), the argument was that NGOs could not match the formal financial institutions, like banks, in terms of financial know-how and scale of operations. It was felt that NGOs would do best to focus on the formation, nurturing and capacity building of the SHGs and leave the financing activities to the banks and other micro finance institutions.

IN POVERTY ALLEVIATION

NGOs in India have been playing a prominent role in the empowerment of poor women, livelihood security and capacity building. However, their efforts to reduce poverty have had limited success, since the root causes of poverty, namely lack of assets and unemployment, lie in the larger realm of the central and state governments. A study by Rajasekhar (2004)[11] revealed the constraints within which NGOs have had to work - lack of technical and political capacity, managerial expertise, trained staff and infrastructure. His study found that the main obstacle faced by NGOs in their efforts to alleviate poverty was the fact that they have had to work in isolation, due to weak support from local government bodies.

PARTICPATION IN WORLD BANK PROGRAMS

The World Bank Operating Manual (1989)[18] lists the main strengths that NGOs can bring to operations supported by the Bank.

- NGOs have the ability to reach poor communities, and remote areas where governments have failed to reach
- NGOs encourage a participatory approach to the design and implementation of development programs
- NGOs use cost effective methods by keeping their fixed costs low
- NGOs study local needs and cater to these needs by adapting existing technologies and using innovative approaches.

Community driven development, which involves working closely with the poor and backward sections, can be accelerated by the intervention of NGOs.

TYPES OF NGOs

NGOs may be classified based on size. This is defined by the number of full-time staff employed by the NGO, as well as the number of branch offices both in the home and foreign countries. Some NGOs such as Greenpeace, Oxfam and the Red Cross may be categorized as multinationals, since they have a large worldwide presence with offices in several countries, apart from multiple branches in the home country. They also employ a huge number of paid, full-time staff. At the other end of the spectrum are the small, one-person or two-person NGOs, which have a limited presence and are run almost entirely with voluntary or part-time staff.

Rajasekhar (2000)[12] classifies NGOs into the following categories:

Grassroots NGOs – These work closely with specific sections of society. They vary both in size and geographical spread and may cover a single project or multiple project locations. They are mainly Development NGOs involved in providing micro credit, fertilizers and technical know-how.

Charitable NGOs – These focused on the needs of the poor, providing food, clothing, shelter and education, as well as on relief work during natural calamities. There is very little participation by beneficiaries in designing or implementing the programs.

Service NGOs – They extend services such as education, health and family planning. The programs are designed by the NGOs often with beneficiaries' participation.

Social action groups – These NGOs mobilize awareness of marginalized sections on social, political and economic issues. For example, Young India Project in Andhra Pradesh, India is involved in mobilizing agricultural laborers for land reforms. These NGOs are also termed as empowerment NGOs. For example, MYRADA, a large multi-state NGO in India, utilizes credit management groups for social and political empowerment. Grama, a Karnataka (India) NGO, provides savings and credit, and enables the people they work with to obtain resources from the government.

Participatory orientation – These practice a participatory approach beginning from the stage of needs analysis and continues right through to developing and implementing the project involving the community.

Often, on the ground, there is no water-tight division among the above categories and many NGOs run projects that involve one or more of the above categories at the same time.

CHANGE OF PROGRAM CONTENT OVER TIME

The nature and focus of NGO activities has changed over time. While NGOs that emerged after the World Wars I and II were more involved with relief work, attention gradually shifted to welfare activities in Third World countries and still later to providing funding and technical services to effective grassroots organizations. The 1970s saw the emergence of NGOs devoted to advocacy of the rights of disadvantaged sections of society and these began public campaigning and parliamentary lobbying in pursuit of socio-political changes. During the 1990s, the trend among NGOs was to get involved in micro-level reform, involving activities such as building rural institutions, redirecting agricultural extension services and bringing about changes in attitudes towards women. The primary objective of NGOs was to bring about change – in values, institutions and technologies.

David Korten (1990) quoted by Misra (2008)[7] identifies four distinct generations of voluntary action. The first generation functions refer to relief work, or helping war victims, as well as welfare services for the poor and the disadvantaged. The earliest NGOs fall into this category. The second generation functions refer to community development, through which NGOs help people become self-reliant and meet their own needs. Third generation functions refer to the efforts of NGOs to bring about reforms in policies and institutions. Fourth generation functions include organizing independent and decentralized initiatives to support a social vision.

According to Clark (1993)[3], the focus of NGO activities has gradually shifted from a "supply side" approach to a "demand side" approach. "Supply side" refers to delivery of services to the community and "demand side" refers to helping the community to articulate its concerns and demands.

STRUCTURE OF NGO SECTOR

NGOs can be identified according to their functional role in the overall structure of the voluntary sector. 'Support NGOs' essentially provide support services in the form of capacity building, technical training in an area of specialty and consultancy with a view to place such specialized services within reach of small and medium sized NGOs which could not have afforded such services in the normal course. They play a crucial role in the growth of the voluntary sector. TNVHA, Tamil Nadu, India is an example of this type of NGO, explained later.

'Funding NGOs' focus on funding the grassroots and support NGOs. Most of the funding NGOs in India raise a substantial part of their resources from foreign sources. Examples include Child Relief & You (CRY) and the Aga Khan Foundation. There are also foreign funded NGOs such as Oxfam and Action Aid, which generate resources from the public and governments in their respective countries.

There are state level NGOs with substantial managerial and other resources that implement projects through NGOs operating at the community level. The program is dis-aggregated and responsibility parceled out to community-based NGOs. Such NGOs may be likened to wholesalers or distributors in commercial marketing of products and the community-based NGOs to retailers

'Umbrella NGOs' are formal or informal groups of grassroots or support NGOs which meet to discuss specific issues or common concerns, share experiences and are involved in lobbying and advocacy. An example of a network NGO is FEVORD–K (Federation of Voluntary Organizations in Karnataka, India).

Tamil Nadu Voluntary Health Association (TNVH) in Tamil Nadu, India is an example of a support NGO providing training services on health issues to staff of NGOs operating at district or village levels. Its activities include holistic health promotion by dealing with other NGOs, providing IEC (Information,

Education, and Communication) material and linking with the government. As per WHO's definition, holistic health promotion includes promotion of both physical and mental health. Apart from health issues, TNVHA also aims at building the capacity of organizations engaged in both social service and social marketing, covering the entire gamut of activities – empowerment of disadvantaged segments through income generating activities, SHGs, work among HIV infected segments, creating awareness of right sexual habits and other health related issues, promoting community management of common resources, promoting conservation of natural resources and environment, delivery of special products or services for community health improvement, promoting change of habits and behavior relating to social, health or environmental concerns and advocacy. TNVHA has over 757 member institutions, including hospitals, dispensaries and community-based organizations and it has grown to this steadily from year to year since 1997.

The relative positioning of the different functional types of NGOs described above can be illustrated as follows

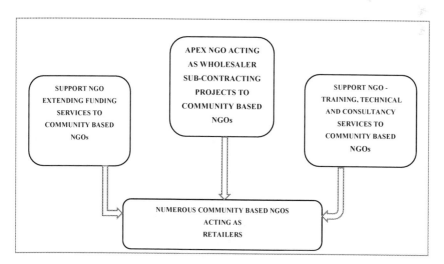

A diagrammatic presentation of various types of NGOs is at the end of this article.

STRATEGIC POSITIONING

White (2001)[17] says that the basis of classification of business organizations is equally applicable to NGOs.

- Static organizations are those with fixed practices and fixed size. These do not change with time. They continue until they are challenged by some new organization.
- Dynamic organizations are those with fixed practices, but whose size may vary with time. However, they decline as new organizations with better practices come into existence and take away their clients.
- Adaptive organizations are those with variable practices and variable size. They constantly seek to improve themselves by adapting their practices, creating new products, retaining their clients and going through several product life cycles. They pose a challenge to static and dynamic organizations.

TYPICAL NGO STRUCTURE

Generally, a typical NGO operating at the provincial, district or village level has the following management structure.

General Body – This includes all the members of the organization and could also include beneficiary members of the community. It is given basic powers such as approval of annual reports and audited statements of accounts, approval of action plans and budgets, consideration and approval of the resolutions passed by the Governing Body.

Governing Body – This is also called the Board of Directors. It includes members elected by the General Body along with office bearers. It is accountable to the General Body and its decisions on pre-defined matters of certain importance have to be approved by the General Body. The Governing Body is responsible for the leadership and management of the NGO. Its responsibilities include appointment of the Chief Executive Officer and Executive Staff, fund raising and use of funds, approval of programs organized by staff, taking care of legal issues, etc.

Executive Staff and Chief Executive Officer – They play an important role, since they are responsible for implementing the programs in co-ordination with the Governing Body. The CEO plays the role of a full-time Administrator, while the Executive Staff are administrative staff in charge of office management and program and field staff in charge of implementing projects.

EXAMPLES FROM THE STUDY[9]

The ten sample NGOs studied by the author represent a variety of organizational types. The Tamil Nadu Voluntary Health Association is the only one, among the sample, operating at the Apex level providing training services to field staff of NGOs dealing directly with communities on health issues. They provide holistic health promotion and educational services. Two NGOs from the sample – Women's Liberation and Rehabilitation Society in Karnataka and Action for Community Organization, Rehabilitation and Development in Tamil Nadu – are community based organizations dealing directly with target beneficiaries. The two deal with empowerment of women and tribals (*adivasis*) respectively. Another five deal with communities directly over a well spread geographical area with a hierarchical organization directed by the apex office. These are as follows – Action Aid engaged in anti-poverty programs, MYRADA in rural development, Samuha in HIV related programs and Agricultural Development and Training Society in empowerment of the working class. The four operate in Karnataka. The fifth is the Tamil Nadu based Social Action Movement dealing with eradication of child labor and education of children.

STATUS OF NGOs IN INDIA

A study carried out in collaboration with the Institute for Policy Studies[6], as a part of a comparative global study provides some interesting statistics on NGOs in India. Due to poor availability of reliable data on the number of NGOs, the size or their activities, and funding sources, we have to depend on private initiatives to estimate the nature and size of the voluntary sector through sample surveys

According to their sample survey, it is estimated that there are 1.2 million NGOs (referred to by them as non-profits) in India. More than half the NGOs are based in rural areas. Of course, several NGOs based in urban areas serve rural communities. Nearly half the NGOs are unregistered. The percentage of registered NGOs is highest in Maharashtra state (74%) and lowest in Tamil Nadu state (47%). An overwhelming majority of those registered are registered under Society Registration Acts. Most of the unregistered NGOs are in rural areas. Indian NGOs are essentially small: nearly three-fourth of all NGOs have only volunteers or at most one paid staff. Only one in 12 NGOs (8.5%) employs more than ten paid staff. There are five dominant activities at the all India level - religious, engaged in social development - 26.5% (the primary identity is that of a religious institution), community/social Service - 21.3%, education - 20.4%, sports/culture - 18.0%, health - 6.6%. Thus "pure" social development NGOs without religious identity are only about 21% of the total. All India estimates of total receipts of NGOs for 1999-2000 were ₹ 17.9 billion ($ 3.6 billion). Four main sources of receipts for NGOs in India were: self-generation, loans, grants and donations. Grants are funds received from government and international sources; donations can be from both Indian and foreign sources, mainly individuals and corporations. More than 50% are self-generated through fees, charges for services etc., grants and donations taken together constitute 40 % of total receipts.

The study concluded that the sector is widespread, the scale huge and significant on several accounts: employment, revenue and types of activities. An institutional sector of such a large size requires strong support from policy-makers, government officials and the political class. Data and system of data collection about NGOs should be organically integrated into the work of the Central Statistical Organization of the Government. Such data should emerge automatically and organically along with other statistics in the country.

NGOs IN A TYPICAL STATE OF INDIA - KARNATAKA

According to the Planning Commission NGO Database, Karnataka has a large number of NGOs that work in the areas of social justice and empowerment. A number of international donors also have their regional offices in Bangalore. Some NGOs are part of state and district level networks, both formal and informal.

According to NGO database, Planning Commission, Government of India, 2004, 33% of the total number of NGOs in Karnataka were involved in rural development, followed by 30% in social justice and empowerment, as of December 2004. With the decentralization of government and greater power given to the local community bodies, NGOs' relationship with the government at that level has changed for the better.

Karnataka state which was part of the Study[9] has an active and heterogeneous voluntary sector that is involved in a wide range of activities. It also has a large number of rural development oriented NGOs. As of 1995, the number of active NGOs engaged in rural development was estimated to be around 500 (Rajasekhar, 2005[12]). One of these, the Mysore Resettlement and Development Agency (MYRADA) is one of the largest rural development NGOs in India with an estimated budget of around ₹ 200 million ($ 4 million) and staff strength of 400.

NGOs IN OTHER COUNTRIES

Ethiopia: For historical reasons the Government has not been well disposed towards the NGO sector. Increasing restrictions are placed on foreign-funding of NGOs. Cooperatives which boosted the country's coffee industry are preferred as a model for development. Ethiopia's coffee industry has recently seen significant growth, thanks in part to indigenous coffee cooperatives - demonstrating, advocates say, cooperatives' superiority to NGO assistance.

It is argued that cooperatives have ownership of development problems motivating lasting change. Others argued that the cooperative model on its own is not capable of achieving long-term sustainability.

Cooperatives were once perceived as an arm of the government and NGOs as agents of foreign influence. The cooperative movement in Ethiopia emerged in the 1950s, during the transition from subsistence farming to commercial agriculture. In the 1970s, under the socialist regime, cooperatives were used to implement a series of radical policies, such as outlaw of private land ownership. Farmers were forced to join cooperatives and give up land for collective use; as a result, cooperatives became very unpopular.

NGOs are foreign-funded and are not member-oriented. "An NGO would bring all things, so that the community remained like beggars, with no role in development." The program often collapsed when NGOs departed, and some NGOs spend up to 75 percent of their budgets on administrative costs, according to critics. (Globalissues) [16]

The Ethiopia experience has several lessons for NGOs if they wish to play a useful role in social and economic development of the countries of Asia and Africa. Heavy funding support from overseas sources induces a feeling of insecurity on the part of governments and the political class that it may give room for outside agencies to play with the country's political stability. Political parties depend heavily on electoral support from the rural masses and any arrangement that leads the population to the perception that benefits are flowing from foreign agencies using NGOs as the conduit is indeed an unsettling feeling. Criticisms of NGO as an institutional instrument are technically valid – that NGOs do not confer ownership as cooperatives can, that they tend to degenerate into giving hand-outs which is an assault on the beneficiaries' self-esteem, and that often the impact is not sustained. These are the corresponding strengths of cooperatives. But NGOs have capacity, technical expertise and ability to mobilize resources. As criticisms of both the NGO and the cooperative models are valid perhaps the answer lies in a synergy combining the two systems that utilizes the best of both.

Bangladesh: A series of natural disasters in Bangladesh during the 1940s and subsequent decades led to the development of what is today one of the world's largest NGO sectors - (Asian Development Bank)[1] and (Transparency International (TI)-Bangladesh)[15]

Moving beyond relief and rehabilitation, new organizations emerged to undertake work in the delivery of services in the fields of health and education. In 1987, the Association for Social Advancement (ASA) was established to serve the poor. This organization played an important role in commercializing microfinance in the country.

NGO policy advocacy on various issues of citizen concern have become common, including environmental conservation, gender equity, trafficking of women and children and good governance.

NGOs have found a niche for themselves in the gap between society and state, and have succeeded in promoting the people's welfare through community level initiatives. NGOs have created job opportunities and have successfully partnered with international development partners to mobilize resources for implementing health, education and literacy programs.

NGOs in Bangladesh are empowering vulnerable sections of the population, in an effort to provide satisfactory resolution to disputes where none was previously available. Bangladesh NGOs recorded rapid growth with a strength of 26,000 NGOs registered with the NGO Affairs Bureau.

A World Bank Report (2003–2004) indicated that 34.1% of the foreign aid ($379.4 million) received by Bangladesh was allocated for the NGO sector. The NGO sector is also an important employment generator. NGOs' entry into commercial ventures has been subject to criticism from the private sector which face uneven competition since NGOs do not pay taxes on their commercial ventures. NGOs argue that they spend commercial income on community development.

Tanzania: The Special Paper (2007)[13] on Poverty Alleviation and the perceptions of Tanzanian NGOs on their role provides a useful picture of the situation of the NGO sector in that country. The following summary of its findings.

The structural adjustment programs adopted by the Tanzanian economy in the 1980s and early 1990s, encouraged NGOs in development. The Tanzania Non-Governmental Organizations Act of 2002 formulated the legislative framework to allow NGOs to operate freely.

The survey found that closer planning and working relationships between the three sectors are emerging, as evidenced by collaboration during the development of the National Strategy for Growth and Reduction of Poverty in 2003-05. NGOs seek to act as a strategic link between the government and local communities to enhance policy outcomes. Additionally, NGOs fill gaps where the government does not provide services.

NGOs complained of pressures with respect to program priorities and compliance. Many respondents also viewed the government/donor relationship as balanced unevenly in favor of donors. Respondents recommended that donors develop projects jointly with NGOs to reflect district/local priorities, and reduce the complexities of funding applications and reporting. NGOs want donors to fund NGOs' core operating costs, personnel and infrastructure to sustain work beyond the terms of individual projects.

NGOs participating in the survey recognized the need to improve their own individual and networking capacities to contribute effectively to policy debate and service delivery, so that the credibility of civil society is strengthened. Viewing the government as an adversary was seen as counterproductive. Many NGOs lack skills and capacity, including the ability to articulate their mission and vision.

Donors are increasingly re-directing development aid to the government, thereby transferring responsibility to the government for promoting civil society.

The area of impact of NGOs cited was input to the Poverty Reduction Strategies (PRS) review, a national consultation process initiated by the Government of Tanzania. Participants felt that many of their recommendations were incorporated into the strategy, especially in areas of disability and gender. NGOs contributed to several other critical areas of policy and legislative change, most notably gender equity, prevention of sexual offences, and land reform.

Several NGOs in Iringa, Morogoro and Kilimanjaro noted that increasing use of condoms and behavior change fostered through awareness programs had reduced the incidence of HIV/AIDS infection in these areas. Progress was being made against the practice of female genital mutilation (FGM)

VALUE ADDITION BY NGO SECTOR

According to E.F. Schumacher, quoted by Misra (2008)[7] the role of NGOs is not to carry out development work in isolation, but through a "participatory approach" - through working with the people. NGOs are essentially grassroots institutions that work closely with local communities. For example, NGOs can communicate with farmers to help them to re-organize their methods of production. On the role of the voluntary sector in society there are different perspectives.

Clark (1993)[3] suggests that the voluntary sector should also strengthen the government's efforts at social development in the following ways. Projecting itself as an alternative to the government is not a wise approach as we have seen from the experience of NGOs in Tanzania.

- Persuading government ministries and official aid agencies to use successful approaches developed by the voluntary sector.
- Making the public aware of their rights under government programs

- Helping to tailor official programs to public needs
- Collaborating with official bodies on operational aspects
- Shaping the local development policies framed by national and international institutions
- Offering training and improved management capacity to the government and funding agencies, thereby enabling them to come up with a more effective development strategy.

The advent of globalization has triggered the worldwide growth of civil society organizations in general and NGOs in particular (Brown et al, 2000)[2]. However, their impact in different countries has not been uniform and has been influenced to a large extent by the degree of openness to globalization and its implications. International NGOs and civil society alliances have been actively involved in disaster relief, service delivery and policy analysis.

CONCLUSION - NGOs ARE SOCIAL CAPITAL

The foregoing survey indicates that the NGO sector can indeed play a useful role filling in gaps between the efforts of the government and the community in accelerating social development. NGOs can complement government's efforts by bringing in additional funds, expertise and single-minded commitment to causes. Experience in countries like Ethiopia shows that the sector is not without its inherent disadvantages. The tendency to replace government efforts, competing with the political class for gaining community loyalty, denial of ownership of programs to the community members and creating a perception of being condescending, are the negative factors. When we speak of the useful role of NGOs it is not to imply that NGO institutions must be present at all levels and that they need to dominate the development scene. NGOs could put their intrinsic strengths to good advantage by operating at the apex level extending wholesaling, funding, training, technical assistance and consultancy services – see diagram earlier in this article. The grassroots could be left free for community institutions, NGOs promoted by local initiatives and cooperatives – the last, as in the case of Ethiopia. Thus, overall, NGOs do have an important contribution to make toward development but the country's context, political sensitivities and the strengths of locally bred institutions would determine the kind of structure which NGOs could fit into to enhance the total effect.

Poteete (2003)[10] uses the term *social capital* to refer to "dimensions of social organization that generate multiple horizontal linkages and foster the development of social trust, collective reciprocity and tolerance. High levels of social capital are expected to facilitate provision of public goods and services and contribute to community well-being". In that sense, NGOs are social capital to be nurtured, appropriately utilized and maintained.

Forms of NGOs

NGOs in community development projects – focus of the author's research study – are in color

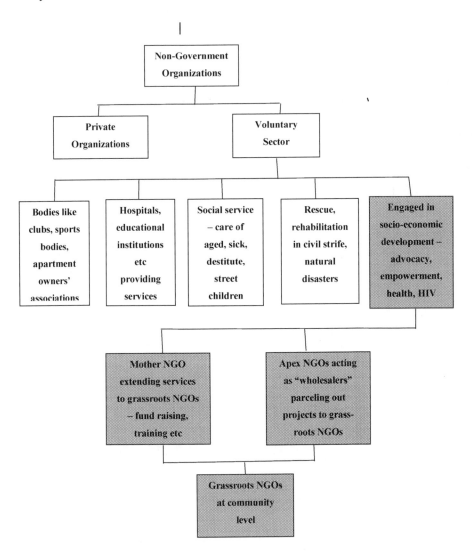

REFERENCES

1. Asian Development Bank, "Civil Society Briefs – Bangladesh", 2008
2. Brown, David L et al, "Globalization, NGOs and Multi-Sectoral Relations", The Hauser Center for Non-Profit Organizations and the Kennedy School of Government, Harvard University, Working Paper No. 1, 2000.
3. Clark, John, "The Relationship Between the State and the Voluntary Sector", The Earthscan Reader on NGO Management, Edited by Michael Edwards and Alan Fowler, Earthscan India, Daryaganj, New Delhi, 1993.
4. Fowler, Alan, "Assessing NGO Performance: Difficulties, Dilemmas and a Way Ahead", The Earthscan Reader on NGO Management, Edited by Michael Edwards and Alan Fowler, Earthscan India, Daryaganj, New Delhi, 2007.
5. Fowler, Alan, "NGO Performance: What Breeds Success? New Evidence from South Asia", The Earthscan Reader on NGO Management, Edited by Michael Edwards and Alan Fowler, Earthscan India, Daryaganj, New Delhi, 2007.
6. Institute for Policy Studies, Johns Hopkins University, USA, 2002.
7. Misra, Rajeeb, "Voluntary Sector and Rural Development", Rawat Publications, Jaipur, 2008.
8. Omana, Julius, "Civil Society in a Conflict Environment: a case of Gulu District in Northern Uganda and Policy Implications for Social Service Delivery", Anaka Foundation, Post Box 868, Gulu, Uganda, 2005.
9. Parthasarathy, Vimala, "Social Marketing Strategies & Traits of Successful NGOs in India - A Strategic Perspective with Reference to Select NGOs in the States of Karnataka & Tamil Nadu, India", doctoral thesis for PhD, approved by Manipal University, Manipal, India, 2013
10. Poteete Amy R, "The Implications of Social Capital for Community Development", World Bank website: worldbank.org, 2003.

11. Rajasekhar, D, "Micro-Finance, Poverty Alleviation and Empowerment of Women: A Study of two NGOs from Andhra Pradesh and Karnataka, Social and Economic Change Monographs", Institute for Social and Economic Change, Bangalore, 2004.

12. Rajasekhar, D, "Non-Governmental Organizations in India: Opportunities and Challenges", Institute for Social and Economic Change, Bangalore, Working Paper No. 66, 2000.

13. Research on Poverty Alleviation REPOA, "Tanzanian NGO's – Their Perceptions", Special Paper 07.21, 2007, website: www.repoa.or.tz

14. Robbins, Richard, "Global Problems and the Culture of Capitalism" (Allyn and Bacon, 2002)

15. Transparency International (TI) -Bangladesh. "Problems in Good Governance in the NGO Sector: The Way Out", October 2007 (www.ti-bangladesh.org/research/execsumngo-english.pdf)

16. Website: http://www.globalissues.org/article/25/non-governmental-organizations-on-development-issues

17. White, Mark, "Three Organizational Types: Evolving from Static and Dynamic to Adaptive", Reproduced in the website of The Global Development Center (GDRC), 2001.

18. World Bank Operating Manual, "Involving Non-Governmental Organizations in World Bank Supported Activities", Abstracted and reproduced in the website of The Global Development Center (GDRC), 1989.

19. Zaidi, S Akbar, "NGO Failure and the Need to Bring Back the State", Journal of International Development, Chichester, Vol. 11, No. 2, March/April 1999. pg. 259.

ARE MARKETING PRACTICES RELEVANT TO COMMUNITY DEVELOPMENT PROGRAMS?

Abstract

The question that the article seeks to answer is whether marketing practices are relevant in development projects to enhance impact. The essential differences between commercial marketing and social marketing constitute the challenges to social marketers that call for adaptation of commercial marketing techniques to community development programs that do not sell a product but sell a change of habit or behavior. The NGO engaged in this activity does not, at the end of a program successfully implemented, derive any monetary benefit equivalent to the profit element in commercial sales. There seems much scope for introducing, through training and consultancy, more systematic and formal marketing practices to make NGOs efforts to achieve higher impact. Commercial marketing practices need to be adapted for application to social development issues. Such practices and related research and monitoring tools also need to be simplified for easy adoption by community level NGOs.

BACKGROUND

The application of marketing principles and practices, conventionally employed in the distribution and popularization of commercial products and services, to social issues is referred to as Social Marketing (SM). Many social development issues find the need to bring about habit and attitudinal changes in order to improve the community's health and economic standards. Such a task is far more daunting and time consuming than launching new products and services in the commercial world. The scholarly opinion of experts backed by experience of many social development projects indicates that application of appropriately adapted marketing techniques does impart a systematic approach to planning and implementation of programs thereby enhancing impact. The following discussion will explain what SM is, list its parallels with commercial marketing, outline how it is different from commercial marketing, indicate the steps for its adoption for social projects and cite examples of its successful application from among the NGOs that formed the subject of the author's study.

SOCIAL MARKETING

The origins of social marketing can be traced to 1969, when marketing scholars, notably Philip Kotler and Sidney Levy, identified the potential for the successful application of commercial marketing principles to non-commercial organizations. Prior to this, marketing was perceived as an exclusively commercial activity, which provided goods and services to consumers for generating profit. However, it also led to some confusion regarding the true identity of marketing. While one school of thought represented by Kotler and Levy defined marketing as a technology, others defined it in terms of the class of behavior towards which it was directed (Luck 1969 and Bartels 1974).

Social marketing deals with the application of marketing principles and practices to social development issues involving behavioural changes among communities towards better health and improved economic status. The origins of social marketing can be traced to 1969, when marketing scholars, notably Philip Kotler and Sidney Levy, conceived the idea of applying commercial marketing principles to non-commercial organizations. Prior to this, marketing was perceived as a pure economic activity, which provided goods and services to consumers for generating profit. However, it also led to some confusion regarding the true identity of marketing. While one school of thought represented by Kotler and Levy defined marketing as a technology, others defined it in terms of the class of behaviour towards which it was directed (Luck & Bartels 1974).

Kotler (1979)[8] referred to *Consciousness 3* to describe the progression of marketing from providing goods and services to a field that included an "organization's relationship with all its stakeholders and not just its consumers".

In explaining *Consciousness 3* Kotler limited *Consciousness 1* to refer to a relationship restricted to market transactions as a business subject and *Consciousness 2* as a broader view that perceived marketing as comprising non-monetary organization-client transactions. *Consciousness 3* visualized a much extended view of the commercial and social organizations' relationship with *all* its stakeholders. Thus *Consciousness 3* at once extended the application of marketing principles (a) to both commercial and social organizations and (b) to relationships with *all* stakeholders and *not just* customers. The term was suggested by Kotler and Gerald Zaltman (1971), when they examined the possibility of applying the "technology" of marketing to social issues. At the same time, Kotler and Levy, who first conceived the idea, considered that implicit in the concept of *Consciousness 3* was a *furthering*, rather than *broadening*, of the field of application of marketing concepts. However, the idea of *furthering* did not catch on in marketing academic circles and the term *social marketing* came to be accepted. Thus, social marketing is essentially the application of marketing practices to maintain and further the *relationships with all stakeholders and not just the consumers* and in respect of not only monetary transactions but *also non-monetary organization-client relationships*. *Social Marketing* (SM) has gained popularity ever since and has been widely researched and taught, especially in the west. The author's study shows that it is often applied with much enthusiasm by NGOs without there being formally aware of the concept of marketing and its usefulness to their context. The following diagram depicts the progressive widening and furthering of the marketing concept.

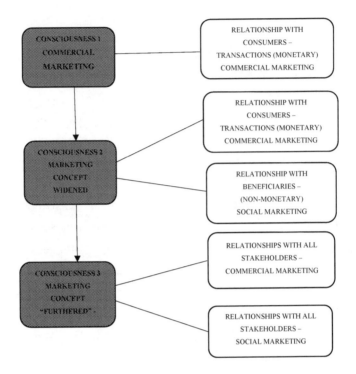

Walsh, D. C. et al (1993)[12] present the case against and for social marketing, especially in the context of improvement of public health. They cite critics of social marketing, notably Larry Wallack (1990), who believe that social marketing reflects commercial interests and values and has not offered any visible benefits in terms of improvement of public health. Other critics have pointed out that a marketing orientation itself is in conflict with the core values of public health. This is because of the negative image that commercial marketing conjures in people's minds caused by the mistaken belief that it is concerned with maximizing profits even at the expense of the consumers' interests. On the other hand, the proponents of social marketing have emphasized that concepts of commercial marketing are not by themselves worthy of condemnation but only their occasional misuse by enterprises that look for instant benefits instead of long term sustained success. They say that marketing techniques are to be adopted when found to produce results consistent with the much broader discipline of morality that demands incorporation of ethical and socially responsible practices.

CORPORATE SOCIAL RESPONSIBILITY

A brief diversion is necessary to distinguish social marketing from Corporate Social Responsibility (CSR). Multinational firms are often accused of irresponsible social conduct in the course of their businesses especially in the post globalization era. Their behavior is described as exploitative of cheap labor, accessible resources and minimalist regulatory regimes. "Multinational firms are criticized for trampling traditional cultures and the diversity of the global village. And they are seen as gravitating to countries where environmental, safety, governance, and employee welfare standards are weak or non-existent". Corporations began adopting CSR with a degree of self-interest either for sustaining their market share or to keep socially conscious investors and consumers happy. It is in this context that CSR has assumed increasing importance as a yardstick for judging the conduct of business houses.

Corporate Social Responsibility as proposed by Milton Friedman in 1962 is summed up in his own words: "The only business of business is business". It, required (a) compliance with laws and regulations of economic activity and (b) respect for the rules of free competition besides the use of resources efficiently in order to offer its shareholders the maximum results. In January 2005 *The Economist*, in its cover story, questioned whether in an intensely competitive global marketplace, companies could afford the luxury of CSR. *The Economist* stated that business' greatest "social responsibility is to create wealth for shareholders, put people to work, contribute revenues to its communities and raise the economic standard of living for the world". It seemed to question whether CSR was any longer sustainable in a competitive world. The way in which companies exercise their CSR behavior must ultimately be reconciled to profit and shareholder concerns and it is a happy situation when CSR and bottom line concerns converge.

Under pressure of public opinion of the conduct of corporations the definition of CSR has expanded such that it requires business houses to mind the consequences of their actions on various interest groups, internal or external, and the effect of their external practices such as environmental protection or health promotion in the community and staff training. Thus CSR is action by corporations with responsibility for the social and environmental consequences of their actions.

Today, going beyond assuming "responsibility for the social and environmental consequences of their actions", commercial organizations are getting increasingly involved in social development, in order to project their image as good corporate citizens. CSR has gained momentum in India over the last few decades. There are several examples of both private and public sector Indian companies promoting social development. Tata and Infosys are examples. The Infosys Foundation, a company linked NGO, has been actively involved in the construction of a super specialty hospital in Andhra Pradesh and in the reconstruction of a school in Karnataka. The Azim Premji Foundation, Wipro's company linked NGO, has been providing elementary schooling to underprivileged children. Yet another example is Apollo Tyres which, in partnership with 36 NGOs, launched the Apollo Tyre Health Care Centre in October 2000, to promote general and sexual health of truckers and transportation communities. The center also provides diagnosis and treatment of Sexually Transmitted Diseases (STD), communication and promotion of condoms.

Commercial organizations have also added a societal dimension to their marketing efforts, which could be referred to as responsible marketing. For example, warning against risks and hazards in usage, incorporating safety features (in cars) and liquor companies advocating moderation in consumption could come under the category of societal marketing.

Thus corporations are discharging CSR in three ways – being responsible for social and environmental consequences of their actions, taking part in social work related to education, health etc. and, thirdly, by responsible marketing.

Social Marketing is the application of marketing principles and practices for social development and emphasises the importance of relationships with all the stakeholders. As such it is different from corporate action to protect their image by demonstrating their concern for the social consequences of their profit making efforts.

CHALLENGES FOR SOCIAL MARKETERS

Social marketing is more challenging than commercial marketing, since most often it is engaged in "selling" ideas for adoption and bringing about sustainable behavioral transformation. Promoting a healthy diet and getting people to change their dietary habits are good examples of social marketing. Any attempt at changing behavior, and in most cases on permanent basis, inevitably faces resistance. In commercial marketing accepting the use of a product also involves change but of a type that allows trial and reversal if the change is unacceptable, without serious consequences. Even after change to the new product, adherence to it for a period of time, comprising many repeat cycles of purchase and use, is enough to meet the commercial objectives of the marketer. So the marketer does not have to seek a permanent irreversible change to his new product. In social issues involving health, drug use etc. not only is change needed but it has to be a permanent self-sustained change in a habit or behavior pattern. Unlike in commercial marketing where the change (say, to a new product) is offered for the choice of the prospective buyer, although subject to "hard- sell" persuasion, in social behavior non-adoption is fraught with risks to health. The target group may not recognize the need to change their diet and even if they did, might offer resistance to the very idea of change as change is unsettling and, therefore, imparts a sense of insecurity and uncertainty. (Bellamy et al, 1997)[2]. The long term consequences may not always be clear.

POSITIVE VS. NEGATIVE DEMAND

Commercial marketers have an active or dormant demand or an inner felt need for products and services, whereas social marketers often have to create demand and acceptance by overcoming negative demand, an inclination for the opposite. Certain practices such as eating unhealthy diet or smoking are strongly rooted in a habit not easily given up. The acute inconvenience of giving up the habit has to be overcome. The challenge lies in making the target beneficiary give up this resistance, the equivalent of paying the price in commercial transactions, but without immediate experience of a benefit as a return. This is like waiting for the value or benefit of the product to be enjoyed in course of time.

Several success stories of overcoming negative demand or resistance and bringing about behavioral change speak of the value of SM. The Washington-Heights Inwood Healthy Heart Program was successful in getting consumers to switch from whole milk to low fat milk in a low income, Latino neighborhood of New York City. The campaign's objectives and strategy were studied by Weschler and Wernick (1992) as quoted by Bellamy. The program aimed to encourage consumers to bring down fat consumption, especially among children, by switching to low fat milk. Initially, there was resistance among the target group to the idea of consuming low fat milk, since it was perceived to be a low quality substitute for whole milk and its availability was also limited. A two-pronged social marketing strategy was developed to influence consumer demand on the one hand and to increase the availability of the product on the other. The promotional strategy consisted of educating consumers about the nutritional benefits of low fat milk as compared to whole milk and explaining the process for making low fat milk. Flyers, posters and other print material, in English and Spanish, were distributed to target consumers. This was combined with consumer sales promotion techniques such as sampling of low fat milk and contests for collecting low fat milk labels. The distribution strategy was to increase availability by persuading educational institutions such as schools and child-care centers to sell low fat milk. The campaign was highly successful in achieving its objectives as evidenced by the following – popularity and high rates of participation in low-fat milk taste tests, large proportion of students in targeted schools who chose low fat milk at lunch and the increased number of availability of low fat milk in 20 out of 28 targeted schools after the program as compared to 6 before the program (Six-Year Report on The Washington heights-Inwood Healthy Heart program Published in American Journal of Public Health February 1996, Vol. 86 No.2)

TANGIBLE IMMEDIATE VS. INTANGIBLE LONG TERM BENEFITS

While commercial marketers promote products and services that offer immediate and visible benefits to consumers, social marketers promote practices for which there are no immediate benefits, but quite often there is immediate intangible cost in the form of inconvenience or dissatisfaction. Eating a healthy diet, exercising regularly and giving up smoking are all examples of change that offer benefits in the form of weight reduction, prevention of cancer, etc. only in the long term.

This essential differential feature of the *exchange* lies at the heart of the challenge entailed in the employment of marketing practices to development programs. The intangibility of *the price* and *the value* derived in return and the immediacy of one and the remoteness of the other have to be faced and overcome and cannot be wished away. In fact, but for viewing the whole exchange process through the marketing prism this central problem of transfer of ideas and practices to the target audience could not be handled scientifically.

In this regard, Bellamy cites Andreasen (1995) and the latter's successful case study of the National High Blood Pressure Education Program (NHBPEP). Started in 1972, this social marketing program was effective in increasing people's awareness of the link between high blood pressure, stroke and heart disease. The social marketing interventions were also successful in encouraging a significant number of people to get their blood pressures checked regularly and to take appropriate treatment. Thus, the program was able to convince people about the long-term health benefits of the behavioral change and to motivate them to sustain the change.

AUDIENCE LITERACY

Commercial marketers generally promote their products and services to middle classes who have expendable surplus, whereas social marketers most often are concerned with illiterate, rural audiences. The task of convincing such audiences becomes more difficult, especially since the media available to reach them with promotional messages are limited. For example, the print medium cannot be used due to low literacy. Mass media allows standardization of the messages avoiding transmission losses and distortions and can reach a large number of people but of this the number that reads or views the message are not all part of the target audience. Reaching out through group meetings is effective in the case of audiences with low literacy but the per capita cost of reach is much higher than that of mass media. Group-reach requires a team of trained staff equipped with necessary display materials, flyers and audio-visuals. Mass media may be suitable for standard products but not for technical explanations and demonstrations that are indispensable for health, family planning and such promotions.

LARGE VS. LIMITED BUDGETS

Commercial organizations operate with large budgets to establish the brand and its market share. It is treated as an investment in creating a brand and the size of outlay is justified by the return of profits it would bring in the short or medium term. They are able to read the outcome of their promotional expenditure by tangible and immediately available indicators like increase in sales or acceptance of a price rise or higher market share. Accordingly, they are able to take sound decisions on the size and content of advertising campaigns. Social marketers depend heavily on external funding for propagating their message. On the one side resources are limited and subject to uncertainty and on the other side the task of habit transformation is more difficult. Thus they are squeezed from both sides. This limits the social marketers' flexibility to experiment and try out different strategies and methodologies. They do not have reliable impact indicators for tailoring their promotional strategy. They are also answerable to a number of stakeholders in the way they use their resources – government, donors, beneficiaries and general public.

SOCIAL MARKETING - ILLUSTRATION

Hoffman (2006)[7] recommends the use of the following eight *P*s in social marketing campaigns by taking the example of social marketing for water management. The *P*s are: product, price, place, promotion, publics, partnership, policy and purse.

Product, in the context of water management, is the concept of usage and conservation of water. The target audience is trained in efficient practices in usage and in storage and distribution for the post rainy season.

Price is the cost of obtaining water in terms of money and also time, effort, self-denial and inconvenience in adopting the special practices. If the target audience perceives the benefit to be greater than the cost, the chances of adoption will be higher.

Place is the delivery system for the training for new practices of usage and conservation. It should be available without the farmers having to travel a long distance. Holding training during the peak season when farmers are busy on the land would be of little value. Holding it far ahead of the season may result in lower memory retention.

Promotion is the use of methods appropriate to the literacy, available media that accessible and cultural inclinations.

Publics are the internal and external stakeholders involved in the campaign. The external publics include the government and policy makers, the beneficiaries of the program and the funding sources. The internal publics are those who are involved in the implementation of the program. The NGO should maintain these relationships to increase the chances of success of their projects.

Partnership, like publics, is an important characteristic of social marketing. The task of bringing about social change is too complex to be undertaken by a single organization. Therefore, social marketers need to enter into symbiotic partnerships with other agencies and organizations with similar goals, so as to achieve maximum impact.

Policy is an external factor outside the control of the voluntary sector. Social marketers should assess the policy environment and try to either adapt to the current policy requirements or constructively lobby for changes.

Purse referring to fund availability in a continuous and timely manner is critical for sustained action. NGO leadership should develop effective fund raising strategies, good relationships and inspire confidence by performance and transparency.

HOW IS MARKETING PRACTICE RELEVANT?

Whether the principles and concepts of commercial marketing can be transferred to social organizations has been the subject of much debate. Kotler and Levy (1969) assert that commercial marketing principles could be applied equally by voluntary organizations engaged in social development and in bringing about changes in social behavioral patterns. Andreasen (2000)[1] has argued that applying commercial marketing principles to the non-profit sector is not a smooth transfer. Other authors such as Bloom and Novelli (1981)[3] have also suggested that the differences between the profit and non-profit sectors make it necessary to adapt the principles of commercial marketing to a social development context. The essential difference between transactions in the profit and non-profit sectors is that the latter are concerned with transactions of a non-economic nature, in the sense that consumers do not pay for the organizations' economic offerings. Andreasen formulated the following hypotheses regarding the applicability of commercial marketing principles to social marketing.

> The more similar the environment and main transaction of the non-profit organization to that of the commercial organization, the more extensively marketing principles can be applied to a non-commercial organization.

While this may sound like stating the obvious, the test is the prevalence of *market-like circumstances* to be able to apply marketing principles to social development. Market-like circumstance requires the presence of a product, service, concept or practice that is transferred to the buyer or adopter in return for an economic consideration or as a discomfort or inconvenience that the adopter willingly undergoes. The latter is in consideration of a benefit, like improved health or freedom from risk of cancer that he gets. The adopter considers the inconvenience worthwhile for the benefit that he derives in due course. An important difference in this exchange process is that in the case of commercial marketing the economic consideration given by the buyer goes to the marketer whereas the benefit of improved health, in social marketing, goes to the community as a whole – in the form of, say, better health, higher productivity, more incomes, improved living conditions. The NGO marketing the program does not get any monetary return, as a commercial organization does, but only sense of fulfilment, winning donor confidence, sustainability and community's esteem.

MARKET-LIKE CIRCUMSTANCES

Stead et al (2007)[11], in their thesis on the development of a social marketing strategy for health improvement in Scotland, argue that ever since Wiebe (1952)[14] concluded that commercial marketing principles could be applied to social marketing campaigns, provided "market like circumstances" exist, social marketing has come a long way. As market-like circumstances, although with some different characteristics, do exist there must be considerable advantage for social projects to adopt – and adapt - various steps in the marketing, planning and implementation process as practiced by commercial organizations.

Extensive survey of scholarly articles, experiences of the voluntary sector and research studies, are forthright in stating that market-like circumstances *are* prevalent in the case of NGOs involved in bringing about behavior change for better health, etc. and in promoting technology (e.g. bio gas), ideas and concepts (e.g. rain water harvesting, self-help groups, building rural institutions, environment conservation). Their activities have the elements of Product, Price, Place (Distribution) and Promotion. Almost all the experts / donors and many NGOs interviewed in the course of the Study[9] stated that marketing practices are relevant for the voluntary sector for greater effectiveness. The responses to the questionnaire also show that all the NGOs interviewed apply several marketing strategies, although many practice them informally and sometimes without being conscious of the fact that they are marketing related.

ARE NGOs AWARE OF THE USEFULNESS OF SM?

The findings of the author's Study[9] based on in-depth study of the functioning of ten NGOs in two leading states of the Indian Union throw some interesting light on the awareness level and related aspects.

Only three NGOs among the ones studied showed clear awareness of the concept of marketing, recognized the relevance of marketing principles to their activity, appreciated the differences between commercial and social marketing and felt the need for adaptation of commercial marketing practices to social development projects. But the general awareness of the applicability of marketing concepts was low scoring only 54% - the satisfactory grade. In contrast, the score for actual application of marketing practices, is surprisingly high in the "good" category at 68%. (In order to judge the values and interpret them, a grading scale based on a popularly accepted model was adopted as follows – 35% or less is poor, 36-50% is moderate, 51-60% is satisfactory, 61-75% is good and above 75% is very good. A fuller explanation of the evaluation procedures is in the Preface) This shows that understanding and appreciation of marketing practices was not high but the NGOs have unconsciously been adopting them implying the need for formal training in application based on a sound understanding of the methodologies.

While the following paragraphs lists some of the important marketing tools practiced successfully by commercial organizations with possible scope for adoption by social marketers, a word of caution is necessary. These practices are not always free of complexities for easy adoption and as such these are more suited for the apex level, "mother" and "wholesaling" NGOs. Community-based NGOs need to be trained on simplified versions of select tools, the relevance of which is readily evident to the smaller NGOs.

MARKETING STRATEGY AND PLAN

Bellamy et al (1997)[2] in their Social Marketing Manual stress the need for social marketers, like commercial marketers, to develop a strategy statement that would include the following components.

- The broad objectives of the social marketing campaign
- A definition of the primary and secondary target audience
- The desired outcome or behavior of the target audience, as a result of the campaign
- The perceived benefits of adopting a particular practice
- The factors that would motivate the target audience to adopt this practice
- The barriers to be overcome in changing the behavior of the target audience

A strategy statement provides a starting point and sense of direction to the social marketing team and helps to tailor the campaign to the specific needs of the target audience. The strategy statement should be developed into a social marketing plan, which includes the type of message, tone of the message, the choice of communication channel, the nature of information and the spokespersons for the campaign. The plan should also specify the objectives, budget, deadlines and responsibility centers for each activity.

TARGET AUDIENCE PROFILE

Smith (2006)[10] emphasizes the importance of defining and distinguishing between different types of behaviors, prior to developing a social marketing strategy. He points out that not all habits are alike. Some are simple, while others are more complex; some are well understood, while others have to be explained; some are supported by regulations (such as drinking and driving):some types of change bring immediate rewards, while others may have only delayed rewards (quitting smoking). Therefore, it is essential for social marketers to research these behaviors and to formulate a strategy that is appropriate to the target.

As with commercial marketing, research is the starting point and basis of successful social marketing. Social marketers, like commercial marketers, have a variety of research techniques at their disposal, which may be used depending on what is to be measured and the decision to be made. These techniques are similar to the techniques used by commercial marketers and include the following as enumerated by Smith (2006).

- Adopter segmentation research – For measuring the demographic, psychographic, psychological and behavioral characteristics of target adopters.
- Positioning research – For measuring perceptions of the social marketing "product" by potential target segments, so as to determine how to position and interpret the "product"
- Product testing – To test the strengths and weaknesses of social products, so as to determine its features to verify if it answers the need of the customer.
- Brand name testing – For testing alternative brand names in terms of recall and comprehension,
- Package testing – For testing alternative packages, to select the best form of packaging if transfer of a tangible product is involved, or the way an idea is presented, which represents its package
- Communication material pre-test – For testing communication messages and execution
- Post communication effectiveness research – For testing the social marketing campaign after its release, in terms of recall, awareness, image and motivation, with a view to determine whether or not to continue the campaign
- Price sensitivity research – To determine the acceptability of the price (the inconvenience of changing over to a new pattern of practices could constitute its cost to the "buyer") of the social marketing product among the target group
- Test marketing – For measuring adoption of behavior among the target group
- Distribution channel research – To determine the best method of delivery of the product/service to target adopters

SEGMENTATION

Social marketers can use the following criteria for selection of their target audience.

- Identify those who are likely to be receptive to and interested in their messages. For example, people in need of hospital based care are likely to be most receptive to information on hospital quality.
- Select the most influential people in the community, who have the power to influence others. For example, opinion leaders or leaders of local communities.
- Reach out to "early adopters." These are people who are open to trying out new products and to new ideas and concepts.
- Identify secondary audiences – for example, if parents are the primary target for creating awareness about health plans for children, social marketers could also target teachers, counselors and school administrators, since they will be in a position to influence parents.

DISTRIBUTION PRACTICES

The standard approach to social marketing, especially in developing countries, is to use the same techniques and outlets as those used in commercial marketing, for promotion and distribution. This is especially true when a project involves the distribution of a tangible product to be used by the target segment – examples are distribution of condoms, or mosquito nets. In such cases the existing retail and wholesale outlets for commercial products have been used in several countries. While this approach is sufficient to reach a mass market, social marketers in developing countries often have to reach specific target groups with a low-income population. Fox (2000)[6] suggests that in addition to the use of traditional sales techniques and distribution systems, social marketers need to discover non-conventional distribution and promotion methods to meet the needs of these segments according to their characteristics and peculiar needs. For example, in some countries, condoms are available not only in pharmacies and drugstores, but also in bars, beauty parlors, gas stations and bus and truck terminals. Fox further suggests some possible alternative approaches that could be adopted by social marketers, briefly explained below.

Community Based Distribution (CBD) Model – In this model, non-professional sales agents are selected from among the general population and trained to serve the needs of the target segment. They are compensated through margins on their sales or number of contacts made, the latter, if the purpose is not to sell but to influence habits. This approach is particularly effective in reaching geographical areas and groups that are not easily accessible. It has been used successfully by some NGOs to complement the traditional outlets.

Community Based Social Marketing (CBSM) – This model is a variation of the CBD model and was first developed and tested in Chennai, India, by International Family Health and its partner NGO, the Indian Institute of Community Health. It involves recruiting sales agents from both the general public as well as specific groups. The agents are trained in reproductive health and are compensated not only through commission on their sales/contacts, but also through a referral scheme, whereby they are compensated for recruiting others as agents. This approach is based on commercial network and multi-level marketing techniques that have been used successfully in the west. It has been successful in reaching specifically defined groups and in HIV awareness and prevention.

Manufacturer Model – By this approach, support is provided in the form of grants for the distribution and promotion activities of a manufacturer. This reduces the manufacturers' distribution costs and time and enables them to devote more time and resources to improve the quality and design of the product.

Targeted Service Delivery (TSD) Model – This approach involves planning social marketing activities so as to distribute products and services directly to pre-determined priority target groups within the population. These groups are identified through research and market segmentation studies. Such specific attention is necessary in situations where the concerned segments are not served adequately by traditional distribution outlets.

OVERVIEW OF SOCIAL MARKETING PROCESS

Walsh et al (1993)[12] have provided a comprehensive overview of the entire social marketing process. They have divided the social marketing process into three phases and described the various activities and elements involved in each phase, as summarized below.

Phase I – Research and Planning

- Planning – Setting realistic and measurable objectives, determining checkpoints for making decisions, reviewing existing research and developing a program and establishing measures of effectiveness.
- Consumer Analysis – Qualitative and quantitative consumer research and segmentation of the market.
- Market analysis – Development of the marketing mix, determination of whether the product is appropriate for the selected target group and analysis of the competition.
- Channel analysis – Evaluation of both communication channels and distribution channels

Phase II – Strategy Development

- Marketing mix strategy – The marketing mix should be translated into a specific strategy for each element, tested in a limited area among the target group and fine-tuned wherever needed.
- Communication – Message strategies and concepts should be developed in keeping with the target group, tested and modified as and when required.

Phase III – Implementation and Evaluation

- Implementation – Getting the commitment of collaborators and determine the exact nature of their involvement in the social marketing program. They also need to train the various people involved in program execution and product/service delivery and activate distribution and communication

- Process Evaluation – This involves assessing the extent to which communication messages have been successful in reaching the target audience, products and services have reached the target and the actual usage of the product or service. Based on the results, modifications should be carried out.

- Outcome Evaluation – Finally, social marketers should assess the impact of the social marketing program in terms of behavioral change and other pre-determined measures of effectiveness. They should also assess the cost-effectiveness of their programs.

The authors suggest that these process elements may be used as a checklist to determine the comprehensiveness of social marketing programs.

COMPETITION IN SOCIAL MARKETING

Competition is a key concept in social marketing, but is different from competition in the commercial marketing sense. In commercial marketing, competitors are all those who offer a similar product or service to the same target segment. In social marketing, competition is in the form of competing behavior of the target group, or stubborn adherence to maintaining current behavior, according to Cahill et al[4]. For example, a social marketer trying to get people to quit smoking, might face competition in the form of the target group continuing to smoke or smoking more, in the conviction that smoking is a stress reliever. Therefore, social marketers should design their programs, delivery, products and prices in such a way as to make the competing habit less appealing, less available and more expensive and also highlighting the benefits of reformed habits in the form of happiness, enhanced ability to earn and higher social acceptance. To make this effort successful Cahill et al emphasize that formative research, or research prior to developing a social marketing campaign, is essential. This involves an in-depth understanding of the needs, wants, fears, attitudes, knowledge, behavior and perceived risk of the target segments. The factors that influence change of practices and the barriers to change should be identified and studied in advance.

WHERE SOCIAL MARKETING HAS WORKED

The application of marketing principles to community development has played a particularly significant role in the improvement of public health in developed countries. The potential of social marketing to build public health was recognized in the UK by the Department of Health (2004) – the White Paper on Public Health describes social marketing as "marketing tools applied to social good" and "used to build public awareness and change behavior". Regarding the question on whether social marketing really works in terms of bringing about behavioral change, the results of a study on the effectiveness of social marketing interventions to influence a change in dietary habits has been cited by McDermott et al, (2005). These interventions were found to be effective in influencing both behavior and perceptions of the benefits of eating healthy food, although their effectiveness in terms of influencing conditions such as blood pressure and cholesterol (which take a much longer time to change) was limited.

There are several examples of successful use of social marketing in India's National Technology Missions. The National Technology Missions for social development were initiated a decade ago and included areas such as immunization, literacy, drinking water and oilseeds. All these involved social change in one way or another, such as creating extra time for literacy classes, giving a child five immunization shots, changing drinking water habits, or cutting down on cooking oil consumption for health reasons.

EXAMPLES FROM THE STUDY [9]

The management of the Tamil Nadu Voluntary Health Association, an NGO engaged in health education and training of trainers based Tamil Nadu, India was of the opinion that commercial marketing practices were very much applicable in their programs, since they were also engaged in the marketing of health products and trying to change mind and behavior. However, commercial marketing practices were applicable to their activity only with suitable changes. According to the management, the main aspect of commercial marketing which had to be adapted was the selling technique which had to be done in reverse order. While commercial marketers highlighted the effectiveness of their products or services to consumers, social marketers explained the consequences of not complying with behavior change. In the case of this NGO, for example, the consequences included risk of contracting AIDS or Reproductive Tract Infection.

Management indicated using an entire range of methods in designing and delivering their programs, such as studying the needs of the community before designing the program, dividing the market into groups based on needs, developing services for specific groups, developing a system for delivery of services, informing target groups about program features, developing a plan of action for a given period, say a year and assessing the effect of the program on the target group. Three criteria they used in selecting their target audience or their member organizations, as mentioned in their annual report for 2008-09, are as follows.

- The organization should have health promotion as an objective
- It should conduct health activities regularly.
- The audited statement of the organization should have a health budget and health staff salary

Social Action Movement, an NGO in Tamil Nadu, India, operates five districts of the state for eradicating child labor, educating them and encouraging them to take up more skilful jobs. Some of their efforts in this direction include freeing child workers from the silk looms, workshops, restaurants, stone quarries and enrolling them in schools, establishing play and study centers for child workers, campaigning against child labor, organizing parents of child workers into self-help groups to avoid using children for earnings and setting up preparatory schools to promote formal school education among tribal children. The NGO also runs a monthly magazine for and by children.

OBSERVATION

Employing a marketing approach enhances the chances of achieving objectives of development programs provided they are appropriately adapted to suit project-specific situations. Even as it is marketing practices are in vogue though not in a systematic manner and without the practitioners having formal awareness or knowledge of this approach. The practice is confined to apex level NGOs and at the grass-roots level the awareness and practice is at a very low level, practically non-existent. There is much need for training and consultancy to bring about systematic use of marketing tools which would go a long way in making NGOs more result oriented and cost-effective. For the community level small NGOs marketing tools should be simplified and tailored to their local needs, understanding and capabilities. There seems to be much scope for mother NGOs offering services to take up consultancy and training in social marketing.

REFERENCES

1. Andreasen, Alan R, "Inter-sector Transfer of Marketing Knowledge", Working Paper, Social Marketing Institute, Connecticut Avenue, Washington D. C., 2000.

2. Bellamy, Hilary et al, "Social Marketing Resource Manual: A Guide for State Nutrition Education Networks", Prepared for the US Department of Agriculture, Food and Consumer Service, Alexandria, VA, USA, 1997.

3. Bloom, Paul N and Novelli, William D, "Problems and Challenges in Social Marketing", Journal of Marketing, American Marketing Association, Chicago, IL, Vol. 45, No. 2, 1981.

4. Cahill, John et al, "Social Marketing – A Resource Guide", Social Marketing National Excellence Collaborative, NY Turning Point Initiative, NYS Department of Health, Albany, NY, year?

5. Cusot, Gustavo and Falconi, Gabriela, International Journal of Business and Social Research (IJBSR), Volume -2, No.-2, 2012

6. Fox, Michael P, "Condom Social Marketing: Select Case Studies", Prepared for the Department of Policy, Strategy and Research, UNAIDS, Geneva, Switzerland, 2000.

7. Hoffman, Jeffrey, "Do we have a Water Problem? The Use of Social Marketing as a Problem Solver", American Water Works Association Journal, Denver, Vol. 98, No. 8, August 2006. pp. 34-36.

8. Kotler, Philip, "Strategies for Introducing Marketing into Non-Profit Organizations", Journal of Marketing, American Marketing Association, Chicago, Vol, 33, 1979. Pp37-44.

9. Parthasarathy, Vimala, "Social Marketing Strategies & Traits of Successful NGOs in India - A Strategic Perspective with Reference to Select NGOs in the States of Karnataka & Tamil Nadu, India", doctoral thesis for PhD, approved by Manipal University, Manipal, India, 2013

10. Smith, William, "Social Marketing An Overview", The Center for Global Health Communication and Marketing, Connecticut Ave., Washington D C, 2006.

11. Stead, Martine et al, "Research to Inform the development of a Social Marketing Strategy for Health Improvement in Scotland", Final Report for NHS Health Scotland and the Scottish Executive, University of Stirling, Institute of Social Marketing, Scotland, 2007.

12. Walsh, D. C. et al, "Social Marketing for Public Health", Health Affairs, Project Hope, Bethesda, MD, Vol. 12, No.2, 1993.

13. Weinrich, Nedra Klein, "What is Social Marketing?" *Weinreich Communications,* Issue of the Social Marketing Quarterly, Connecticut Ave., Washington D C.

14. Wiebe G D, "Can Brotherhood be Sold Like Soap?" Publishers Brian Cugelman, 1952

RELATIONSHIPS – KEY TO SUCCESS

Abstract

It may not be an exaggeration to say that NGO activity and mission is all about relationships. It is relationships with government for a conducive environment, with donors for uninterrupted funding, with partners for mutual support for a common cause and with the community to help them for sustainable transformation. Types of relationships, common friction points and how they are being overcome have been covered, though briefly, in this article. Using India as an example, the evolving changes in the government's policy towards the voluntary sector has been traced – from grudging acceptance to a strong mutually reinforcing relationship. Explanations have been supported by a few examples and experiences.

BACKGROUND

The nature of the relationship between government and NGOs varies from country to country ranging from one of mutual distrust to that of harmonious partnership complementing each other according to relative strengths and deficiencies. NGOs get financial and technical assistance from domestic and external funding agencies and philanthropists. The less developed a country the higher are the chances of a large portion of the total fund flow from external sources. With reasonably good supply of funds and technical training reinforced by a relatively higher accountability to funding agencies, many NGOs are able to acquit themselves well in accomplishing set objectives compared to local government bodies entrusted with similar responsibilities. Public agency staff are often not paid as well as those of NGOs and are often saddled with other unrelated responsibilities. All these affect their performance. In such a situation, people of the community look up to the NGO leadership for help and guidance in times of need giving rise to a relationship of mutual trust. Political parties suspect the larger influence of NGO leadership over local populations as a source of rival influence in times of elections to local, state or central bodies. This complex tends to prevail in less developed economies where domestic resources are scarce and poverty is acute.

In such situations, building strong trust and supportive relationship with government bodies at all levels constitutes a challenge to the voluntary sector; without it success can last awhile but cannot be sustained. Competitive popularity will not ensure long term sustained engagement. The type of legislative and policy environment is a reasonably good indicator of the terms upon which the government is willing to work with NGOs in furthering community welfare. Against this background this article will examine types of relationships and prevailing policy provisions compared to needs.

PARTNERSHIP FOR IMPACT

Facilitating a collaboration between the government and NGOs has been identified as one of the characteristics of an enabling policy environment. In this regard, it would be important to first identify areas where the government and voluntary organizations could partner together for joint action. In India, issues such as eradication of poverty, population, education and health are potential areas for collaboration. Joint action must not degenerate into a situation in which the government formulates programs, NGOs merely implementing them. The ends of effective implementation and achievement of desired impact would be well served if the government takes advantage of NGOs' knowledge of the area and its people to involve them actively in framing policies and programs as well as in monitoring and evaluation. Another aspect of collaboration is to identify areas where NGOs and the government may sometimes have to work independent of each other according to their relative strengths in respective subjects or communities in order to create an enhanced total effect. A healthy partnership is based on mutual respect and recognition of the fact that the other partner may have to function independently in some areas.

The impact of NGOs on social development varies in different countries and even within each country. Impact in the country as a whole is dependent on the enabling atmosphere created by the government and the degree of trust it has in the NGO sector's ability to deliver. The impact could sometimes be higher in some segments even when the overall atmosphere is not altogether favorable. The credit for such performance of individual NGOs defying the overall constraints is often due to good leadership. Some individuals heading NGOs and those at the head of local government bodies with which the NGOs have day-to-day relationship, are highly motivated and are, by their dedication and creative initiatives, able to maximize impact within prevailing limitations.

FRICTION POINTS

Due to political polarization an NGO may fall in the opposition camp, while the government or ruling party may see itself as the voice of the people. This could create conflict between the two. NGOs may at times prefer to remain isolated from the government in order to avoid unwanted control over their activities. NGOs can focus on key issues and prioritize them, while the government may want to handle a number of issues at the same time according to political expediency. This could create conflict of priorities and interests. NGOs, which are highly dependent on foreign funding, may be looked upon with suspicion by the government as an opening for foreign agencies to interfere in local affairs.

POLICY SETTING FOR RELATIONSHIP

The ideal policy setting is a non-interventionist environment where legal restrictions are minimized and NGOs have the freedom to select their funding sources and associate with anyone they desire. However, such an environment does not obtain in the real world because it presupposes ideal NGO managements that act strictly within their stipulated mission and have the ability and integrity to put funds provided to them to best possible effect. A favorable policy environment is one which promotes collective growth of NGOs and includes regulations to ensure that funds are being used for the intended purpose. A good balance of regulation and freedom is characterized by the following features.

- Regulations which help growth of NGOs, but at the same time enforce financial discipline and control corruption
- Taxation policies which encourage private philanthropy and NGO's income generating activities for the income to be ploughed in to social development.
- Government's willingness to partner NGOs in special programs
- Recognition of NGOs views in framing policies
- Encouragement to NGOs in priority areas of development through training programs or funds

RELATIONSHIP IS A CRITICAL FACTOR

Raval et al (2007)[7] consider that relationship-based social marketing strategies are more successful than transaction-based strategies in terms of achieving sustainable behavioral change. This is an important feature of social marketing as compared to commercial marketing. Relationship marketing is based on building relationships with stakeholders with the objective of integrating the entire marketing process and bringing about customer loyalty and retention. The authors cite the need for relationship-based marketing, quoting Kotler and Armstrong (1997): "Build good relationships and profitable transactions will follow." Similarly, the authors quote another dictum from Kotler and Armstrong: "Build mutually fruitful relationships with the recipients and stakeholders and desired behaviors will follow." Relationship-based approach to social marketing is necessary and unavoidable for the following reasons.

A relationship-based approach in social marketing makes it more likely that the behavior change will be sustained over the long run. Sustainability of impact is a basic objective in social marketing.

One of the tasks of the social marketer is to try to influence the policy environment, so that it facilitates, rather than hinder social marketing programs.

In order to do this, social marketers need to maintain good relationships with policy makers, regulators and legislators.

Since social marketing programs have a long-term objective, they are likely to be successful only if long term relationships are built with other related organizations.

The theory of exchange is as applicable to social marketing as in commercial marketing and calls for a more intensive human inter-action and, therefore, relationships assume importance.

Given that social marketing's goal is sustainable behavioral change, there is need for continued support and long-term interventions on the part of social marketers. This also calls for constant interaction between providers and customers, or the beneficiaries of the program, through various "touch points". Therefore, it is essential to build enduring and deep relationships with participants and target recipients.

Today, many NGOs and other social organizations operate on a global level and work in different cultural contexts. The nature of relationships vary among different cultures. Cultural anthropologist Edward Hall, (1976), quoted by the authors, distinguishes between relationships in "high context" and "low context" cultures. He argues that in high context cultures, where relationships are individual centered, such relationships tend to be deeper and longer lasting, but take longer to develop than in low context cultures. Social marketers need to be aware of these differences and build relationships accordingly. For example, a social marketer in China needs to be aware of the concept of *guanxi*, which refers to a deep relationship at a personal level that is built over a long term.

RELATIONSHIP TYPES

Raval et al (2007)[7] have categorized different types of relationships. The characteristics of the different types are not mutually exclusive. More than one characteristic may blend with each other according to the demands of the situation and the style of the participants in the partnership.

Process based relationships refer to relationships which are built in four stages – "before, during, after the relationship and in some cases, the dissolution of the relationship". Empathetic and supportive relationships are built based on society's value systems and ideas of what is right and wrong. Love-hate relationships arise out of interdependence between two parties that have opposite goals. For example, two social organizations may compete with each other in trying to bring about behavioral change among the youth, but collaborate to increase government funding for NGOs or to change tax rules. Platonic and dormant relationships are implicit and not readily obvious during normal situations but which surface only during times of crisis. Obligatory or reciprocal relationships are between two parties that are expected to fulfill mutual obligations and reciprocate each other's efforts on legal, cultural or moral grounds. Affinity-based relationships, in the context of social marketing, mean building relationships with affinity groups or groups that can enhance the reach and effectiveness of programs and messages. For example, a social marketer trying to promote the concept of eating a healthy diet could build relationships with grocery stores and food manufacturing companies and persuade them to promote the idea of eating healthy food in their marketing campaigns. Horizontal relationships refer to relationships with peers or those organizations working with similar objectives, activities and clients. Vertical relationships on the other hand are built with the objective of shortening the supply chain and achieving vertical integration. For example, the same NGO could form an alliance with a manufacturer of condoms to obtain the products directly and at less cost. Multiple level relationships mean cultivating relationships at more than one level with customers. Symbiotic relationships refer to those between two parties that depend on each other to achieve their results. Such a relationship benefits both parties. Technology-driven relationships refer to new dimensions to social marketing relationships with the emergence of new technologies such as the internet and data mining.

NGOs IN GOVERNMENT'S PLANS – INDIA EXPERIENCE

In countries like India the country's Five Year Plans are an important source of information on what role the government visualizes for the voluntary sector in the development plans for the economy over a five year period. The Plan document sets out targets for different sectors, estimates the investment and revenue budget costs required to meet targets, identifies the sources of investment, private and public sectors and foreign sources, and estimates the contribution of the different economic and institutional sectors. The policy indications in the Indian Five Year Plans since 1980 are summarized as it may perhaps serve as a guide for other developing countries for defining the role of the NGO sector in a graduated and progressive manner to ensure its organic integration into the macro-economic plan.

The recognition of the role of NGOs by the government dates back to the First Plan document, which mentions their involvement in community and social development. The Sixth Plan (1980-85) visualized useful roles for NGOs in the following areas - optimum utilization and development of renewable source of energy, including forestry, family welfare, health and nutrition, education; "health for all" programs; water management and soil conservation; social welfare programs for weaker sections; implementation of minimum needs program; disaster preparedness and management; promotion of ecology and tribal development; environmental protection and education.

The Seventh Plan enlarged the role in rural development to supplement the efforts of the government. NGOs were expected to "disseminate information, make communities as self-reliant as possible, to show how village and indigenous resources could be used, how human resources, rural skill and local knowledge grossly underutilized at present could be used for their own development..." Involvement of NGOs in development planning and implementation was initiated in the Seventh Plan.

The Eighth Plan focused on building community institutions through voluntary organizations, in areas such as education, health, family planning, more efficient use of land and minor irrigation. These institutions would be accountable to the community.

The Ninth Plan's primary objective was to promote and develop people's participatory bodies through voluntary sector initiatives.

The Tenth Plan[5] emphasizes the importance of including civil society, namely voluntary and non-profit organizations, in the developmental effort. The Tenth Plan evolved a nine-point formula for involving the voluntary sector in community and welfare programs. The most important of these are summarized.

- Involving the NGOs in planning and implementing developmental and welfare schemes
- Helping them develop core competencies and professionalism
- Encouraging the growth of the sector in states where they are weak or where the state machinery is found wanting
- Involving them in designing and evaluating monitorable targets of the Tenth Plan.

The Planning Commission also played an active role in bringing together NGOs, Central and State level Ministry representatives in periodical all India conferences where papers were presented on the problems and prospects of the NGO sector.

It is seen that from Plan to Plan every five years there has been a progressively more meaningful role assigned to the voluntary sector leading to a vision for the sector as outlined in the formula listed above. The step-by-step approach demonstrates how a partnership between the voluntary sector and the government can be built gradually with unfolding experience. The extent to which the voluntary sector had *actually* been assigned these expanding roles, how well it was able to acquit itself and what obstacles were encountered, are interesting aspects for research and evaluation.

LEGISLATIVE ENVIRONMENT

NGOs need to have an understanding of government regulations in order to function effectively and within the boundaries of Law. The government acts as a regulator, whereby the government tries to control NGOs and make them accountable to it, as a funder to ensure that government programs are made efficient and effective.

There is no specific single legislation in India for governing and regulating the conduct of the voluntary sector. An NGO could register under any one of four laws. It can be registered under the Indian Trusts Act, 1882 or the Charitable and Religious Trusts Act, 1920. A Trust is a body which can include three or more members entrusted with the responsibility, on trust, as the name implies, of running and managing the affairs of the institution under them. They are not owners but trustees. The NGO can opt to register as an Association or Society. This form of voluntary organization comprises seven or more members. It may be registered under the Societies Registration Act, 1860 at the state, district or national level. This is by far the best form of an NGO, since it provides for internal democracy and participation, thereby securing the confidence of philanthropic agencies and facilitating fund availability. The NGO could register as a Co-operative under the Co-operative Societies Registration Act, 1962. For this the cooperative must have members with shares who elect the Managing Committee and Chair Person. As a non-profit company NGOs are permitted to register under the Companies Act of 1956. However, on account of the provisions on disclosure and reporting under the Act, NGOs tend to prefer to register under the earlier alternatives.

The perceived disadvantages of the current legislative framework are identified by the expert group with which the author had interviews: (a) the sector is subject to a variety of legal requirements since NGOs do not fall under any one legal entity; (b) new NGOs are at a disadvantage for getting funds, since they are required to be an FCRA (Foreign Contribution Regulation Act) agency for a minimum period of four years; and (c) the regulatory authority is divided as more than one law governs NGOs and as such it is not strong enough to monitor and enforce legal requirements or gather national data on the activities of the Third sector (as the NGO sector is referred to indicating its importance in the economy).

As part of the Study[4] experts in the voluntary sector were subject to in-depth interviews during which their perceptions of the legislative environment in India were explored. With the exception of two respondents, the rest considered that there was no distinguishing legal identity for NGOs engaged in development activities. They are clubbed with various other bodies that are not concerned with social development. There is no national parent body or licensing authority for NGOs. There is no general legal framework that binds NGOs and makes them accountable to a central authority. Only in special cases like watershed development are there MOUs between individual departments of government and NGOs, which confers some identity on the participating NGOs. One of the suggestions is that there should be some unique ID number / registration for NGOs across the states and that their track records should be available for review and reference.

Creation of a single identity would, according to the experts, have the following advantages: avoiding duplication and wastage of scarce funds; improving targeting; a financial and progress reporting system can be enforced; giving opportunity to private-public partnership; establishing accountability to government / district authority / funding agency; and affording scope for identifying successful models for replication or scaling up.

FOREIGN FUNDING OF NGOs

The Foreign Contribution Regulation Act monitors the flow of funds to the voluntary sector. The government's role as a funder began with the Sixth Plan (1980 – 1985). Since then, this role has been rapidly expanding, with the government increasing its funding to NGOs through various Ministries at the Central and State levels.

The regulations in India are indicative of the precautions that governments like to take while encouraging foreign funding of NGOs in the country. Apart from security and drug trafficking considerations, several reports of misuse of funds for religious conversions and similar purposes that run counter to government policies have made it necessary to bring overseas funding under regulation. Ministry of Finance of the Government of India has spelt out the following criteria for foreign funding of NGOs.

- Any country may provide grants directly to NGOs, provided they are meant for projects of economic and social importance only.
- Grants to NGOs will be governed by the Foreign Contribution Regulation Act, 1976 and only those NGOs registered under the Act are eligible to receive assistance from other countries. Those NGOs that are not registered need to get prior permission from the concerned authority under the Act before receiving external funds.
- The recipient NGOs will be required to fill out and submit a prescribed form along with their proposals, to the Department of Economic Affairs (DEA).
- The external development partner country has to provide information to the DEA at a specified time during the year on the amount of funding to various NGOs and the status of projects.
- The partner country may transfer funds directly to the NGOs after approval by the DEA and may also set up their own mechanisms for monitoring the progress of the projects.

A new regulation was passed in 2005 known as the Foreign Contribution (Management and Control) Act which faced resistance from Indian NGOs. It was seen as restricting the functioning of NGOs in several ways. First, NGOs objected to a clause in the Bill which made renewal of the certificate of registration mandatory, once granted – which introduced an element of potential discontinuity in flow of funds. Second, NGOs felt threatened by the clause which granted the registering authority the right to cancel the certificate at any time since this would place them under constant fear of closure. The process of appeal had not been spelt out clearly.

CAPART MODEL

CAPART (Council for Advancement of People's Action and Rural Technology) is an example of a collaborative effort between the Government of India and NGOs. It was set up in 1986 by the Government of India recognizing the need to supplement its own efforts to promote rural development and employment. Since the government's programs were not having the desired impact in rural areas, it was felt that NGOs could play a role in rural development through direct implementation or through interventions around specific issues.

CAPART has initiated programs in rural areas directly through a nodal NGO scheme, i.e. by appointing NGOs in each state and district. Selection of nodal NGOs is done by CAPART, based on the recommendations of the concerned State government. Monitoring, evaluation and selection of NGOs is done directly by CAPART headquarters and its regional offices. Nodal NGOs are expected to ensure adequate follow up of CAPART's various programs in rural areas. This enables the state governments and CAPART to reach the remotest areas and identify those which have not benefitted from these programs. The primary objectives of the nodal NGO scheme are as follows.

- To create a network of development practitioners in each Block and District, so that NGOs have adequate representation at the grassroots level
- To implement projects on a need based and location specific approach
- To provide ready information on implementation and impact of projects in rural areas
- To work in an integrated manner for development of rural areas

The nodal NGOs have to meet CAPART's conditions for financial assistance. They can either implement the programs directly, or by appointing grassroots NGOs, using the resources of the State government, CAPART's and their own experience and knowledge. The previous track record and experience of the grassroots NGO in rural development is an important criterion for selecting and sponsoring NGOs for taking up CAPART sponsored programs.

It is the responsibility of the nodal NGOs to provide adequate marketing and technical knowledge to the grassroots NGOs, facilitate the implementation of projects and resolve the problems faced by the local staff. In addition, they have to report progress on implementation of various schemes to CAPART on a regular basis, provide ready information on the status of projects and be open to monitoring and inspection by CAPART.

On CAPART's side, the major responsibilities include development of a monitoring mechanism, setting up a cell to monitor the information provided by nodal NGOs and appointing an external agency to evaluate the project at 6-month intervals. The diagram of the model shows the role of each entity in the white boxes.

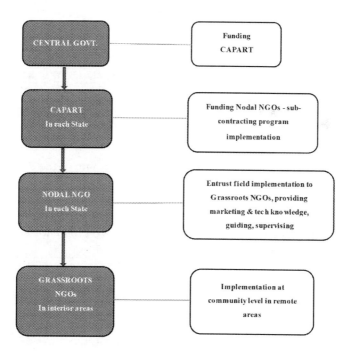

The nodal NGOs implement CAPART's programs in the following priority areas - life skill development, rain water harvesting, sanitation awareness in rural areas, professional scheme for rural youth, primary food and vegetable processing, addressing malnutrition, income generation among the rural poor, promoting computer skills, innovative rural technologies, which address concerns of the rural poor, establishment of village knowledge centers, creation and maintenance of database of NGOs in the Block/District specified.

An outcome of the nodal NGO scheme is a database of NGOs, building a platform for NGOs to share their success stories and problems, and ensuring transparency, sustainability and accountability in project implementation.

From 1993 to 2003 CAPART increased its assistance from ₹ 545 million ($ 11 million) for 4000 NGOs, to ₹ 3 billion ($ 60 million) for over 10,000 NGOs. As an indicator of the vigilance on fund utilization by the beneficiaries it may be mentioned that, for instance in one year alone in 1998, CAPART blacklisted 248 NGOs on grounds of corruption, misuse and false claims.

Operating through nodal NGOs as intermediaries to provide all important inputs, CAPART is a useful model for developing countries. It is an example of how a symbiotic relationship could be built between the voluntary sector and the government. A critical review of the shortcomings and flaws in this model should be taken into consideration, for suitable correction and adaptation, when transplanting this model elsewhere. Here are some of the drawbacks of CAPART.

The over-extended role of the NGO sector in operational decision-making of CAPART is highly problematic in a funding organization. There has been considerable NGO meddling in the functioning of CAPART, indicative of the growing clout of the NGO sector. Equally, the overpowering presence of government at policy and managerial levels has led CAPART to the governmental pattern of functioning affording no room for flexibility and creativity necessary for handling a vast range of development programs spread throughout the country. "Redesign of governance and management structures to rationalize stakeholder participation and include elements of good governance is, therefore, strongly indicated". Procedural lapses, out-of-turn favors, *quid-pro-quos* and frequent changes in top management, as is the practice in government departments, has led to a sense of instability and *ad hoc* decision making.

NGOs' GROWTH

Taking India as a test case, the question is whether the Plan documents envisioning a growing role has enabled the voluntary sector to grow. NGOs did not really take off in a big way until the 1990s, largely due to the earlier attitude of the government taking upon itself the responsibility of providing a range of welfare services expecting NGOs to play only a supplementary role. From the sixth Plan period, as we have noted elsewhere in this paper, government began to realize the ineffectiveness of its "top-down" approach to development and began to collaborate with NGOs on a number of schemes in the areas of rural development, literacy and education. This marked the beginning of the emergence of the voluntary sector.

In terms of sheer numbers, NGOs that are active in rural areas run into thousands covering half of the villages in India. Apart from numbers, Indian NGOs enjoy increased funding, are equipped with professionally qualified and trained workers, people's organizations at the village level and work closely with marginalized groups such as women and backward classes. This vast social infrastructure enables them to provide better services, to encourage the poor to access resources provided by the government and to empower them so that they are in a position to enter village decision-making bodies such as *gram panchayats*.

Rajasekhar believes that Indian NGOs have improved their overall image and are now better equipped to influence government policies at various levels. This, in turn, has led to the government changing its previously hostile attitude to NGOs and in taking into consideration the opinions of prominent NGO leaders in framing policies. This transformation is reflected in the Plan documents and is also evident from the fact that several NGO leaders are represented in key government committees and decision-making bodies.

In such a scenario, NGOs are able to play a pivotal role through policy advocacy, lobbying and mass mobilization of the poor. Opportunity thus exists for different types of NGOs including developmental and advocacy NGOs.

Even after the full-fledged emergence of NGOs, the relationship between the government and the voluntary sector has not been free of problems. Both look upon each other as competitors, with the government trying to exercise undue control over NGOs and NGOs tending to shift the focus of their activities too often, depending on where the funds are available and divert funds meant for social development.

BANGLADESH EXPERIENCE

The Asian Development Bank has played a significant role in recognizing NGOs in Bangladesh as significant players in the development process and cooperates with them in a joint endeavor. As a result NGOs are involved in ADB-financed Loan Projects. ADB has assisted the NGO sector to improve impact, sustainability and quality of its services. Bangladesh, along with Pakistan, boasted the largest number of new loans, ten of them, approved in 2007, involving NGOs and other civil society groups compared to any other ADB member country. ADB maintains an ongoing dialogue with advocacy NGOs interested in the Bank's operations, frequently drawing upon NGO suggestions to improve the effectiveness, quality and sustainability of projects.

Bangladesh NGOs provide value-added services in promoting sustainable development through the following.

- innovation - identifying new approaches and models for specific development activities and drawing upon their close knowledge of local communities
- accountability - helping ensure that project components are implemented as envisaged and planned
- responsiveness - encouraging the implementation of projects to respond to local needs

- participation - serving as bridge between project authorities and affected communities, and providing structures for citizen participation
- sustainability - nurturing continuity in project work.

ADB's resident mission in Dhaka acts as a focal point for relations with NGOs in Bangladesh. The resident mission often organizes roundtable discussions and briefings with NGOs.

The attitude of the Bangladesh government toward the NGO sector, as manifested in its successive Five Year Plans and other official documents, has generally been positive. The government recognizes NGOs' creative role in overcoming gaps in delivering services to communities. NGO service delivery creates competition between government organizations and NGOs thereby addressing issues such as cost-effectiveness, transparency and accountability of the use of public funds.

Palli Karma-Sahayak Foundation (PKSF) established in 1990 is a state-run micro-credit funding institution. It works as an apex microcredit funding and capacity-building organization for eradicating poverty by providing microcredit to poor people through its partner NGOs. In English, the organization's name means "rural employment support foundation". ADB and other major international financial agencies have provided resources to PKSF.

Under the ADB-financed Primary Urban Health Care Project, essential primary health care services were contracted through NGOs or private providers via competitive partnership agreements. The project covered the city corporations of Chittagong, Dhaka, Khulna, and Rajshahi particularly the slums located in populous areas inhabited by poorer city dwellers. Completed in 2005, the project had a significant positive impact on the primary health, family welfare, and nutrition of the urban population, and particularly women and children.

Bangladesh is an example of tripartite cooperation among the NGO sector, the government and international funding agencies.

STUDY FINDINGS

The author's Study[4] based on in-depth understanding of the functioning of ten NGOs in two leading states of the Indian Union throw some interesting light on relationship aspects of social marketing and related aspects. For various traits and sub-traits of NGOs an evaluation was carried out and converted to comparable score values as explained in the chapter on Preface.

The results of the correlation analysis for testing the hypotheses show that many independent variables have a spurious correlation with the components of the dependent variable, namely, marketing effectiveness. Although this is not unexpected - because many of the independent variables are not directly connected with components of the dependent variable, except in select situations – these had to be tested to be able to confirm or reject the assumptions. It also serves the purpose of isolating the *specific* independent variables that have correlation with *specific* components of the dependent variable. With Policy (dependent variable), the only independent variable that has a non-spurious association is Relationship. The responses from the NGOs interviewed during the survey clearly supports this finding, since most of them indicated that cooperative relationship with the government at various levels is necessary for ensuring a favorable policy and functioning environment.

The same is true of Relationship having a non–spurious correlation with Publics (Stakeholders). Good relationship should lead to stakeholder involvement (Publics). Relationship-based social marketing has been heavily emphasized in expert and scholarly articles as elaborated in the Literature review, in contrast to transaction-based functioning.

The correlation analysis indicates that Relationship as well as Funds (independent variables) have a meaningful correlation with Program (dependent variable). Study of the sample NGOs indeed goes to show that these two factors have played a part in influencing the effectiveness of Programs.

Relationship also has a non-spurious correlation with Partnership (Networking). Striking strategic alliances and fostering and maintaining them are important tasks for successful social marketing, which can be accomplished only with leadership, quality management and sound relationships. The observation ratings of NGOs in the sample show that in most cases where leadership gets a high rating networking has also received high scores.

Overall, Relationship, Funds, Type of Leadership and Quality of Management have emerged as independent variables that have non-spurious correlations with one or more of the seven components of the dependent variable – Relationship being the most prevalent factor.

Having said that Relationship is the most prevalently significant factor among the independent variables influencing the effectiveness of the NGO, we may examine the level of commitment to this factor in the selected sample. In order to judge the values and interpret them, a grading scale based on a popularly accepted model was adopted as follows – 35% or less is poor, 36-50% is moderate, 51-60% is satisfactory, 61-75% is good and above 75% is very good. A fuller explanation of the evaluation procedures is in the Preface.

Government Relations: From the evaluation of the selected NGOs it is observed that the combined overall score for all aspects of Policy (government relations) is 81%, which falls in the highest category of 'very good'. The collective score on the first sub-trait (of Policy) for interactions with the government is a full 100%, indicating that so far as relations with government is concerned all of them pay full attention to this aspect. The collective scores on the other sub-traits – frequency of interactions, relationship at more than one level of government and having cooperative relations - are also in the upper end of the very good category (97%, 83% and 90% respectively). The relationship with the government in a majority of cases is of a cooperative nature. In a few cases it was pointed out that the relationship was largely governed by the nature of the issue and the individuals in office on the government side.

Stakeholder Relations: Stakeholders include donors, lenders and community. The combined overall score of all NGOs for all aspects of Publics (stakeholder relations) is 68%, which falls in the 'good' category. While the collective scores on the sub-traits of being in touch with stakeholders "constantly" and coordinating with them actively falls in the 'very good' range with 93% and 78% respectively, the score on the other sub-trait – keeping stakeholders informed of program aspects – is just about 'satisfactory' at 51%. It seems to indicate that while the NGOs are in touch with stakeholders there is room for greater accountability to them in the form of formal periodic progress reports comparing actual progress with targets measured quantitatively as far as possible.

Partner Relations (Networking and Alliances): The combined overall score of all NGOs for all aspects of Partnership (relations with network and alliances) is 64%, which falls in the 'good' category. The combined overall score of all NGOs for the sub-traits - having networking/alliances, such arrangements aiming at enhancing marketing effectiveness, the basis for such arrangements being one of active cooperation, using a participatory approach in working with the community, having a flat management structure to promote internal participation and formulating plans iteratively with the community - fall under different categories of effectiveness. Participatory approach in dealing with the community and iterative planning with the community, register scores as high as 93% and 90% respectively, which are in the upper end of the 'very good' range. However, the scores relating to alliances for marketing effectiveness and which are based on active cooperation are only at the 'moderate' level (40% and 50% respectively), below even the satisfactory level. Having a flat management structure and having a network/alliance register scores in the 'satisfactory' category (60% and 60% respectively).

The indication seems to be that stronger marketing alliances are needed to supplement and strengthen the NGOs' own skills. Existing alliances/networks/ partnerships seem to need a relationship of much closer coordination and cooperation.

The author's research indicates that while relations with government were good there was room for better reporting and higher accountability towards stakeholders and for stronger networking and strategic alliances.

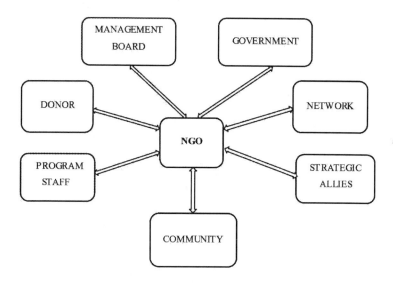

RELATIONSHIP – EXAMPLES FROM STUDY[4]

The NGO based in Tumkur district, Karnataka, India covers 2500 villages of Tumkur District, 35 wards under Tumkur Urban, 35 wards of Bangalore Urban, Hassan District and Kolar District. The main activity is women's empowerment through the formation of Self Help Groups (SHGs), the primary target being below-poverty-line (BPL) women in villages and towns. The management is in touch with the state government, district authorities and local government bodies at the community level on a regular basis and the relationship with the government was co-operative and one of mutual support. They also mentioned having strategic partnerships with different government departments for the purpose of rural development. Regarding other stakeholders, management was of the opinion that the three stakeholders most important for their operations were the target community, community based organizations and community opinion leaders. The interaction with funding benefactors was once in three months and their relationship with neighboring NGOs operating in the same area/activity was described as one of active cooperation towards common goals.

The NGO based in Chennai engaged in training implementing NGOs receives funding from several domestic and international donors such as UNICEF, USAID, the MacArthur Foundation, the Gates Foundation, the State and Central Governments of India and the corporate sector. Their activities include both social service and social marketing. Their social marketing activities include empowerment of disadvantaged segments, work among HIV affected segments, creating awareness of right sexual habits and other health related issues, promoting community management of common resources, delivery of special products/services for community health improvement, promoting change of habits and behavior relating to social, health or environmental concerns and advocacy. In the choice of theme for their major projects, designing and implementation of their programs, there is consultation with state/central government, local government bodies, community leaders, the general community, donors, mother NGO and internal management, including field staff. Management said that they were in touch with the target community on a daily basis. The management interacted with the government once a month and were in touch with all levels of the government – state, district, local and central and that the relationship was co-operative, supporting each other mutually. The management ranks stakeholders in order of importance as follows – 1) government 2) Donors 3) Target community followed by others. Management also interacted with funding agencies once a month and relationship with neighboring NGOs operating in the same activity/area was one of active co-operation towards common goals. Management was of the opinion that such a relationship was essential for NGOs' growth.

FUTURE OF INDIAN NGOs

Based on various studies carried out among a number of Indian NGOs Rajasekhar (2000)[6] considers that the biggest opportunity for Indian NGOs is to play a central role in participating in community development filling the space provided by the government's inability to fully cope with the problem of unemployment and poverty even after several decades of efforts in this direction. In spite of economic reforms and liberalization policies, poverty continues to be a problem. NGOs have the opportunity to play a pivotal role through policy advocacy opening the door for both developmental and advocacy NGOs.

The challenge lies, according to Rajasekhar, in playing a dual role in dealing with the government. On the one hand, NGOs need to collaborate with the government on development schemes and on the other they have to advocate policies that are pro-poor. To play this dual role effectively, Rajasekhar suggests that NGOs should become self-reliant generating their own resources, instead of depending on outside sources of funding.

Development and advocacy efforts require large monetary and technical resources and the NGO sector, particularly NGOs operating at the community level, do not have such resources nor the opportunity generate them as they are not paid for their services by the beneficiaries. The sector's dependence is not limited to funds. The author's Study[4] indicates that what NGOs need even more urgently is capacity building through technical assistance, training, consultancy (for research and impact monitoring and measurement systems) and equipment. The most valuable input that grassroots NGOs can bring to the table is their intimate knowledge of local needs, aspirations and culture, their emotional proximity to the community members and dedication to the cause. These cannot be supplied by outside sources. It seems that relationships that bind the NGO structure should not be considered in terms of dependence but as one of inter-dependence and synergy. Instead of chasing the mirage of financial self-reliance smaller NGOs should strengthen their institutional capacity and reliability and maintain a holistic relationship with the communities they serve. Such values will be sought after by apex NGOs and funding agencies.

REFERENCES

1. Asian Development Bank, "Civil Society Briefs – Bangladesh", 2008
2. Minutes of the First Meeting of the Tenth Five-Year Plan (2002-07) - Steering Committee, on "Voluntary Sector", Government of India, Planning Commission, March 16, 2001.

3. National Policy on Voluntary Sector, Voluntary Action Cell, Planning Commission, Government of India, 2007.

4. Parthasarathy, Vimala, "Social Marketing Strategies & Traits of Successful NGOs in India - A Strategic Perspective with Reference to Select NGOs in the States of Karnataka & Tamil Nadu, India", doctoral thesis for PhD, approved by Manipal University, Manipal, India, 2013

5. Planning Commission, Approach Paper to the Tenth Five Year Plan (2002-2007), Planning Commission, Government of India.

6. Rajasekhar, D, "Non-Governmental Organizations in India: Opportunities and Challenges", Institute for Social and Economic Change, Bangalore, Working Paper No. 66, 2000.

7. Raval, Dinker et al, "Application of the Relationship Paradigm to Social Marketing", Competition Forum. Indiana, Vol. 5, No. 1, 2007. pp. 1- 8.

8. Report of the Steering Committee on Voluntary Sector for the Tenth Five-Year Plan (2002-07), Planning Commission, Government of India.

WEAK ACCOUNTABILITY RETARDS
GROWTH OF THE VOLUNTARY SECTOR

Abstract

Accountability in a NGO is more complex than it appears at first look. It has several dimensions – financial, technical, institutional, marketing and in terms of impact. There are several stakeholders towards whom accountability flows – donors, strategic partners, networking allies, government, beneficiary group and community. What is to be accounted for in respect of each is a different aspect of the NGO's operation. How to keep accountability from getting overdone, constricting managerial space for creativity and a say on project design and implementation is also an important consideration. A natural inclination for benefactors is to ensure that the assistance extended is well spent and in that anxiety they may tend to overwork accountability obligations to the point of expecting too many details, and too many reports too frequently. The situation is compounded if there is more than one funding source. Standardization, simplification and reporting by exception would be mutually beneficial – to the funding agencies and the recipients. In general, there is not enough accountability downwards. Ultimately, however, there can be no compromise on the need for transparency and integrity in the functioning of the NGO to impart confidence to stakeholders – especially the donors.

SIGNIFICANCE OF ACCOUNTABILITY

NGOs, like all organizations, are answerable to their stakeholders to merit continued support to sustain their activities and accomplish their mission year after year. Accountability is another word for answerability. Accountability, in a narrow sense, might suggest that responsibility ceases once the recipient of support in cash or kind has shown that it has been utilized partially or fully and has shown the unutilized balance. It carries the connotation of being limited to each transaction whereas organizations like NGOs are continuously in the process of receiving support in various forms – funds, equipment, training, technical assistance - and are expected to utilize them for achieving pre-defined social objectives. The term accountability could lend itself to the interpretation that it *only* has to show that the NGO has spent it in part or full and *not* how well it has been spent. The reality is that lenders of support want to know that it has been used as agreed and that it has had the desired effect. In other words, the recipient NGO should account for the output as well as the outcome. An example could be that a hundred training camps have been conducted and condoms have been supplied - representing the output. The output is meant to produce an outcome. The number of people adopting the practice is the impact or outcome. These are the quantitative and qualitative dimensions of accountability – the *effort* dimension and the *result* dimension. Another possible misunderstanding is that accountability is *only* to account for support received in the form of funds. Support could be as equipment, material, expert staff, technical assistance, vehicles or even intangibles like a favorable legal or policy environment. This understanding widens the definition of stakeholders to whom the NGO becomes accountable. Donors are increasingly looking for results and value for money before financing projects and this places the burden of accountability on NGOs and planners. In summary, accountability is not transaction-centric but relationship-centric; it is both in terms of utilization and the result obtained; being a response to all forms of support it is accountable to all its stakeholders thereby having the responsibility to identify its stakeholders and their stake.

DEFINITIONS OF ACCOUNTABILITY

Set against the fore-going parameters of accountability we may look at various definitions of accountability offered by scholars. In the Development Dossier on "Debating NGO Accountability" produced by the UN Non-Governmental Liaison Service, Bendell (2006)[2] says that NGO accountability must be understood in the broader context of democratic accountability. He describes the latter as a form of accountability that involves the entire society and not just individual organizations. More specifically, democratic accountability is "the quality of being accountable to those with less power who are affected by one's actions or decisions." In other words, NGOs must be accountable to those they affect who are less powerful. A question that, naturally, arises is whether by insisting upon accountability towards the *entire* society we are running the risk of spreading it so wide and thin that it may degenerate into a ritualistic accountability to many as opposed to a meaningful accountability to the critical few.

Another definition of accountability has been put forth by Brown and Moore (2001)[1]. Since accountability involves "a promise to perform", it may be defined as "a relationship between two or more actors". This definition implies accountability to several parties – (a) donors or funding sources for the effective and appropriate use of funds; (b) beneficiaries for the effective delivery of services; (c) staff for enabling them to perform their roles in fulfilment of the organization's objectives; (d) partners for keeping commitments made while developing and executing joint projects; and (e) to the government for keeping in concert with its policies.

Williams (Financial Times, 2005)[11] has laid stress on the governance and transparency aspects of accountability among NGOs. He believes that only the large international NGOs currently conform to international standards of financial management, record keeping and auditing. The smaller NGOs need to improve their standards of governance. The author gives NGOs a low rating compared with intergovernmental and UN bodies such as the UNHCR, WTO and the World Bank. This is based on the results of a survey (2005) conducted among international NGOs, intergovernmental bodies, MNCs and public sector companies worldwide. NGOs were found to provide inadequate information to their stakeholders and the public. For sound management practices and governance standards to percolate down to the smaller NGOs, systems, practices and disciplines need to be simplified, adapted and made understandable.

TO WHOM IS THE NGO ACCOUNTABLE?

Edwards and Hulme (2007)[4] define accountability as "the means by which individuals and organizations report to a recognized authority and are held responsible for their actions." It seems confined to one single "authority" whereas most organizations have several entities that have invested a stake in them in some form or the other in expectation of achievement from which they derive a material benefit or an intangible sense of fulfilment. In a way, it would be ideal if the NGO were to have a single authority to whom they can be held accountable whereas they are accountable to donors – often several – partners, local government bodies, state government and community. When there are several sources of funding, the periodicity, content, format and method of reporting are different for each stakeholder making it difficult particularly for grass-root or district level NGOs to comply with accountability obligations. Often they are not familiar with sophisticated reporting requirements. When commercial organizations borrow sums that are large enough for more than one bank to share the lending, the lenders from a consortium and the borrower is held accountable to the lead institution of the consortium. This not only makes accountability easier for the borrower but also secures the lenders' interests by ensuring that the borrower does not play off one bank against the other. Unfortunately, a system of donor consortium is not feasible as the NGO projects are for relatively small sums compared to the size of corporate borrowings. But "mother" NGOs specializing in funding smaller NGOs engaged in project implementation can indeed play the role of a consortium and as a single window source of financing making accountability effective and simple. Funding NGOs are, in that respect, a much better way of routing funds from individual and corporate philanthropists for community development projects whereby those giving the funds could delegate the responsibility of project evaluation or accountability to NGOs specializing in multi-functional supervision.

Currently, an NGO's accountability runs in different directions – downward accountability to beneficiaries and grassroots constituents, upward accountability to donors and the government, lateral accountability to partners, internal accountability to staff and volunteers or external accountability to the community.

The workshop held on the "The Future of Civil Society Accountability", held at the World Social Forum, at Porto Alegre, Brazil, organized by Hauser Center for Non-Profit Organizations, January 30, 2005 (Workshop Report - 2005)[12] defined NGO accountability by distinguishing between internal and external accountability. Internal accountability refers to the accountability to staff of the organization and is a measure of the degree of internal democracy of the organization. Developing internal accountability includes building leadership within the organization. Internal leadership needs to be trained at different levels in terms of acceptance of responsibility, tactical planning, implementation, mid-course corrections, periodic feedback and seeking guidance at critical stages.

DOES ACCOUNTABILITY IMPINGE ON AUTONOMY?

As NGOs are dependent on assistance from outside agencies, their accountability to those who have provided it with resources in several forms, namely, funds, infrastructure, technical assistance, vehicles, equipment etc. tends to be predominant over other accountabilities. They are accountable for two major aspects – one, in the sense of accounting for resources received and spent and two, how effectively the resources produced impact with reference to objectives stated in terms of social change. Accountability is the basis for assessing the reliability of NGOs in order to determine whether they merit continued assistance. In that sense, the nature and type of accountability systems and internal monitoring mechanisms not only form an important part of the NGO organization structure, but are also essential to ensure organizational sustainability.

Observations in the debate on accountability versus autonomy are interesting for the reason that they throw light on the degree of accountability necessary and practicable without restricting managerial space for effective and timely action. Misra (2008)[8] defines organizational autonomy as "freedom to make decisions with the optimal degree of discretion." In the context of the Third World, Misra is of the opinion that NGO accountability should be downwards, but that autonomy should be with respect to upward relationships. He suggests the following "keys to autonomy" of NGOs. First, there must be a clear organizational commitment to the idea of the NGO's autonomy. Secondly, NGOs must have financial support from multiple sources, so that they are not dependent on any single donor for funding. On this aspect, one may, argue that multiple funding may be a safeguard against major dislocation but the consequent answerability to multiple sources with conflicting demands may affect managerial effectiveness and may also give scope for misuse of public funds for want of a single source of supervision of fund usage. Thirdly, NGOs must develop grassroots organizations. Autonomy is enhanced by in-house technical expertise, managerial excellence and strategic knowledge about development.

Accountability and autonomy often provide the basis for grievance and friction between the benefactor and the beneficiary organizations. The latter argues that accountability is constraining their decision making freedom and ability to respond speedily to changing field situations. The former justifies, for example, the periodicity and content of reporting formats as a means of ensuring that unmonitored managerial freedom does not lead to inefficiency and/or misuse. It is not a question of choosing one or the other – accountability or autonomy. Both the concepts are valid and needed; but they need to be balanced since too much of one is bad for the other, affecting organizational effectiveness. They are not antithetical as they may seem. They are incompatible if the brake and the accelerator in an automobile are considered incompatible. The presence of the brake facilitates safe acceleration and speed. Accountability and autonomy thus provide the organization the necessary check and balance to make for stability and growth. A balance between rigid accountability and total autonomy has to be achieved.

In the case of private corporations, there is a clear ownership of the corporation by the stockholders on the one side and the management responsible for delivering results on the other side, strengthened in this relationship by the fact that the latter's salaries are paid by the owners. Reward and punishment are possible. The management is accountable to the General Body of stockholders and in the management the CEO, COO and CFO are held responsible if the outcome does not meet expected standards. In the case of an NGO there is no owner who can crack the whip to demand "performance or else!" At best the donor can stop the fund flow. Donors and funding agencies give grants and are not owners. The promoter of the NGO is dependent on donors for running the show but is not the owner. While the promoter can sack his staff for non-performance, the promoter himself/herself is not so easily sacked. It is only the donors collectively that can enforce accountability by threatening to stop funding. The other stakeholder who can intervene forcefully is the government that can withdraw recognition under the concerned law but the wheels of government grind slow and more so in developing countries. In a government regulated environment punishment for misconduct or recognition for good work comes long after the occurrence of the cause. In the commercial world by changing the management or the concerned officer, the corporation can be put back on track and in this process ownership continues while the management changes. It is not so in NGOs which do not have a continuing, supporting and committed entity based on ownership stake. As such, enforceability through accountability is not a sufficiently strong mechanism in the voluntary sector. By its nature, the success or failure of an NGO ultimately depends on the integrity and dedication of the promoter-leader. Leadership is critical for NGOs and this came out clearly in the author's research findings.

REGULATION AND ACCOUNTABILITY

NGOs in India are open to register themselves under any one of the following Acts of the government – The Indian Trusts Act of 1882, The Societies Registration Act of 1882, The Cooperative Societies Registration Act of 1962 or The Companies Act of 1956. The Trust Act is meant to define the relationship between the Trustees and the beneficiary/beneficiaries. Under clause 19 the beneficiaries can call for an account of the "amount and state of the property". As any NGO invariably has a large number of beneficiaries it is difficult for them to take concerted action to call the management of the NGO to account. The Societies Act is meant for literary clubs and such cultural organizations. The Cooperative Societies Act envisages a body of subscribing membership primarily meant for village cooperatives of farmers for collective procurement, marketing and processing of produce or for dispensing seasonal farm credit. The Registrar of societies has powers to inspect the books upon receipt of complaints. The Companies Act is meant for corporates where accountability is established through a General Body of stockholders who are the owners and the management.

The Foreign Contribution Regulation Act (FCRA) was established with a view to control the foreign funding received by Indian NGOs. All NGOs depending on foreign funds are subject to government surveillance by the Home Ministry. The object of this piece of legislation is to ensure that foreign funds are not diverted to drug trafficking, gun running or for religious conversions. Inefficiencies and fraudulent practices in use of money are outside the scope of this legislation.

NGOs that have been successful in attracting foreign funds have not been able to effectively communicate the message that the funds are being used for laudable causes. As a consequence, the public is not only ignorant about the work being done by these NGOs, but also has an image that these NGOs are wasteful and extravagant in their expenditure and that they use funds for extraneous purposes.

Thus it is seen that none of these legislations provide a good fit for the structure and needs of an NGO. By offering different options to NGOs for a legal status, accountability towards government and the public has become weak. NGOs have become important players in the development of the economy and are large in number as well as by the volume of funds routed through them for community development. Their current status warrants the enactment of a special legislation to govern the structure and conduct of affairs of the voluntary sector in social development.

The laws governing the functioning of NGOs are an important instrument available to the government to enforce accountability. However, the usefulness of this instrument is largely confined to cases of fraud or diversion of funds. In actual practice this is further restricted to extraordinary cases of misdemeanor often after much public outcry and publicity. The government is neither legally equipped nor is it suited to act in cases of inefficient use of funds or failure to achieve objectives with the resources entrusted to the NGO.

Transparency in dealings and decisions is demonstration of accountability. The person affected by a decision/action and the person the use of whose resource is involved should know the rationale and implications of the decision/action. Vaidyanathan (Business Line, 2005)[10] says that the time has come for greater transparency from the "third sector" of the Indian economy. Today, the third sector (NGO sector or the voluntary sector) is as significant to the economy as the first sector (government) and the second sector (corporate sector) in terms of size, resources and capacity for impact. Hence he feels that it is only fair that the third sector should also show the same degree of transparency, by disclosing their practices and the manner in which their funds are being used.

RECIPROCITY OF ACOUNTABILITY

Accountability is reciprocal especially in the voluntary sector. An example is in the relationship between the donor and the NGO. Once the objective is agreed upon the donors ensure smooth timely fund flow and the NGO, in turn, is responsible for cost-effective use of funds and to ensure that the objectives are met. Thus there is a mutuality in the stakeholders-NGO relationship of accountability. This is summarized in the following Table adapting the model designed by Keating and Frumkin (2000)[7] Here the NGO management is the implementing stakeholder on the one side and all the other stakeholders on the other side.

Stakeholder	Stakeholder's perception of accountability from NGO Management	NGO Management's perception of accountability from stakeholders
Donor	Effective use of funds and non-fund resources to achieve agreed objectives - ensuring there is no diversion – "free of cost" or "prescribed basis of pricing" for services is adhered to – ensure sustainability of impact in the post-project phase – sound leadership from the Promoter	Timely provision of adequate resources free of complex/time consuming formalities – adequate managerial freedom
Government	Monitoring for ensuring that funds are not used for non-authorized purposes – ensuring that there is no incompatibility with public policies and schemes	Single reporting authority – providing a facilitating policy and legal environment – tax exemption for generated surpluses if they are ploughed back into social projects
Target Beneficiaries	Voice in designing the Program – program contents are culturally compatible – make adoption of new behavior worth the change – timely and proper quality of delivery of services - adequate number and frequency of contacts	Full and collective cooperation in attending group meetings and training sessions – help of opinion leaders and persuaders – providing info on adoption rate and on hurdles –providing community support by way of effort and material
Strategic Partners	Performing respective roles – free exchange of information, data, experiences – coordinating implementation – work towards long term relationship – present a unified face before public, beneficiaries and other stakeholders	Pro-active support to achieve agreed objectives – understanding and support tin times of stress
Field and executive staff	Training to handle the "marketing" – adequate support facilities and tools – participation in designing the program – realism in objectives and targets	Timely reporting and feedback – observance of systems – integrity in use of time and resources – commitment to achieve objectives
NGO Promoter	Dedication and integrity from the management – cooperation and understanding from donors	Providing leadership – maintenance of relationships with donors, partners and government

The Table maps out the mutual accountability among the stakeholders of an NGO. A reciprocal and inter-related pattern of accountability among the management and the stakeholders towards each other considerably enhances the effective functioning of NGOs. Each participant performing its role responsibly in achieving the common objective is accountability to the common cause.

RECOMMENDED PRACTICES FOR ACCOUNTABILITY

In the course of the in-depth interviews with experts it was suggested that transparency on fund deployment, maintenance of proper records, annual reports and reports of program progress with monitoring data and involvement of stakeholder in decision making are sound practices for ensuring a high standard of accountability.

Resources should be used effectively to produce the desired effect. This calls for periodic observation of the impact on the beneficiary and timely modification of strategies

The fact that resources are well used should be communicated to stakeholders systematically, supported by quantitative data and at agreed periodicity. Contact at other times, if there is a major problem, should not be shunned. Reports should present a balanced picture mentioning in particular likely obstacles and problems, how they would be overcome and what additional assistance may be needed. Reports should be terse, quantitative as far as possible and supported by pictures wherever it would be useful for better understanding.

Accountability is the means by which the stakeholder feels reassured that things are going well according to or close to the plan. Poor governance cannot be covered by honest accountability. Good performance is necessary.

The institution's reputation of being a good deliverer of services and user of scarce resources should be built and projected. Image can be built only on the foundation of good performance. Good advertisement does not sell a bad product nor a good product sell without communicating its goodness.

Good governance can be established by applying principles and practices of social marketing.

Performance measurement is necessary to give meaning to accountability. Generalities in accountability are of little use to the stakeholder. Accountability based on good performance ensures continuity of support. Continuous and timely flow of resources is critical for sustainability of the organization and its impact on society. A good deliverer of services sustained over the years acquires an image and is sought after. Public relations should be used as a tool to build that image and, of course, continued sound performance is necessary to sustain that image.

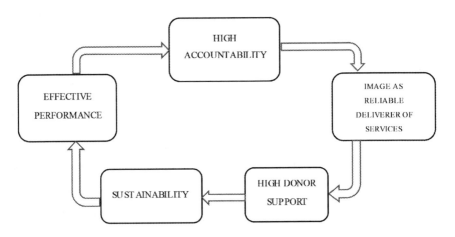

RULES OF GOVERNANCE

As seen in the earlier section, good governance is a core necessity to sustain the NGO and its mission. Drucker, Peter (1990)[3] suggests "do's and don'ts" of managing performance in non-profit organizations. The most important rule is to focus on information and communication, rather than build an organizational hierarchy. If information is freely available and flows without delay, he sees a flat organizational structure as being more suitable for non- profits than a multi-layered structure. Other guidelines recommended by Drucker for non-profits such as building mutual trust, clarity of relationships and establishing mutually understood goals and deadlines are strikingly similar to those that any marketing organization that wants to be successful would want to adopt.

He emphasizes the importance of setting clearly understood, high performance standards and realistic goals. Only if goals and standards are clearly established can the quality of performance be adjudged and accountability demanded from those entrusted with tasks.

Performance and accountability are on one side of the coin. On the other side is a constant flow of information and images that strengthen the stakeholders' perception of the NGO. This calls for "image marketing". Image maintenance with donors is in effect "backward marketing" analogous to backward integration in business. Effective performance and periodic accountability are the equivalent of a good "product" in commercial terms and image building of the NGO is like advertising that "product" to the prospective buyer, the donor. To the voluntary sector, its very existence and sustainability is dependent on its image with prospective funding agencies.

REASONS FOR WEAK ACCOUNTABILITY

While weak accountability in the voluntary sector could affect fund flow and threaten its continued growth, it is necessary to examine the underlying reasons for this weakness. Multiple demands of accountability, complex and varying reporting formats prescribed by different stakeholders, lack of clarity in defining goal posts, insufficient training on performance measurement and weak internal management processes are hurdles to be removed to make accountability a spontaneous and meaningful function and a useful indicator of progress to guide management decisions.

The Study[9] shows that emphasis seems to be more on upward accountability, while downward accountability to the beneficiaries seems to be inadequate. Even in the case of upward accountability, while it is adequate in terms of number of reports, timeliness etc., the standard of presentation offers much scope for improvement - making it quantitative, more comparative with targets and benchmarks, more transparent, more focused on impact (outcome) and more objective covering aspects such as cost-effectiveness and goal achievements/ failures.

EXAMPLES FROM STUDY[9]

A rural development NGO in Karnataka (Agricultural Development & Training Society) has as its main activity empowerment of the working class by building a people's organization, the *Coolie Sangha*, at the village, cluster and taluk levels. The Coolie Sangha Units (CSUs) are membership based organizations comprising small and poor peasant families of agricultural labor, migrant workers, self-employed artisans and small farmers. They have a socio-political presence in 31% of the villages that comprise Chickballapur district, covering 18% of the population in 5 taluks, Karnataka state, India. Their population coverage with functioning Coolie Sangha Units is as high as 33%. According to the management, the most innovative feature of their programs was the Carbon Device Mechanism (CDM), a new concept created by ADATS and implemented through biogas, afforestation and woodstoves. They have completed two projects in the last three years, while six projects were currently in progress. Regarding the issue of accountability, the management named the following stakeholders whom they kept informed about the organization's performance and results – Board of Trustees/Board of Management, their staff and their main funding agencies. The procedures that they had for reporting to these stakeholders included regular meetings in the form or reporting meetings every Monday and monitoring reports or Management Information Systems (MIS). Various reports and monitoring studies are available on their website detailing activities, progress, income, expenditure (project-wise) reflecting high degree of transparency.

DEEPAM's (Deepam Educational Society for Health, Tamil Nadu, India) keeps the following stakeholders informed about the organization's performance and results – Board of trustees/Board of Management, their staff, the main funding agencies and government/local bodies. The procedures they had for reporting to these stakeholders included management information systems for all projects, with each donor having their own format, annual and quarterly reports, annual general meeting for the Board and monthly review meetings for the staff during which they identified gaps and engaged in problem solving.

OVERVIEW OF ACCOUNTABILITY ISSUES

Accountability is not only for efficiency but also for effectiveness, that is, to present that outputs have been delivered according to plan and that outcome has been achieved as expected. Mutual accountability is a key element of the aid effectiveness agenda reflected in the Paris Declaration, Accra Agenda for Action and Busan Partnership for Effective Development Co-operation. In the case of the NGO sector in which services are delivered with the help of funders and others extending technical assistance, training and equipment and within a pro-active policy environment provided by the government accountability is a two-way obligation. An example could be that donors in return for good service rendered by the NGO, are accountable for timely and adequate release of funds free of excessive documentation, procedures and legal sophistications. The mutuality aspect of accountability is illustrated in the Table in the earlier part of this article. As there are many stakeholders in a NGO accountability, reporting could become onerous and complicated. Reports limited to presenting only critical numbers and highlighting only exceptions could help to simplify accountability leaving enough space for managerial freedom. The absence of meaningful regulations on NGOs has also led to poor standards of transparency and accountability, affecting their fund raising capacity. In such a scenario, only a few NGOs with a sound reputation and track record are able to attract funds.

Finally, indispensable pre-requisites for accountability are clear objectives, good performance, output-outcome performance measurement system and sound communication,.

REFERENCES

1. Brown, David L and Moore, Mark H, "Accountability, Strategy and International Non-governmental Organizations", The Hauser Center for Non-Profit Organizations and the Kennedy School of Government, Harvard University, Working Paper No. 7, 2001.

2. Bendell, Jim, "Debating NGO Accountability", Published by UN Non-Governmental Liaison (NGLS), Geneva, Switzerland, 2006.

3. Drucker, Peter, "Managing the Non-Profit Organization", Harper Collins Publishers, 1990.

4. Edwards, Michael and Hulme, David, "NGO Performance and Accountability: Introduction and Overview", The Earthscan Reader on NGO Management, Edited by Michael Edwards and Alan

5. Fowler, Earthscan India, Daryaganj, New Delhi, 2007.

6. Eighth V Year Plan Chapter 6, NGOs and their networks, Planning Commission, Government of India.

7. Keating, Elizabeth K and Frumkin, Peter, "Reengineering Non-Profit Financial Accountability: Toward a More Reliable Foundation for Regulation", The Hauser Center for Non-Profit Organizations and the Kennedy School of Government, Harvard University, Working Paper No. 4, 2000.

8. Misra, Rajeeb, "Voluntary Sector and Rural Development", Rawat Publications, Jaipur, 2008.

9. Parthasarathy, Vimala, "Social Marketing Strategies & Traits of Successful NGOs in India - A Strategic Perspective with Reference to Select NGOs in the States of Karnataka & Tamil Nadu, India", doctoral thesis for PhD, approved by Manipal University, Manipal, India, 2013

10. Vaidyanathan, R, "NGOs: To Whom are they Accountable?" Business Line April 21, 2005.

11. Williams, Francis, "Audit Culture Learns from Corporations", Financial Times, London, May, 2005

12. Workshop Report, "The Future of Civil Society Accountability", Workshop held at the World Social Forum, at Porto Alegre, Brazil, organized by Hauser Center for Non-Profit Organizations, January 30, 2005.

VOLUNTARY ORGANIZATIONS SHOULD PASS THE SUSTAINABILITY TEST

Abstract

The ultimate test of the success of an organization, the NGO, lies in its durability and continuity fulfilling its objectives year after year and creating a lasting impact on the community in accordance with its vision. Sustainability is not mere continuity and survival. The many dimensions of sustainability are explained followed up with suggestions of possible strategies for ensuring and maintaining financial, technical, programmatic, institutional and impact aspects of sustainability. Experiences of sustainability in other countries and illustration of the practices of NGOs studied by the author are described. It concludes that the organization's sustainability is dependent upon the caliber of leadership and that sustainability is an on-going process and not a static destination.

INTRODUCTION

The successful establishment of an NGO is reflected in its durability as an organization and the permanence of its impact on the client group/community it has chosen to serve. Sustainability is how biological systems endure and remain diverse and productive. The concept of sustainability has assumed much importance because of irresponsible use of scarce, exhaustible natural resources to support rising living standards. It takes an organization, small or big, effort, skill and money to build and equip itself to be able to fulfill certain objectives and cannot afford to exhaust itself to extinction upon completion of one project or one cycle of performance. As time passes, with repeated performance, it acquires special expertise in its field of operation. A valuable social institutional asset like this cannot be allowed to wither away. Although outside support is needed in the form of resources and technical assistance, the initiative and responsibility for securing that support lies with the leadership of the NGO.

DEFINITIONS OF SUSTAINABILITY

The word sustainability is derived from the Latin *sustinere* (*tenere*, to hold; *sus*, up). *Sustain* can mean *maintain*, *support*, or *endure*. Durability through ability to support itself for continuous effective action year after year, program after program, makes an organization sustainable. Durability calls for endurance of stresses and strains and capacity to survive internal and external challenges without loss of strength. The resources to overcome hurdles while retaining the capacity to pursue its mission over time are derived from external sources as well as from internally-generated human resources, innovations, skills and initiatives. The greater this capacity is derived from internal sources the higher is the sustainability. One living on ventilator support is not the same as a person living by his own ability to breathe. External supports like pain relievers, vitamins, oxygen, and expert surgical intervention are necessary but the basic health must be good. The degree of self-reliance in respect of financial and technical resources and presence of decision-making and monitoring systems are an indicator of sustainability.

Sustainability can be viewed in four stages. First, funding in the hands of good leadership is the *basic means* by which the organization can function to fulfill its mission. The basic means comprise money and leadership. Second, money in the hands of a dedicated leader can create the *mechanism to deliver* the services or output - namely, the organizational structure, managerial systems and technical competence. The delivery mechanism comprises institutional strength and technical competence. Third, appropriate marketing strategies and tools comprise the program and its implementation methodologies which can be called the *output*. Fourth is the *outcome* – are the effects of the NGO's projects of a lasting self-sustaining nature? The effects may, by design, be confined to a target group or aimed at involving the whole community in a way that community institutions take over the replication of the model program to cover the whole community. Thus an NGO has to have the following to become and remain sustainable – fund flow, leadership, institutional effectiveness, technical competence, marketing effectiveness and permanence of beneficiary/ community impact. A brief review of some of the definitions to see if they capture the essentials features of sustainability follows.

A widely quoted definition of sustainability in the context of sustainable development is that of the Brundtland Commission of the United Nations, 1987: "sustainable development is development that meets the needs of the present without compromising the ability of future generations to meet their own needs". This definition focuses on the outcome or impact. Future generations should be able to meet their own needs by virtue of the development now carried out.

Cannon (2007)[3] identifies the following types of sustainability – benefit, organizational, financial and community sustainability. She defines benefit sustainability as "a continuation of the benefits that result from an activity, with or without the programs or organizations that stimulated the benefit in the first place." In other words, the NGO may no longer exist or the program may be discontinued, but its program activity continues to have a favorable and lasting impact. This again is an outcome-centric definition wherein the emphasis is on the lasting nature of the impact.

Financial sustainability, according to Cannon, is a part of organizational sustainability. It refers to the organization's ability to raise resources on its own, rather than being dependent on external funding and particularly on foreign funding. The definition is focused on self-reliance to raise the means to accomplish.

Community sustainability implies that the NGO would enable the community to bring about the transformation – thus placing emphasis on the whole community, rather than on individual beneficiaries. Communities will be empowered to set up community-based organizations that can provide essential services. Or, communities will be in a position to lobby the government for the provision of services.

One aspect of sustainability or the other may be emphasized as being the most critical by different stakeholders depending on their stake in the NGO. For example, donors may attach more importance to organizational sustainability, while members of the community will be more concerned with community sustainability.

O'Sullivan et al (2007)[7], in their technical report on "Moving Toward Sustainability: Transition Strategies for Social Marketing Programs", prepared for USAID, distinguish between two dimensions of sustainability – institutional sustainability and programmatic sustainability. Institutional sustainability is "the ability of a social marketing program to continue operations with little to no outside support." This definition of sustainability refers to the financial aspects of a social marketing program. Programmatic sustainability on the other hand has been defined as "using the 4 Ps of marketing to reach maximum efficiency" and refers to the market impact of the social marketing program. Both the output and outcome viewpoints of sustainability have been brought out in this definition.

Sekher (2000)[10] offers an alternative definition of sustainability in the context of environmental problems and natural resource management. According to the author, sustainability is "the continued and effective administration of the resource, leading to asset creation (forests) benefiting the entire community." This includes two aspects of sustainability – sustainable use of the resource and sustainability of the collective system of management of the resource. The author emphasizes the importance of a participatory approach that involves the local communities for achieving resource sustainability. This definition emphasizes the effective use of natural resources and can be applied equally to effective use of monetary and human resources.

SUSTAINABILITY ASPECTS

From the foregoing discussion we can derive five aspects of sustainability for NGOs. The first aspect of sustainability relates to the ability of the NGO to pursue its mission without break for which continuity of fund flow is indispensable. This implies the ability of the NGO to find financial resources in a continuous and uninterrupted manner from one or more sources. This is achieved by several methods, such as avoiding over reliance on a single or very few sources for assistance, tapping the proximate and local sources, or self-generation of funds through contributions from the target community by way of payment for services and inspiring confidence among funding agencies in the ability of the organization to deliver results.

The second aspect is technical sustainability implying that the capability of its technical and field staff is maintained at peak level at all times through training and motivation.

The third component of sustainability is marketing (programmatic) effectiveness. This in effect means that marketing and communication strategies and methodologies should be carefully designed and applied to achieve a lasting impact on the target beneficiary groups. Strategic involvement of the community and adoption of participatory approaches adds further value to the impact by creating community ownership to take forward, with minimal support, the replication of the program to other groups, eventually to cover the entire community. If the programmatic effectiveness is not there, sustainability in terms of financing, institutional framework and technical competence would be of little avail.

The fourth dimension is institutional sustainability. The organizational structure and management systems and processes should be such that at all times it is able to meet changing field needs and conditions. It should have the capacity to adapt and change according to the demands made on it.

The fifth criterion is that the changed practice (for example, giving up smoking or adoption of prescribed sexual habits) among the target beneficiary group should be sustained without the support of the organization in the post-program phase. In other words, the change in practice and habit should be permanently imbibed not by external prompting but through conviction in the beneficial experiences of the change – called the impact sustainability. This is not only a permanent benefit to that group but it also releases the organization's energies and resources to the advantage of another group in that or a neighboring community. Such replication leads, in due course of time, to the coverage of the whole community or creating a core model group in different communities. Sustainability of the impact can also be extended over the whole community by replication. In this case, the community is involved in planning and executing the program and in the course of it they get committed to the idea and purpose of change and also are able to develop trainers from among those with aptitude within the community to replicate the program on their own with only some minimal technical guidance from the implementing NGO. In short, the community gets trained and equipped and assumes ownership for bringing about the social change. This is a high order of manifestation of sustainability which makes the NGO concerned become a force multiplier.

The following is a diagrammatic representation of the sustainability criteria of an NGO.

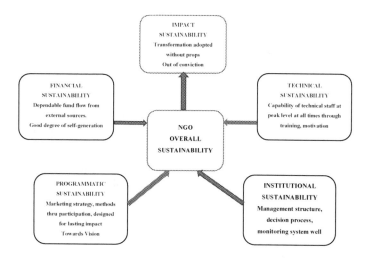

SUSTAINABILITY INDICATORS

In the following tabular form the attributes by which each aspect of sustainability of an NGO can be recognized and the measures needed to achieve each are illustrated. These are indicative and alternative package of practices can be developed to suit specific situations.

Sustainability	Indicators	What is needed to become Sustainable
Financial	Adequacy of funds for current objectives Timely availability of funds Provision for new schemes, expansion Funds for revenue as well as capital expenditure Fund availability not subject to procedural complexities Overheads and cost of delivery reasonable and kept under control	Gradually build self-generation through pricing services or from income by non-project activities like rental, interest, market services like surveys etc. Develop multiple sources for funds but not too many as to multiply time-consuming administrative/reporting work Local and nearby fund sources may be easier and quicker to access Fund generation through strategic, symbiotic partnerships as they are likely to be more durable

		Low overheads and cost-effective delivery – closely monitored Good track record of performance, financial integrity and transparency attract donors Sound documentation and data base to make convincing cases for funding Uncomplicated reporting system - quantified for critical parameters and compared with budgets/targets Inspiring leadership and public relations
Technical	Knowledge of product/services, communication abilities of staff, periodically updated knowledge and skills Adequacy of staff Has access to technical resources and training if needed Program objectives consistently achieved according to target and time-line	Clarity of objectives of respective roles Research support Training periodically Supervisor guidance and demonstration Constructive feedback Motivation through monetary and non-monetary recognitions Participatory process in design and implementation Sufficient availability of well-designed material for program activities and related equipment Adequacy of transport and infrastructure
Programmatic	Field staff are clear about objectives, the desired impact and their role They are adequately trained and equipped	Pre-project appraisal and research of target group profile Evolve strategy by participation of beneficiaries and field staff Choose communication theme and media Train field staff, provide material, equipment and transport Monitor at intervals for desired impact, to modify design as necessary
Institutional	Durability Ability to withstand crises and challenges from within and without Growth in size and through related diversification	Organization structure tailored to match field conditions Structure flat, not multi-layered Designed to create proximity to beneficiary group Delegation of authority appropriate for speedy reaction Inculcate cost-effectiveness as a part of culture

		Participatory decision making process System and process driven management Communication flow to help unified purposeful action by all members Management by Objectives with clarity of jobs, key result areas and indicators Build people to move to higher responsibility through a succession plan Inspiring leadership Seeking help of outside experts for objective assessment or problem solving
Beneficiary	Observance of new behavioral pattern and habits even without prompting and urging by outside agency Total assimilation of above through conviction of benefits Willing to seek help when there is need for advice	Program design effectiveness maximized through participatory approach, pre-implementation survey/research and post-design tests Monitoring to identify implementation problems or design defects Seeking feedback and suggestions from field staff as they are closest to beneficiary Highlight benefits from adoption and ensure such benefits are large enough to offset the pain/insecurity of change
Community	At the end of the program must be able to take over and replicate it targeting another group – with minimal guidance from NGO Aim of community should be to make the change total community-wide In short, community accepts ownership of program and its objectives	Involvement of community, its leaders and opinion makers Train trainers choosing the latter in consultation with community Keep in touch with community through supply of material, technical assistance, special day celebrations and keeping record of progress

SUSTAINABILITY IMBALANCES

It is possible that in a majority of cases NGOs may not have a high degree of sustainability in respect of all the parameters discussed in the earlier paragraphs. If sustainability levels are not uniformly good and there are variations, what would be the impact on the NGO? Possibilities are visualized and summarized in the following table – but taking only the financial, technical, programmatic and institutional aspects as only these constitute the "effort" side, the impact on the group / community beneficiary being the result side.

	Possible Sustainability Situations	Likely Impact
1	Financial – High Technical – High Institutional – High Programmatic - High	Beneficiary impact is likely to be high as communication and marketing strategies are rated high suggesting that they have been designed to facilitate adoption – sustainability is confined to beneficiary group or at the community level depends on the choice of strategy.
2	Financial – Low Technical – Low Institutional – Low Programmatic - Low	Beneficiary impact is likely to be poor – situation is not good – may call for revamp of organization, leadership and strategy
3	Financial – High Technical – Low Institutional – Low Programmatic - High	Beneficiary impact is likely to be poor despite programmatic quality being high and this situation is indicative of poor leadership that has not paid attention to technical and institutional aspects (which represent the delivery mechanism) despite the security offered by a high financial sustainability and good program
4	Financial – Low Technical – High Institutional – High Programmatic – High	The organization is languishing for want of dependable fund flow and the impact at the field level is likely to be poor. A good organization is wasting for want of funds. A good case for a donor to enter. What is the leader doing when he has a good case to sell?
5	Financial – Low Technical – Low Institutional – High Programmatic – Low	A good managerial structure and process is of little use without funds and ability to upgrade the technical capability of field staff and evolve a sound strategic plan. Indicates poor leadership. Calls for leadership change
6	Financial – High Technical – Low Institutional – High Programmatic - High	Beneficiary impact likely to be poor because of lack of technical capacity. Fund flow should not be wasted and must be used for getting results. Urgent action needed on upgrading technical competence. This is a quick job and can be accomplished in a relatively short time with a good consultant. Examine how good the marketing leader is. If action is delayed donor may withdraw.

| 7 | Financial – High Technical – High Institutional – Low Programmatic - High | Similar to no 6 but here the leader is responsible in having failed to address the organizational structural and management process problems. Urgent corrective action is needed. Much can be done with imaginative reforms internally before the outside consultant comes in for help. Financial support cannot sustain without organizational and technical competence. But the field staff may be still able to create impact despite the poor institutional backing – likely to lose trained staff due to low morale |

SUSTAINABILITY CONTINUUM

Using the concept of the *continuum* it is possible to map the deficiencies of any NGO. Such an evaluation enables a comparison of existing practices with ideal practices (say, the last column in the first Table above) and constitutes an objective basis for formulating a plan of action to correct sustainability deficiencies within a time frame. O'Sullivan et al (2007)[7]offer a comprehensive definition of sustainability – "the ability of a social marketing program over time to manage its technical, financial, institutional and market-related activities to maximize efficiency, self-financing and self-governance without reliance on external support." Based on this definition, the authors have developed a "sustainability continuum", with four components of sustainability - technical, financial, institutional and market sustainability. Technical sustainability according to the authors is "the ability of the organization to fulfil the core mission of social marketing." Financial sustainability is defined as "the degree to which the costs of the social marketing program (including overheads) are covered, typically through revenues generated by the sale of products." Institutional sustainability is defined as "the management skills and infrastructure required for the social marketing organization to operate efficiently over time." Market sustainability refers to "the ability of social marketing programs to adapt and innovate to respond to market changes over time."

Each of the above components in turn is divided into three levels of sustainability – beginning, intermediate and advanced levels or as low, medium and high. Indicators of the level of sustainability for each component are also included in the authors' design of the continuum. The idea is that the continuum and its indicators could serve as a guide to both donors and program managers for assessing the progress of their projects and the capacity of the NGO.

STRATEGIES FOR FINANCIAL SUSTAINABILITY

Based on the inputs and experiences of several NGOs, Srinivas (2007)[11], quoting World Bank, *Working with NGOs: A Practical Guide to Operational Collaboration between the World Bank and Non-Governmental Organizations*, Operations Policy Department, World Bank, 1995, has summed up some specific strategies that have been successful in raising funds.

- It is easier to raise money for a single event than for a long term program, break up a long-term program into several parts to raise funds for each part.

- Develop a diversified range of funding sources, including both local and international sources that can contribute different amounts at different stages of the program.

- Identify both close and distant donors. Generally, distant donors tend to provide more funds than donors who are located close by.

- Communicate needs clearly to the donor. While negotiating with the donor, it is also important to understand the donor's perspective and the reasons for the terms imposed on the use of the funds.

- Look for contributions in kind. This could be in the form of advice, technical knowledge, managerial expertise, equipment etc. This helps to build long-term, lasting relationships between the NGO and the donor.

- Display professionalism and transparency regarding objectives and programs, when dealing with donors. This builds a positive image of the organization.

- Since donors in developed countries may be reluctant to provide funds to smaller NGOs, seek the help of apex NGOs that specialize in funding services.

- Since fundraising is time consuming, different responsibilities involved in fundraising, such as identifying donors, negotiation, writing reports and proposals should be distributed among staff members.

SCOPE FOR INCENTIVIZING NGOs

To examine the possibilities for incentivizing NGOs it is necessary to recapitulate the principle of exchange underlying marketing activities – be it commercial marketing or social marketing. It is said that the test is the prevalence of *market-like circumstances* to be able to apply marketing principles to social development. Market-like circumstance requires the presence of a product, service, concept or practice that is transferred to the buyer or adopter in return for an economic consideration or as a discomfort or inconvenience that the adopter willingly undergoes. The latter is in consideration of a benefit, like improved health or freedom from risk of cancer that he gets. The adopter considers the inconvenience worthwhile for the benefit that he derives in due course.

An important difference in this exchange process is that in the case of commercial marketing the economic consideration given by the buyer goes to the marketer in the form of sale proceeds from which, after recovering all costs, he derives a profit for his efforts. In social marketing, however, the benefit of improved health goes to the individuals and to the community as a whole – in the form of, say, better health, higher productivity, more incomes, better living conditions. The individual is compensated for undergoing the inconvenience of change. That is, for his/her "cost" he/she gets the benefit. In the case of social marketing the consumer pays and gets a value but the essential difference being that, in commercial marketing, the consumer's cost becomes the seller's monetary benefit. That monetary benefit helps the seller to reinvest, grow, increase self-reliance and become sustainable. The NGO marketing the program does not get any monetary return, as commercial organization does, but only sense of fulfilment, winning donor confidence, sustainability and community's esteem. The question is: does the lack of a tangible return to the successful NGO cause low motivation to achieve goals and deny it a legitimate source of revenue to increase its self-reliance?

NGOs have costs that are fixed and incurred regardless of the number of projects (FC), and variable costs that are directly related to a specific program and incurred only when there are programs (VC). VC has to be fully to the account of the donor for the specific program. The donor has to compensate the NGO, in addition, an appropriate share of the NGO's FC (also called overheads or management costs) depending on the number and size of the programs he entrusts to the NGO. Thus, the NGO recovers its FC by implementing one or more programs according to its capacity. If the program results are achieved the NGO gets *only* its costs and there is no reward for fulfilling targets of output and outcome. If the NGO gets extra money or kind in return for implementing a number of programs successfully it can use it for training or buying equipment to strengthen the technical capacity or improving management processes. Such an element in the compensation structure, separately earmarked, seems necessary to motivate successful NGOs and help them to raise their level of sustainability. In the absence of such an incentive, the good, the bad and the ugly are treated alike. A cardinal principle of marketing is that one pays according to the quality of product or service. If marketing principles are applicable to social development the provider of service should be no exception for getting a compensation for good performance instead of just cost reimbursement.

FINANCIAL SUSTAINABILITY – SIMULATION

With the observations in the previous section as the basis, a simple simulation of costs can be attempted to determine the level of activity and order of returns needed to build financial sustainability. (Table). The actual situation is indeed more complex but this simplification enables a view of the parameters for sustainability in clear relief. The amounts in the Table are not any specific currency but indicators of amounts.

	FINANCIAL SUSTAINABILITY – SIMULATION		
A	Fixed Cost p.m. (amount of money)	-	10000
B	Fixed Cost p.a. (amount of money)	A x 12	120000
C	To incentivize NGO it should earn FC x 1.5 times	-	1.5
D	Should earn - (amount of money)	B X C	180000
E	Margin from donor 15% for FC + 5% as incentive - both on project cost	-	0.2
F	Projects Needed to earn 180000 at 20% - (amount of money)	D / E	900000
G	Project/s size should be x times of FC p.a.	F / B	7.5
H	Surplus of earning over FC (amount of money)	D minus B	60000

The following inferences can be drawn from this model where the NGO has a Fixed Cost (overheads) of 10,000 per month or 120,000 per annum. If a given NGO has a higher or lower FC the numbers will change accordingly but not the basic logic. The NGO should earn, over and above variable costs that are reimbursable, a suggested minimum of 1.5 times the annual FC. Only then can it spend it on FC and keep the balance as surplus (see H) for capacity maintenance/building. If the margin allowed by donor is 20% and FC is 120,000 per annum it has to get projects valued 7.5 (G) times the annual FC value i.e. 900,000 (F) – to be sustainable. So, NGOs should watch the overheads and should try to get a minimum of 7.5 times the annual expenditure on Fixed Costs or try to keep their FC lower. Similarly, the higher should be the total project value, if the compensation is lower than 20% assumed in the above simulation.

TECHNICAL, PROGRAMMATIC AND INSTITUTIONAL SUSTAINABILITY

Technical, programmatic and institutional sustainability aspects are combined into the McKinsey Model (7S Model), which, to explain, a brief digression is needed. The premise behind the McKinsey model is that for organizations to function effectively they have to rely on the interdependence of the seven variables:

- Structure: The organizational map/chart (line of authority and responsibility)
- Strategy: The plan leading to the allocation of resources (project selection)
- Staff: The people employed (teamwork, empowerment, participation)
- Style: The management style of the organization (management commitment)
- Systems: Procedures, guidelines and control mechanisms (management of activities)
- Shared Values: The goals shared by all employees (everyone involved)
- Skills: The strengths and capabilities of all employees (knowledge, tools, techniques
available)

The structure and strategy (equivalent to the Institutional aspect) have been classified as hardware variables and the remaining five (staff, style, systems, shared values, and skills) – constituting the technical and programmatic components - have been classified as software variables. This approach offers a useful checklist and guide to NGOs to direct their attention to areas that are weak by their own self-assessment.

SOCIAL SCIENCE APPROACH FOR IMPACT SUSTAINABILITY

Bellamy, Hilary et al (1997)[2] prepared a social marketing guide for State Nutrition Education Networks, where they suggest that social marketing can bring about sustainable change by using an interdisciplinary approach. Social marketers should draw concepts from a number of social science disciplines such as social anthropology, behavioral science, health education, mass communication and commercial marketing.

Social anthropology is the study of customs, norms and values in different cultures. The authors believe that it can help the social marketer in understanding the cultural barriers to change and in developing messages and products that will help the target audience to overcome these barriers and adopt a particular practice.

The authors suggest that social marketers should first try to understand the motivations and barriers faced by their target audiences while adopting a particular practice. This would involve doing formative research to understand the attitudes of the audience. The authors emphasize the importance of the "Stages of Change Model", developed by Prochaska and Di Clemente (1983), according to which individuals go through different stages when deciding whether to change a particular behavior – pre-contemplation, contemplation, preparation, action and maintenance. They are of the view that formative research would also help to determine which of these stages the audience is going through, so that messages could be tailored accordingly. For example, if the audience is in the early stages of the model, the messages would have to educate them about the benefits of the change, for example, giving up smoking or changing dietary habits. Therefore, the model can be used by social marketers to understand and segment their audiences and to tailor their messages according to the needs of the audience. All this is aimed at sustainable change.

The PRECEDE (Predisposing, Reinforcing and Enabling Constructs in Educational Diagnosis and Evaluation) model suggested by the authors includes predisposing, enabling and reinforcing factors that influence behavioral change. Predisposing factors refer to knowledge, beliefs and behavior before the social marketing intervention is introduced. Enabling factors refer to the community and environment of the target audience. Reinforcing factors are the positive and negative consequences of change. The authors cite the Health Belief model of Andreasen (1995), which is based on the assumption that behavior is influenced by four beliefs – "perceived susceptibility to a given health problem, perceived severity of the problem, perceived benefits from acting and perceived barriers to taking the action." Social marketers can use this model to try and change beliefs and perceptions of their target audiences regarding health or any other issue. Both the models may be adopted by social marketers, not only in the area of public health, but in other areas as well.

Sustainability assessment studies should be carried out periodically, preferably by an independent expert, to identify and correct factors affecting the NGO's / project's sustainability.

Action Aid, which is one of the NGOs studied by the author, indicated that the time taken to create a sustainable impact in a particular area or segment and move to another area or segment is 5–6 years. Two factors were mentioned as helping to sustain the impact without continued major support from the organization – enactment of enabling laws and policies, community leadership's mobilization. The method adopted to measure the post program impact was the "appreciative enquiry" technique - appreciative enquiry vs. deficit evaluation (i.e. what was done and how).

SUSTAINABILITY DEFICIENCY SYMPTOMS
Some symptoms for identifying weaknesses in the overall sustainability of the organization may be useful in addressing problems before they assume a serious dimension. High fixed costs, inadequate senior level attention to funding needs, neglect of capacity building, incoherent management and, above all, weak leadership are symptoms of an oncoming crisis. These symptoms have been put to the test in the course of the survey of ten NGOs of South India.

Fixed Costs: While the Study was able to collect an indicative range of administrative expenses (fixed costs, as an indicator of efficiency in operation) from the NGOs interviewed, due to the reluctance of the respondents to divulge information on donors and donations (for assessing continuation of social programs), it was not possible to put to a statistical test the hypothesis that high fixed costs of NGOs adversely affect the effectiveness and continuation of social programs. However, a similar hypothesis test conducted in the USA among 2359 NGOs over a few years utilizing information from IRS sources available in the public domain, came to some interesting conclusions. *Strategic Positioning and the Financing of Non-profit Organizations: Is Efficiency Rewarded in the Contributions Marketplace?* Frumkin and Kim (2000) [6]. The Hypothesis read: Non-profit organizations that have low administrative to total expense ratios and that appear efficiently managed will have more success raising contributed income than organizations that have higher administrative expense ratios. The results of the regression model in that study indicated that "reporting low administrative to total expense ratios and positioning an organization as efficient does not lead to greater success in garnering contributions. In none of the six fields of activity did we observe a statistically significant effect of efficiency on contributions..... They indicate that non-profit organizations that spend more marketing themselves to the donating public do better at raising contributed income". The situation could be different in developing countries where funds are difficult to come by and have to be spent to maximum effect.

Among the ten NGOs that formed part of the Study[8] administrative cost to total expenditure five were in the 10-20% range and four in the 21-40 range, one not reporting. The best among them was 13%. Experts and donor representatives with whom the author had in-depth interviews indicated that 8-20% could be considered as efficient in the Indian situation. It appears that a significant number have fixed costs that are above the efficiency threshold. Only a detailed study of the accounts and the way expenses are classified by each NGO as variable, semi-variable and fixed costs would reveal a correct picture. Fixed costs are those that have to be incurred regardless of the volume of program activity. Variable are those expenses that are directly linked to activity and are not incurred if there is no program. Semi-variable are costs of full time field staff entirely meant for programs and if there are no programs for several months together their services can be dispensed with. Donors do not like to subsidize high overheads and avoidable expenditures incurred by the NGO because of inefficiency or lack of prudence.

The following paragraphs set out the findings of the Study in response to the questionnaire for in-depth interviews with NGOs in regard to sustainability aspects. In order to judge the values and interpret them, a grading scale based on a popularly accepted model was adopted as follows – 35% or less is poor, 36-50% is moderate, 51-60% is satisfactory, 61-75% is good and above 75% is very good. A fuller explanation of the evaluation procedures is in the Preface.

Funding Effort: The combined overall score of all NGOs under the Study was 70% falling in the 'good' category. The collective scores on the sub-traits - being in regular contact with donors, spending significant time on fund raising, fund raising capacity having minimal obstacles and possessing enough experience in the related field or target groups to be able to attract funds - fall in the 'very good' range with 80%, 80%, 83% and 93% respectively. Most of the NGOs spent time on and off throughout the year to maintain the fund inflow. Most of them cited the lack of contacts and differences in approach between the NGO and the donor as the main hurdles to fundraising.

Capacity Building: The combined overall score of NGOs for all aspects of capacity building indicated an 'unsatisfactory' score of 39%. The highest collective score on the sub-traits was just about 'satisfactory' for building field staff capacity and taking assistance from outside agencies. Training staff in technical competence (43%) and future plans for capacity building (23%) were in the 'below satisfactory' and 'poor' levels respectively. Overall, the low scores and wide variations indicate the inadequate efforts with regard to capacity building.

Management and Leadership: The combined overall score of NGOs for all aspects of Management and Leadership is 65%, which falls in the 'good' category. The collective scores on the sub-traits can be considered under two broad heads – Leadership, Management. On Leadership there are 5 sub-traits of which 3 are in the 'very good' category and 2 in the 'good' category, indicating a generally high quality of leadership among the NGOs interviewed. The leadership's clarity and direction, transparency and articulation and communication are the 3 sub-traits that have scored 97%, 83% and 80% respectively. The leadership's grasp of the institution's strengths and weaknesses and the threats and opportunities in the environment and the marketing approach of the leader scored 70% each.

As regards the quality of management, we can consider it under the following heads – organizational aspects of management, cost, accountability and transparency. Equipping field staff to handle their responsibilities and having clearly demarcated functional departments are the organizational aspects that score 53% and 70%, placing them in the 'satisfactory' and 'good' categories, respectively. The accountability aspect is central to the continuity of the NGO and its image of credibility. Accountability is at three levels – upward accountability to donors, Board or Trustees and government; lateral accountability to the media and the public about progress; and downward accountability to beneficiaries and staff. The scores on the above are 63% (good), 10% (poor) and 30% (poor) respectively. While upward accountability is good, perhaps due to the compulsions of fund raising, the poor scores on lateral and downward accountability leave a lot to be desired. Transparency has three dimensions – first, making transparent reports disclosing practices and fund use; the second, quality of websites (ranging in quality from being available, static, updated, informative, disclosing financials) and the third, regular meeting with stakeholders. The first scored 63% (good), 60% (satisfactory) and 80% (very good) respectively.

From the foregoing, we may summarize, overall, that leadership quality is of a high order, organization is functionally well structured, overheads affording scope for control, upward accountability is in practice and transparency in its various forms is generally up to the mark. However, these observations on the basis of average scores conceal lower levels of practices at the individual NGO level. This is particularly evident from the poorly maintained and static websites of many NGOs. The following aspects revealed deficiencies – efforts on equipping field staff to handle responsibilities, independent audit of programs and lateral and downward accountability.

Overall Sustainability of the studied NGOs: The combined overall score of all NGOs for all aspects of sustainability is 50%, which falls in the 'moderate' category which is below 'satisfactory' category. The collective score on the sub-trait of not having any major difficulty in fund flow is 80% in the 'very good' category. This means the NGOs in the sample have had no major impediment in securing funds. However, on the other two important aspects of financial sustainability – dependence on one or very few sources for funds and ability to meet at least about 10% of requirements through self-generated funds – the scores are only in the 'poor' and 'moderate' categories (33% and 40% respectively). Organizational sustainability has two aspects – ensuring adequacy of infrastructure like equipment, space, vehicles, computers, etc. and installing and improving systems, processes and controls by taking appropriate expertise – and these have scored in the 'good' and 'moderate' categories respectively (63% and 50% respectively). Continuous attention to internal systems and controls is an important need by taking outside help whenever required to sustain the organization.

EXPERIENCES – OTHER COUNTRIES

Based on the findings of a research study conducted to determine the impact, sustainability and cost effectiveness of two NGOs in India and two NGOs in Bangladesh, Fowler, Alan (2007)[5] offers certain observations regarding sustainability. The Indian NGOs in the study were found to focus more on benefit sustainability rather than on community sustainability - making the local community responsible and self-reliant in the future. The Bangladesh NGOs on the other hand, were found to be more concerned with organizational sustainability. The findings from the study of Indian NGOs revealed mixed results – while one of the NGOs was successful in achieving community sustainability, the other one failed to build self-reliance among women's groups, which continued to depend on the NGO for basic raw material supplies, production and marketing of the final products.

. Agha, S. et al (2005)[1] examined contraceptive social marketing in four middle income countries – Morocco, Dominican Republic, Peru and

Turkey – implemented through the manufacturer's model. The purpose was to determine whether social marketing efforts would continue to have positive results even when donor support was fully or partially withdrawn in these countries. The findings revealed that effective social marketing practices could help to maintain increased sales of contraceptives in all countries, even after donor support was discontinued. The authors generalize these findings by suggesting that the sustainability of the social marketing organization does not depend on the size or continuity of funds from donors. Further, social marketing organizations can also bring about sustainable behavioral change through effective strategies. However, they believe that sustainable change can be achieved, provided certain conditions exist – the absence of competition (e.g. from the government), partnership with the private sector and the willingness of the private sector to continue funding social marketing activities after donor support has been withdrawn. Sustainability in the foregoing case could be due to the medium of a tangible product, whereas behavior change without involvement of a tangible product, market sustainability may be more difficult to achieve.

EXPERIENCES – SOME NGOs OF STUDY [8]

An APEX NGO in Tamil Nadu, India (Tamil Nadu Voluntary Health Association) is engaged in training frontline NGOs on health aspects and it receives funds from several sources, with the bulk of funds coming from their own generated surplus. The break-up of funds as indicated by the management is as follows – a) Domestic state government – 15% b) Domestic central government – 10% c) Domestic institutions – 10% d) Overseas – Institutions and Individuals – 25% e) their own generated surplus – 40%. They mentioned however, that the funds received from overseas and the central government had now reduced. Fund raising activities were carried out continuously throughout the year and some of the factors mentioned by management that affected their fund raising capacity included lack of necessary contacts and changes in government and donor policies. They had income generating programs such as sponsors, ads and sale of books and that these activities generated an income of approximately ₹. 500,000 ($10,000) per year accounting for 20% of the total fund generation. They had income from other sources to make up to 40%.

Regarding the sustainability of their programs, they could not move the program and resources to another area/segment when they were satisfied that a sustainable impact had been achieved in a chosen area/segment, the reason for this being that they had to work with their member NGOs. Besides they had to build the capacity of their members on health issues, which is an ongoing process. The created impact was sustained without any continued major support from them, thanks to two factors – 1) district level structure (coordination committee, volunteers, resource center) which is sustained source of support and 2) link with local health bodies/officials by co-opting them as committee members. The post program impact was measured and known through methods such as surveys, questionnaires and meetings with members.

As regards the sustainability of the organization, three factors were cited: 1) leadership and effective management 2) clarity of objectives and 3) program implementation.

Mysore Resettlement and Development Agency (MYRADA) was established in 1968 with the purpose of helping the Government in resettling Tibetan refugees. After the Tibetan program ended, MYRADA moved out of resettlement in 1982 and shifted its focus to the poor and marginalized in rural areas. Currently, their main activities in the area of socio economic development include building poor people's institutions and promoting Self Help Groups (SHGs). They have rural development programs in three States of South India and provide on-going support to programs in six other States. They also promote the Self Help Affinity Groups in Cambodia, Myanmar and Bangladesh.

The management engaged outside experts for special assignments and assistance in designing reporting systems and for conducting management audits. Their field staff was able to handle its responsibilities since the staff had learnt by experience and were also periodically trained internally. They undertake capacity building of their member NGOs and provide several types of assistance, including training their field staff, training their supervisors/

managers, fund raising, preparation of their plans and proposals, supplying promotional material, financial assistance for infrastructure/equipment, progress monitoring, reporting systems, participatory methods and leadership training.

The main domestic source of funding was the State government which accounted for 25% of the funds received. The time spent on fund raising activities was mentioned as on-and-off throughout the year. Regarding the sustainability of the organization, the factors considered by management to be most critical for its successful operations are clarity of objectives, program implementation and contact with the community. They have a unique system of Sustainability Budgeting. The objective of the sustainability budget is to work towards sustainability in the core organization sector as well as to make all the Program, Project Officers and staff review their approach to finance management. Over seven years there were indications that foreign donors will move to the North, therefore MYRADA needed to raise funds from local sources and to build a corpus project level to sustain core staff. This meant that the Project Officers also had a role to play since the local governments at the district level had resources which could be mobilized. In 2010 the Program Project staff drew up an annual budget covering expenditure *as well as income under each sector*, so that there is a framework to manage their budgets. The capital of the Project Corpus was invested and the interest earned from this corpus fund was used to meet the salaries and allowances of the core staff. The income from Training for member NGOs was charged for to cover the costs of salaries of training staff and maintenance of the Centers.

LEADERSHIP NEEDED FOR SUSTAINABILITY

Drucker, Peter (1990)[4] emphasizes the role of the Board in building organizational sustainability in non-profit organizations. Apart from defining and helping to achieve the organization's mission, ensuring effective management and assessing performance, the Board should bear the responsibility for fund raising for the non-profit organization. This implies that it is the responsibility of the Board to build financial sustainability, which is a part of organizational sustainability. In addition to fund raising, the Board's task is to provide leadership and a sense of direction to the organization as a whole. Sustainability is a continuous process, not a static destination.

REFERENCES

1. Agha, S et al, "When Donor Support Ends: The Fate of Social Marketing", Paper in Global Research Brief, US AID, PSP-One, Bethesda USA, 2005.

2. Bellamy, Hilary et al, "Social Marketing Resource Manual: A Guide for State Nutrition Education Networks", Prepared for the US Department of Agriculture, Food and Consumer Service, Alexandria, VA, USA, 1997.

3. Cannon, Lisa, "Defining Sustainability", The Earthscan Reader on NGO Management, Edited by Michael Edwards and Alan Fowler, Earthscan India, Daryaganj, New Delhi, 2007.

4. Drucker, Peter, "Managing the Non-Profit Organization", Harper Collins Publishers, 1990.

5. Fowler, Alan, "NGO Performance: What Breeds Success? New Evidence from South Asia", The Earthscan Reader on NGO Management, Edited by Michael Edwards and Alan Fowler, Earthscan India, Daryaganj, New Delhi, 2007.

6. Frumkin, Peter and Kim, Mark T, "Strategic Positioning and Financing of Non-Profit Organizations: Is Efficiency Rewarded in the Contributions Marketplace?", The Hauser Center for Non-Profit Organizations and the Kennedy School of Government, Harvard University, Working Paper No. 2, 2000.

7. O'Sullivan, Gael et al, "Moving Towards Sustainability: Transition Strategies for Social Marketing Programs", ABT Associates and USAID, 2007.

8. Parthasarathy, Vimala, "Social Marketing Strategies & Traits of Successful NGOs in India - A Strategic Perspective with Reference to

Select NGOs in the States of Karnataka & Tamil Nadu, India", doctoral thesis for PhD, approved by Manipal University, Manipal, India, 2013

9. Raval, Dinker et al, "Application of the Relationship Paradigm to Social Marketing", Competition Forum. Indiana, Vol. 5, No. 1, 2007. pp. 1- 8.

10. Sekher, Madhushree, "Local Organizations and Participatory CPR Management: Some Reflections", Institute for Social and Economic Change, Bangalore, Working Paper No. 61, 2000.

11. Srinivas, Hari, "Fund Raising Realities and Strategies: Lessons Learnt at the NGO Café", GDRC Special Feature Website: gdrc.org., 2007.

12. VanSant, Jerry, "A Composite Framework for Assessing the Capacity of Development Organizations", A Paper prepared for USAID, http://www.g-rap.org/docs/ICB/USAid, 2000.

WHAT DO DONORS WANT OF NGOs? SOME EMPIRICAL EVIDENCES FROM INDIAN NGOs

Abstract

This article is based on a Ph.D. research study of the voluntary sector in India, of which nongovernmental organizations are a part. The perceptions, assessment and recommendations of donors and experts on various aspects of NGO functioning were examined in depth as one of the components of the research, in the backdrop of social marketing objectives. The study covered the most important aspect of the application of marketing principles to socioeconomic development, besides identifying important issues governing the operating effectiveness of NGOs and the traits and qualities that make them eligible for donor support on a sustained basis. The results suggest that in the Indian context, level of funding significantly influences performance of NGOs. While the program component of social marketing effectiveness had a significant relationship with level of expenditure, there was, however, no relationship between level of expenditure and social marketing effectiveness as a whole. A significant conclusion of the paper is that NGOs should project a more positive image of their performance and credibility to donors. The paper also suggests that systematic outcome measurement is critical to assess NGO performance. The article appeared originally in Elixir Online Journal (2001)[10] and we are grateful to the Journal for permission to re-publish it as part of this book. The original article has been supplemented with some useful information on the experiences of Bangladesh and Tanzania.

INTRODUCTION

NGOs make up the voluntary sector, also known as the "third sector" of the economy, which has shown tremendous growth in many countries. This has been triggered by several factors including greater availability of funds for development programs, insufficient capacity of governments to address social concerns and the voluntary sector's ability to work closely with target communities.

A recent Ph.D. Study[9] conducted across two states in southern India shows that the growth of this sector had its roots in the pre-independence period and reached a peak after Independence, with the recognition of the role of voluntary organizations by the Fifth Five Year Plan Document. During the 1990's, NGOs' role and collaboration between government and NGOs were emphasized by the Planning Commission in the Seventh Five Year Plan Document. In addition, Indian NGOs began to make their presence felt at the global level and were given a prominent role in poverty reduction and development of civil society by the World Bank's New Policy Agenda. The Seventh Plan indicated a bigger role for the voluntary sector in rural development, by supplementing the efforts of the government. The Eighth, Ninth and Tenth plans emphasized the importance of building people's institutions through voluntary sector initiatives. The Tenth Plan also recommended a nine-point strategy for involving the voluntary sector in community and welfare programs, which included help in the development of core competencies and professionalism.

A study carried out in collaboration with the Institute for Policy Studies, Johns Hopkins University, USA (2002)[6], estimated that there are 1.2 million non-profits in India. The study also indicated that NGOs involved in socio-economic development through the transfer of ideas and concepts for social behavioral change are only about 21% of the total number of NGOs. All India estimates of total receipts of NGOs for 1999-2000 were ₹ 179 billion ($ 3.6 billion). The four main sources of funds for NGOs in India are: self-generation, loans, grants and donations. Grants include funds received from government and international sources; donations may be from both Indian and foreign sources, mainly individuals and corporations. Grants and donations taken together constitute two-fifth of total NGO receipts.

The rapidly increasing scope for the voluntary sector to play a vital role in socio-economic development calls for a critical examination of the sector's capabilities and shortcomings, with special reference to the tools it adopts to maximize impact at the community level. Marketing practices of the commercial sector have been successfully adapted to socio-economic development projects in other countries. Examples of these are: i) the application of social marketing to build public health by the Department of Health, UK, ref: their White Paper 2004 and ii) Drucker's (1990)[3] mention of the successful application of market segmentation by the American Heart Association. Therefore, the functioning of this sector offers much scope for research in India. The current article is a part of the research on select NGOs in Karnataka and Tamil Nadu (the two economically progressive southern States of India) and deals with donor and expert expectations and perceptions of NGOs in terms of pre-requisites for receiving assistance.

IS EFFICIENCY A CONSIDERATION?

The question of whether funding agencies tend to favor non-profits that show greater operational efficiency has been examined by Frumkin and Kim (2000)[4]. Operational efficiency implies that the organization is cost effective and has low administrative expenses and fixed costs. The authors base their conclusions on a study of a large sample of non-profit organizations over an eleven-year period. There was found to be no significant difference between NPOs that projected themselves as cost efficient and those that did not, in terms of the amount of contributions received from individuals, foundations and corporates. Therefore, the authors suggest that efficiency is not a dominant factor. While this may appear irrational, it is possible, although the authors' study does not mention it specifically, that even at a higher cost, extensive coverage and sustainable impact might have clinched funding decisions. In other words, it is not enough to be efficient without being effective.

WHY IS DONOR PERCEPTION IMPORTANT?

Unlike the commercial sector, which has a non-returnable equity capital, the success of the voluntary sector depends on continuous flow of funds from benefactors. This is one dimension of sustainability, i.e., financial sustainability, identified by Cannon (2007)[1], which relates to the sustained ability of the NGO itself to continue to pursue its mission. A second aspect of sustainability according to Cannon is benefit sustainability, or "a continuation of the benefits that result from an activity, with or without the programs or organizations that stimulated the benefit in the first place." Financial sustainability is the bedrock upon which rests organizational sustainability and benefit sustainability of any NGO.

Since the financial sustainability of the NGO depends largely on donors, how donors view NGOs and what they expect from this sector are of prime importance. In order to attract continued assistance, it is important for donors to have a positive perception of the NGO and of the sector as a whole. The current study reveals some interesting findings on this particular aspect.

WHAT NGOs WANT OF DONORS - TANZANIA EXPERIENCE

The Special Paper (2007)[11] on Poverty Alleviation and the perceptions of Tanzanian NGOs on their role provides a useful picture of the situation of the NGO sector in that country. The following summary of its findings is based on a liberal use of the contents of this valuable Report.

Over 90% of organizations surveyed are donor funded, and three-fifths of respondents receive funding for 60 to 100% of their activities. Relations with donors were often initially described as cordial and smooth. Tanzanian NGOs largely receive project based funding, and respondents were critical that only limited resources are made available for NGOs' core operating costs, personnel and infrastructure. Participants strongly argued that project-only funding is unsustainable in the long-term; that when this funding is withdrawn, activities often cease abruptly and prematurely. NGOs also complained of pressure from donors concerning program priorities and compliance with inflexible funding conditions. Respondents further suggested that the over-emphasis by donors on advocacy work to the exclusion of service delivery was imbalanced compared to the needs.

Participating NGOs made the following recommendations to donors:

- Develop projects jointly to reflect local priorities. NGOs possess grassroots knowledge and expertise.
- Display greater openness about funding agendas. Announce priorities in advance (for example, once a year) so that qualified NGOs can apply, and those that do not have necessary experience will not waste time and resources writing doomed proposals.
- Reduce the complexities of the application process. Complicated bureaucratic requirements for funding applications and reporting are often unnecessarily difficult and restrictive.
- Provide more technical assistance, including capacity training in the preparation of joint proposals.
- Introduce a 'priority list' approach to funding, whereby donors advertise topics or projects being considered for funding nationally. NGOs then submit proposals to demonstrate relevant expertise and capacity, and receive funding for specific portions of the project. Donors could then link disparate organizations through civil society networks to work jointly on these projects.
- Increase funding for transport and infrastructure to expand the presence and services of NGOs in more remote, rural areas.

RESEARCH METHODOLOGY

Both secondary and primary research was done to assess donor perceptions and expectations. The secondary sources included scholarly and research articles, websites and reports of international institutions such as the World Bank. The primary research included both quantitative research in the form of a survey using structured questionnaires, as well as qualitative research through depth interviews. The study covered twelve donors (both Indian and international) and experts. The respondents were given the option of completing the questionnaire online, or through a face-to-face interview.

In addition to the questionnaire developed for the experts and donors, a guideline was designed for conducting one-to-one depth interviews with the experts/donors. The purpose of these interviews was to incorporate "phenomenological" research into the qualitative research design, whereby the experts were asked to describe their personal experiences of phenomena related to the NGO sector. These interviews included probing questions to gain additional insights into the sector from the experts. The responses to these questions were analyzed separately and integrated with the quantitative data.

The integration of quantitative and qualitative research techniques has been advocated, especially for socio-economic situations, by Weinrich (1996)[15] in a scholarly article. According to the author, research on social marketing would not be complete with gathering data of a quantitative nature alone, since it is concerned with behavioral change. Qualitative methods such as depth interviews provide deeper insights into complex behaviors and motives.

Secondary Research has thrown light on donor perspectives. Several scholarly and research articles have dealt with funding and donor perspectives. NGOs in developed countries are the biggest source of funds to Indian NGOs. They tend to fund projects that focus on community development and on specific sectors such as agriculture, health and education.

Donors also have different preferences regarding the mechanism through which funds are distributed to Indian NGOs. Some donors prefer to go through an intermediary agency that identifies and evaluates projects. Others pool their funds and distribute them through an intermediary agency. Some international NGOs set up in-country offices, staffed with local experts, which play the role of an intermediary agency. Many donors have also tried to fund NGOs directly, without the intervention of an intermediary.

According to Holcombe et al (2004)[5], the tendency among donors, especially internal funding agencies, is to provide assistance for projects whose impact can be measured. Measurable results indicating achievement of goals would undoubtedly induce greater confidence among donors that their money is being effectively used.

The World Bank's Practical Guide to Operational Collaboration with NGOs (1995)[19] spelling out its policy on NGOs regarding funding issues, is indicative of their expectations from this sector, which are as follows:

- NGOs are generally cost-effective. They should not, however, be viewed as a "low-cost alternative" to other types of implementing agencies.
- NGOs should not be expected to provide services free of charge, or at lower than market rates (unless according to a co-financing agreement).
- NGO involvement could be in various forms -e.g.: informal unpaid advisor, paid consultant, or contractor.
- Mutually acceptable fees and overhead costs should be established.

The World Bank estimates that NGOs have huge potential to contribute to the success of its projects due to their participatory approach. NGO involvement can contribute to the sustainability and effectiveness of Bank-financed projects by introducing innovative approaches and promoting community participation. NGOs can help expand project uptake and reach and facilitate greater awareness of diverse stakeholder views. NGOs can provide particularly valuable input during project identification and design.

The World Bank's Operational Directive (1989)[18] expects local NGOs to work within the framework of the policies of the relevant government. They should also try to create a harmonious working relationship between governments and donors. Corruption and inefficiency in use of funds have been one of the main obstacles to receiving funds from international donors. A World Bank report (1995) on the status of health projects being implemented in

India cites corruption and fake NGOs as the main reasons for delay in execution of projects. The Bank has been known to withhold funds for the health sector, after detecting misuse of funds previously granted. According to Collings (2008)[2], one of the biggest impediments to fundraising efforts by NGOs in emerging countries in general is their poor image and lack of credibility. There are several instances of retired government officials setting up NGOs to attract State funds, which are at times diverted for purposes outside the objective.

Secondary research shows that in India for example, there is much scope for the voluntary sector to avail of a substantially higher share of resource availability from the World Bank and other international sources with proper project identification, convincing presentation of proposals, track record of efficiency and an image of greater reliability and accountability.

FUNDS SIGNIFICANTLY INFLUENCE NGO PERFORMANCE

The above mentioned hypothesis of the study in India under reference implies that the amount of resources in terms of funds or expenditure determines both the quality and quantity of output, as measured by the quality and number of training sessions, for example. Based on an extensive survey of available literature and research studies, specific hypotheses related to factors affecting performance effectiveness of socio-economic projects were developed as part of the larger study, using the Log Frame (Logical Framework) Model. This Model is used by international financing institutions for assessing performance of socio-economic projects and has three components – a) Input, or what is put into the organization (for example, resources), b) Output, or what the organization puts out (for example, number of brochures or training programs) and c) Outcome, or impact created by the Output (for example, number of loans received, or women starting businesses).

Statistical Test of Hypothesis

Statistical tests including regression, correlation, t test, F test and co-linearity were carried out to test the hypothesis stated earlier, as well as the other hypotheses that were relevant to the larger study, using the SPSS 17.0 statistical software package.

Since information on the amount of funds was unavailable in precise and reliable terms, the expenditure by each of the NGOs was taken as being indicative of funds made available. This is a reasonable and safe assumption, since NGOs spend most of what they receive and, in any case, do not have the means to access borrowed funds from lending institutions. Data was also unavailable on both output and outcome (impact). Therefore, social marketing effectiveness, in terms of seven components (Program, Promotion, Delivery of Services, Policy, Purse, Publics and Partnership), on which information was available, was adopted as indicator of output and determinant of outcome. Thus the hypothesis was interpreted with reference to the *components of Outcome* and *not* to *Outcome as a whole.*

The significance value in the coefficient analysis being <0.2 for Funds (0.087) indicated that Funds as an independent variable, has a non-spurious correlation with Program. F Value (4.563) being >1, the null hypothesis that there is no relationship between the independent variable and Program (dependent variable) was rejected at the 0.12 level of significance. Therefore, the above hypothesis was restated as follows –

Input significantly influences Outcome (where Input is expenditure and Outcome is social marketing effectiveness).

Null hypothesis: There is no relationship between expenditure and social marketing effectiveness.

Alternate hypothesis: Level of expenditure significantly influences social marketing effectiveness.

The other relevant statistical indicators that were taken into account to arrive at a conclusion regarding this hypothesis were as follows – (a) coefficient of multiple determination, denoted as $_R^2$ which measures the multiple correlation or linear relationship among more than two variables, the value of "R" indicating the multiple correlation / causation between the set of independent variables and the dependent variable (b) adjusted $_R{}^2$, calculated to remove the "spurious" effects of independent variables on the dependent variable, with large differences between R^2 and adjusted R^2 indicating that some independent variables have a spurious effect on the dependent variable. (c) standard error of estimate, which shows the degree of variability of effect for sample data (NGOs in this case), of the many independent variables.

Based on the statistical indicators described, the alternate hypothesis was accepted and may be restated as: Level of expenditure significantly influences *program aspects* of social marketing effectiveness.

The program aspects of social marketing effectiveness include adaptation of program design to cultural needs, introduction of innovative features in program design, involvement of stakeholders in theme selection, program design and implementation. However, there was found to be no relationship between the level of expenditure and components of social marketing effectiveness *other than program aspects*.

The result of the test of this hypothesis would be of significance to funding agencies and NGOs, as it indicates that the size of expenditure by an NGO, consequently funding, is critical for the effectiveness of the *program aspects* of social marketing. Although this result is specific to India, it may also be of relevance to developing countries.

QUESTIONNAIRE

Regarding the applicability of marketing methods, all the 12 respondents representing the donor group unanimously agreed during the interviews that all marketing practices are relevant to socio-economic development activities.

The respondents also emphasized the importance of building stakeholder relationships, particularly with the target group and government at different levels, which were ranked as the most important stakeholders of an NGO.

As for the current legislative framework, 10 out of 12 respondents were of the opinion that there is no distinguishing legal identity for Indian NGOs. There is no national parent body or licensing authority, nor is there a legal framework that binds NGOs and makes them accountable to a central authority. Only in special cases like watershed development, there are MOUs between individual departments of government and NGOs, which confers some identity on the participating NGOs.

Experience in the given area of activity was named by 7 out of the 12 respondents interviewed as the most important trait of an NGO, followed by financial capabilities, which was named by 6 respondents.

The importance of assessing performance effectiveness in terms of a specific formula was recognized by a majority of the respondents. Periodic measurement of impact (outcome) as well as output was suggested by 6 out of 12 respondents for assessment of performance effectiveness.

The respondents were almost unanimous in their opinion (11 out of 12) that for administrative expenses, a range of 8-20% was a reasonable limit.

Leadership and management and clarity of objectives were ranked first and second respectively as the most crucial factors for organizational sustainability, that is, the organization's continued and successful operation.

The consensus among all 12 respondents was that management aspects have not reached a satisfactory level, since NGOs have systems in position, but do not pursue them as an important component of the management process. This is evident from the average rating of various management aspects – approximately 3 on a 5 point scale. However, this was an observation on NGOs in general and not specific to any of the NGOs that formed part of the sample for this study.

A majority of the respondents among the donors and experts interviewed emphasize the need for a distinguishing legal identity for NGOs engaged in socio-economic development. They are of the opinion that there is no national parent body or licensing authority for NGOs. There is no general legal framework that binds NGOs and makes them accountable to a central authority. One of the suggestions that emerged from donors/experts is that there should be some unique ID number / registration for NGOs across the states and that their track records should be available for review and reference.

Experience in the related field / target group and money management capabilities, including past record of spending and governance were considered important considerations for funding. With the exception of one respondent who suggested a limit of 30%, the suggestions from all others ranged from 8 to 20% as a reasonable limit.

FINDINGS FROM DEPTH INTERVIEWS

The first question asked of respondents was whether NGOs applying marketing practices with suitable adjustments to the development sector are able to attract more committed assistance from funders than those that lag behind in this aspect.

The majority - 5 out of 6 respondents - was of the view that funding, especially foreign funding, is influenced by many different factors and that the application of marketing principles to NGO activities is not of prime importance.

According to one of the experts, the Regional Director of an international NGO, donors give more consideration to factors such as the goal of the project and the selection of the appropriate target audience, rather than to the method or approach used to achieve that goal. Partnership with the private sector is another factor considered by overseas donors.

Another expert, the Program Director of a mother NGO involved in AIDS prevention and cure had a similar opinion and felt that there was no experience of either domestic or foreign funders favoring NGOs that apply marketing principles. A third expert, a medical doctor with an NGO working in the area of HIV pointed out that NGOs working in the area of public health have managed to attract funds due to their success in building relationships, rather than to the application of marketing principles. His opinion was based on his experience in the area of health care.

A senior manager with a bank that provides funds to NGOs engaged in rural development was of the view that factors such as the credibility of the NGO play a more important role in the decision to grant funds, rather than the application of marketing methods.

An expert with an NGO involved in the area of counselling believed that all NGOs unconsciously applied marketing practices and that those applying them in a systematic manner tended to attract more funds than those who did not. High recall and visibility of the NGO, according to her, were factors that were given greater importance by funding agencies.

In the course of the depth interview, the respondents were also asked to recall and describe actual incidents of success and failure among NGOs, in which they were involved in one way or another. Based on these incidents, some of the factors which could lead to success, according to the respondents, were generation of own funds without dependence on outside sources, effective marketing techniques and innovative media such as counselling centers for promoting awareness of HIV. For projects to be successful, it was essential to have appropriate institutional partnerships or linkages (e.g. Self Help Group-bank linkage) and to develop models that have high replicability in other areas.

The most common failure factors that were cited were as follows – mismanagement of funds, an able leader disassociating himself from the project and less emphasis on commitment and more on formal education in staff selection.

CONCLUSIONS

Building the Donor Constituency is a Marketing Function – "Upward Marketing": Corruption and poor efficiency in use of funds have been one of the main obstacles to receiving funds from international donors such as the World Bank. According to a World Bank report (1995)[19] on the status of health projects in India, corruption and fake NGOs are some of the primary reasons for delay in implementation of projects. Instances have been reported of the Bank withholding funds for the health sector, after detecting misuse of funds previously granted. According to Collings (2008)[2], one of the biggest obstacles to fundraising efforts by NGOs in emerging countries is their poor image and lack of credibility.

According to Drucker (1990)[3], fund raising is today better known as "fund development", since it involves cultivating a long-term relationship with the donor, rather than a single transaction, or receiving a single contribution. The first step is to make the donors aware of the organization's mission and goals. These need to be defined and spelt out clearly. The next step is to get the donors involved in the organization's activities, so that they develop a sense of commitment, reducing the externality character of the relationship. A separate strategy should be developed for each donor, depending on the nature of the donor's needs and sensitivities. Personalized communication, annual reports, periodic progress reports and special reports on timely alert on critical problems and how they are being tackled would all go a long way in building long-term relationships.

The tendency among donors, especially internal funding agencies, is to provide funding for projects that produce results that can be measured. Measurable results indicating achievement of targets would undoubtedly induce greater confidence among assisting agencies. Considering the difficulty of measuring the outcome of many of the social development schemes much attention is needed to this aspect while designing programs.

Availability of funds in adequate measure and timeliness impacts program efficacy. Therefore, NGOs should conduct affairs in a manner that induces confidence in prospective and existing donors to release funds without interruption.

The findings indicate that from a donor viewpoint, the application of marketing principles is not of prime concern. This need not be interpreted as marketing practices being irrelevant or unimportant. Other over-riding factors related to the functioning of NGOs are more of a source of concern to donors. These include caliber of leadership, quality of management, clarity of objectives, experience in the related field and financial integrity.

Considering that poor image is a major stumbling factor for donors to participate in NGO projects in a much larger measure, it seems necessary for the voluntary sector to enhance project performance through imaginative adaptation of marketing practices, establish a systematic link of accountability to donors and project themselves as reliable, efficient organizations committed to community development. There is much scope for brand building by Indian NGOs. NGOs need to make vigorous efforts to project a more positive image of the organization to potential donors. Image building should be based on performance, credibility, experience, financial capabilities and good achievements.

There seems to be need for a distinguishing legal identity for NGOs engaged in socio economic development. One of the suggestions that emerged from donors/experts was that there should be some unique ID number / registration for NGOs across the States and that their track records should be available for review and reference.

Although many NGOs have systems in position, the impression among donors/experts was that they do not pursue them as an important component of the management process. Demonstrating capability through quantified performance indicators would go a long way in convincing donors that the NGO is result oriented and in attracting assistance. Evaluating output performance (in terms of efforts in the form of training, brochures, leaflets, meetings, etc.) and performance in terms of outcome or impact are both equally important. The first is for short-term measurement of efforts made to create impact. The second is meant to measure the long-term outcome of the effort. Training in outcome measurement methods may be needed.

The results of the hypothesis test, the questionnaire and the depth interviews are specifically related to the two states of southern India covered by the study. It is possible that these may have some relevance to developing countries, offering scope for further research in this area.

REFERENCES

1. Cannon, Lisa, "Defining Sustainability", The Earthscan Reader on NGO Management, Edited by Michael Edwards and Alan Fowler, Earthscan India, Daryaganj, New Delhi, 2007.

2. Collings, Simon, "Fundraising in Emerging Markets: Challenges and Opportunities", Target Marketing, Philadelphia, Vol. 6, No. 5, May 2008. pp. 38-40.

3. Drucker, Peter, "Managing the Non-Profit Organization", Harper Collins Publishers, 1990.

4. Frumkin, Peter and Kim, Mark T, "Strategic Positioning and Financing of Non-Profit Organizations: Is Efficiency Rewarded in the Contributions Marketplace?", The Hauser Center for Non-Profit Organizations and the Kennedy School of Government, Harvard University, Working Paper No. 2, 2000.

5. Holcombe, Susan H et al, "Managing Development: NGO Perspectives", International Public Management Journal, Stamford, Vol. 7, No. 2, 2004. pp. 187-206.

6. Institute for Policy Studies, Johns Hopkins University, USA, 2002.

7. Jalali, Rita, "International Funding of NGOs in India", Paper presented at the Annual Meeting of the American Sociological Association, Washington DC, 2006.

8. O'Sullivan Gael et al, "Moving Towards Sustainability: Transition Strategies for Social Marketing Programs", ABT Associates and USAID, 2007.

9. Parthasarathy, Vimala, "Social Marketing Strategies & Traits of Successful NGOs in India - A Strategic Perspective with Reference to Select NGOs in the States of Karnataka & Tamil Nadu, India", doctoral thesis for PhD, approved by Manipal University, Manipal, India, 2013

10. Parthasarathy, Vimala, "What do Donors Want of NGOs? Some Empirical Evidences from Indian NGOs?" Elixir Online Journal Arts 39 (2011) 5093-5097, 2011

11. Research on Poverty Alleviation REPOA, "Tanzanian NGO's – Their Perceptions", Special paper 07.21, 2007, website: www.repoa.or.tz

12. Srinivas, Hari, "Fund Raising Realities and Strategies: Lessons Learnt at the NGO Café", GDRC Special Feature Website: gdrc.org. 2007.

13. Steering Committee for Tenth Five Year Plan (20022007), Voluntary Sector (2001), Minutes of the First Meeting of the Tenth Five-Year Plan (2002-07) -Steering Committee, on "Voluntary Sector", Government of India, Planning Commission, March 16, 2001.

14. Valadez, Joseph and Bamberger, Michael, "Monitoring and Evaluating Social Programs in Developing Countries", Economic Development Institute of the World Bank, EDI Development Series, 1994.

15. Weinrich, Nedra Klein, "Integrating Quantitative and Qualitative Methods in Social Marketing Research", 1996 Issue of the Social Marketing Quarterly, Washington D C.

16. World Bank, "Working with NGOs: A Practical Guide to Operational Collaboration between the World Bank and Non-Governmental Organizations", Operations Policy Department, World Bank, reproduced in the website of The Global Development Research Center (GDRC), 1995. pp. 7-9.

17. World Bank India – Representatives of Civil Society Organizations Dialogue, Lessons Learnt from NGOs Working on Bank Operations, New Delhi, September 2007.

18. World Bank Operating Manual, "Involving Non-Governmental Organizations in World Bank Supported Activities", Abstracted and reproduced in the website of The Global Development Center (GDRC), 1989.

19. World Bank, "Working with NGOs: A Practical Guide to Operational Collaboration between the World Bank and Non-Governmental Organizations", Operations Policy Department, World Bank, 1995. pg.29.

20. World NGO Conference -Report of the First Preparatory Meeting Held at UNU Headquarters, Tokyo, September, 23-24 1996. "NGO Development: Focal Issues", Research reproduced in the website of The Global Development Center (GDRC).

CULTURALLY ADAPTED SOCIAL MARKETING (CASM) - SOME MODELS AND EXPERIENCES FROM INDIAN NGOs

Abstract

Social marketing strategies need to be adapted to the local cultural context, since beliefs, customs and practices stand in the way of behavioral change. This is especially true of countries like India with diverse cultures. The extent to which NGOs are aware of the need for adaptation of marketing practices, the perceived importance of social and cultural features of the target community and examples of adaptation of practices are covered in this article. The examples are drawn both from secondary research and the primary research through questionnaire-guided in-depth interviews with the CEOs of ten select NGOs from two states of South India. The examples of cultural adaptation offer some insights into how local barriers had been overcome and these may bear relevance to NGOs placed in exceptional cultural situations in other parts of Asia and in African countries

INTRODUCTION

Developing countries today are grappling with a number of basic issues such as poverty reduction, availability of critical resources such as clean drinking water for all, awareness of and prevention of AIDS, and family planning. Tackling these issues involves catering to the most primary imperatives and is in contrast to the situation in developed countries which address higher order issues such as promotion of healthier diets, quitting smoking or drugs and traffic discipline. While governments in developing countries have been playing a role in socio-economic development, the enormity of the problems requires the additional contribution and initiative of the private and voluntary sectors to supplement governmental efforts. The root cause of the problem is that although funds and technical resources have been invested, the impact has not been felt at the grassroots level, due to improper study of the target segment, their behavior, needs, aptitudes and socio-cultural characteristics. This is where the voluntary sector, comprising NGOs that have presence at the communities, can step in and make a difference by their intimate understanding of the local community.

WHAT IS CASM?

Most social development issues involve bringing about behavioral change. Beliefs, habits and practices vary from community to community. The impact of cultural factors on behavioral change is not given adequate attention by social marketers. The concept of Culturally Adapted Social Marketing (CASM) suggests that social marketing strategies should be understood and adapted to prevailing cultural norms. The best of programs at times fail to produce the desired effect and subsequent deeper study showed that some critical aspects of the program had overlooked some cultural aspect or had come into direct conflict with it. CASM involves an in-depth study of the target segment in the form of Culturally Adapted Social Market Research (CASOMAR), which is conducted during different stages of the program. The three stages of CASOMAR are: (i) formative research during the design stage to determine the target audience; (ii) process research during the implementation stage to determine whether the project features are in harmony with local cultures and are going according to the plan; and (iii) accountability research during the final stage of the project to assess the impact and the extent to which the program had succeeded in adaptation.

According to Jha (1999)[7], social marketing is all about behavior change. Bringing about change involves a sacrifice or inconvenience initially, until the benefits are felt later (e.g. quitting smoking) and for that reason, often meets with resistance. For example, the practice of family planning in tradition-bound societies like India was frowned upon and is now accepted even in villages thanks to successful communication of the benefits of a small family, specifically through the woman of the house. Such resistance to change is strongly rooted in culture. Therefore, social marketing strategies must be adapted to cultural values, rather than try to change them. The concept of CASM is based on the differences between application of marketing practices in the commercial and social spheres. CASM involves the use of marketing and communication strategies that can overcome cultural barriers to social behavioral change.

CASM is critical for the successful implementation of socio-economic development projects. This is especially true of developing countries like India, characterized by cultural diversity. The implication is that programs need to be adapted at the finer grassroots level to suit the needs of broad cultural segments, as well as smaller sub cultures based on religion, ethnic groups, age, gender and geographic differences.

SECONDARY RESEARCH - CASM SUCCESS STORIES

A few case studies in developing countries have indicated that the adoption of the CASM concept has led to more effective social marketing.

Healing Hands International, a grassroots NGO, used a model of agricultural development to reduce hunger and establish economic viability in Ethiopia. Duke and Long (2007)[5] identified two factors – training and establishing trust through social networks - that led to the successful implementation of their program. One of the factors which led to the success of the new agricultural program was the fact that HHI selected persons with agricultural training as well as an understanding of cultural differences. The agricultural model used by HHI involved the following four steps.

Step 1: Building trust and social networks by distributing medical aid, food and educational resources - this involved setting up and maintaining schools, hospitals and orphanages with the necessary infrastructure, cultivating relationships with important local contacts, and working closely with USAID and other humanitarian organizations This helped them to build relationships.

Step 2: HHI was successful in bringing about food security in famine stricken Ethiopia, by using the social networks built in step 1 to work with Ethiopian farmers. They conducted Food Security Workshops during which farmers were trained in "survival gardening" techniques. This involved helping the farmers to identify and make use of neglected resources already available in the area.

Step 3: This involved encouraging farmers to expand both their survival gardens and drip irrigation systems to bigger plots of land of about five to ten acres in area to enable them to produce surplus crops that could be sold in the community.

Step 4: The purpose of this last step in HHI's agricultural model was to bring different small farmers together by forming village clubs or co-operatives to facilitate bulk purchase of seeds and raw materials, pool resources and share capital costs.

Having successfully implemented the four step model in Ethiopia, HHI also introduced it in Malawi and other developing countries.

Fox, P Michael (2000)[6] draws lessons regarding the success of social marketing from selected case studies of condom social marketing in Haiti and Mozambique. Since selling condoms to rural audiences was one of the main cultural barriers encountered, the distribution strategy used to market condoms in these countries was adapted through an innovative approach – community-based distribution. In this model, non-professional sales agents were recruited from the general population, trained in sales of condoms and rewarded through small margins on their sales. The CBD approach was quite successful in opening up new sales areas and outlets and in educating people about AIDS. The program was also cost effective, since the benefits of using community-based distributors exceeded the costs incurred in appointing and rewarding them. The lesson to be drawn from this experience is that use of low cost, innovative methods can lead to success of social marketing, besides overcoming cultural barriers.

Promotion of condoms was also found to have maximum impact when the promotion strategy was adapted by using a combination of media, including mass media, interpersonal channels and local media. The case studies were selected from six developing countries – Haiti, Mozambique, India, Cameroon, Kenya and Columbia and present six applications of different techniques of condom social marketing to prevent the spread of HIV/AIDS. In all the countries, social marketing was found to be successful in removing the "stigma" associated with the use of condoms, indicating that it can be effective in helping people to overcome social and cultural resistance to certain types of products or practices.

Population Services International (PSI) is a multinational organization, funded by USAID and the Bill and Melinda Gates Foundation. It works mostly in Sub Saharan Africa and S.E. Asia. It sells and promotes products and services that address major causes of death in developing countries, such as condoms, insecticide treated bed-nets for malaria prevention and birth control to prevent unwanted pregnancies. PSI's promotion strategy includes mass media advertising and interpersonal communication, the latter involving training people to talk to the target audience about condoms, safe sex, etc.

Y.R. Gaitonde, India, is a company-linked NGO established in 1993 and is involved in four core areas of AIDS awareness and prevention – education, care and support, research and training. Its main sources of funding are the Ford Foundation and USAID. The activities of the organization include providing support materials for information on AIDS, organizing workshops and developing a network of HIV infected people. Its marketing communication strategy involves the use of art forms such as street plays and folk music to spread awareness. Its programs have been highly successful and are reported to have won international acclaim from the UNICEF, the WHO and the Red Cross.

A study mission in Tanzania (2003), taking into consideration the local terrain, infra-structural limitations and poverty level, proposed a scheme of providing bullock carts for transport of crop and inputs. It was proposed under the project to fund the purchase and distribution of bullock carts for villages in areas that have the cattle population for draught but not the resources to buy the cart. The assistance would be in the form of a grant to NGOs who are active, well organized and successful with the same or similar schemes. Women-organized NGOs were spoken to by the mission and they were enthusiastic to participate in the pilot scheme (Tanzania Association of Women Leaders in Agriculture and Environment – TAWLAE). The grants would be used for buying and distributing carts to select villages – 4 per village per district – through a selection of applicants in consultation with the village elders. The carts would be given on easy terms of repayment spread over four years. The TAWLAE would hire them out and use the proceeds to pay back the loan. The scheme would be spread over three districts that form a compact area to ensure close supervision. An additional sum was provided in the budget to meet supervision expenses. The NGO would use the recovered money as a revolving fund for further assistance. The coverage would be 256 carts costing approximately $ 120,000 which would cover two rounds – one in PY1 and the second in PY 4 if the first round was successful.

Aravind Eye Care System[9], started in Madurai, South India in 1976, has become the largest provider of eye care for the poor in the world. It conducts eye camps in remote villages and extends free eye care and sight-restoring surgeries free of cost to thousands. It is a non-profit organization and its patient services are entirely self-funded through a unique differential pricing model under which patients are given the option of choosing the free-of-cost option or the moderate price option or the full price option. The choice is not questioned or verified for income eligibility as is normally done in other hospitals.

Aravind's marketing concept is again original in its thinking. The founder-promoter designed an innovative business model that treats the poor "not as passive beneficiaries of charity but as customers in an economic market place. The restoration of sight is not the end point but viewed as a vital step in a larger chain of interconnection". The woman with restored sight is able to work in the fields again, her child has a better chance of going to school, then, a better chance of finding a job that will break the cycle of poverty. Their marketing concept targets those least able to pay.

As regards cultural adaptation, Aravind has set new standards. Their delivery design is meant to take the screening service nearest the homes of the poor – say, in the local school class room. Village camps are announced by loudspeakers fitted to auto rickshaws well in advance of the camp date as other means of communication like leaflets and TV do not reach the interior villages. Aravind doctors tell those needing surgery to come to the nearest hospital but surprisingly not many were turning up although the surgery was free of cost. Aravind realized that delivery of medical screening at the door step was not proving to be enough. It was found on research that the patient had to pay a bus fare, lose a day's wage and pay for food and medicines. And also because women in the villages, were unaccustomed to go to hospitals unaccompanied by an escort from the family. Aravind decided to take the bold step of giving transport to and fro, surgery, accommodation, food, post-operative medication and a follow-up visit at the village, all free of cost. Acceptance rate for surgery went up from 5% of those screened and marked for surgery to 80%. The number of patients brought in through its outreach camps was about 76,000 a year. The cost went up too and this had to be met by cross subsidizing and reduction in the cost per surgery by introducing the assembly line system hitherto unknown in eye surgery hospitals. Each surgeon was given a set of para medical staff/nurses who attended to all the peripheral functions, releasing the most valuable time of the surgeon for the actual surgery. This lowered the unit cost of surgery substantially.

FINDINGS OF STUDY[10]

The responses to the questionnaire on the application of marketing principles, their adaptation, the importance of cultural factors and actual examples of cultural adaptation revealed the following.

Only three out of the ten NGOs in the sample were of the view that marketing practices were largely or very much applicable to NGO activities. However, they were unanimous in their opinion that these practices were applicable only with changes to suit socio-economic activities.

Two aspects of commercial marketing requiring adaptation that were named by these NGOs included - first, the selling technique (social marketing requires emphasis on the consequence of non-compliance with behavioral change, as opposed to commercial marketing, which focuses on the benefits of compliance by using the product) and second, the approach towards the target group, since their cultural and economic situation was different as compared to commercial marketing.

A majority of the NGOs surveyed (9 out of 10) rated social and cultural features of the target community as 'important' or 'extremely important' in affecting their programs. However, only 7 NGOs grasped the full significance of cultural adaptation, as indicated by actual examples named by these NGOs of how their practices were adapted to suit the social or cultural needs of the community.

A Karnataka based NGO, whose main activity is reduction of the incidence of AIDS, adapted its media strategy based on a study of the cultural features of its target group in two different geographical areas – Raichur and coastal Karnataka. Raichur being a more permissive society, open discussions were held with the target group on safe sex practices to prevent AIDS. However, in coastal Karnataka, which was more conservative but more literate, the NGO used printed material to convey the same message.

Another Karnataka based NGO whose focus is on rural institution building and which also works among HIV affected segments, designed its programs differently for two different segments – MSMs (men having sex with men) and FSWs (female sex workers).

Use of the interpersonal channel itself was adapted based on the nature of the problem. For example, an NGO involved in empowerment of the working class held separate meetings for men and women in its target group to deal with gender related issues. While the meetings with women discussed issues like women's health and child marriage, the meetings with men focused only on land and property-related matters.

Similarly, an NGO involved in women's empowerment conducted individual meetings with women to deal with harassment issues, but spoke to opinion leaders of a particular caste to resolve caste issues.

An NGO involved in promotion of the concept of holistic health adapted its promotion strategy for Reproductive and Child Health (RCH) to its target group comprising women in rural areas. The NGO used street theatre instead of flip charts showing explicit details and visuals, to explain the concept and to avoid offending cultural sensitivities. They also did not conduct workshops during the festival season when the target group was not available.

Another NGO, also engaged in health promotion, adapted its promotion strategy for RCH by having separate sessions for mothers and daughters, men and women and by making the visuals culturally sensitive.

An NGO that focuses exclusively on the development and advocacy of the *adivasi*s, a backward community of original inhabitants in the Nilgiri hills, adapted its communication strategy to the needs of this community. All their communications were in the local dialect, oral medium, since the elders of the community were more comfortable with the oral, rather than the written medium. Secondly, since the *adivasi*s had their own language, all the NGO's field teams were drawn from the community, stayed in villages and spoke the *adivasi* language.

The NGO in Tamil Nadu engaged in imparting Social Health Education, is concerned with behavioral change through the "self-empowerment model", rather than being disease focused. The concept was borrowed from a sociologist from the UK and aims at enhancing social and life skills. The NGO organizes training modules and educational materials for the promotion of Reproductive and Child Health and prevention of RTI/STI/HIV/AIDS in slum areas, hospitals, industries, schools and colleges.

CONCLUSIONS

Awareness of the relevance of marketing practices to NGO activities seems to be low among the NGOs in the sample. Although the NGOs are aware of the need for adaptation of marketing principles, there seems to be lack of knowledge regarding the specific aspects to be adapted. Systematic training in marketing techniques and practices and adaptation of practices to socio-economic activities using outside experts may contribute to greater effectiveness. While there is an instinctive appreciation of the need to adapt delivery and communication methods to suit local habits and practices there is lack of formally trained understanding of the methodologies for cultural adaptation. Only four of the NGOs surveyed – three in the health sector and one involved in advocacy – seem to be effectively adapting their strategies to suit the cultural needs of their target groups.

Social marketing also seems to be considered synonymous with media, since the examples of cultural adaptation given are all related to promotion/communication strategy. CASM is all about fine tuning the program design, communication and delivery of services to cultures as well as sub cultures within a culture. This requires effective market analysis and an in-depth study of the target segments. More specific targeting of the different segments through more localized program design, delivery methodologies, communication messages and media, is required, taking into account social and cultural factors.

Although there have been a few success stories of CASM across the world, the results of the study indicate that it is not practiced in the areas covered to the extent that is desirable. Being a relatively new concept, it could form the subject of more detailed research, possibly a cross-cultural study in different developing countries, to assess its role in enhancing social marketing effectiveness.

The Aravind model of uniquely designed practices described earlier in this article, show how this NGO has been able to craft its marketing practices – production, delivery, communication, pricing, pre and post "sale" services - to suit every twist and turn of local cultural needs. From these experiences, there are two valuable lessons to be learned on culturally adapted social marketing. One, that the NGO was able to grasp the implications of the cultural and economic setting that determined the "exchange" balance between cost to consumer and the value she derives by the "purchase". The offer of sight restoration, strangely, in the environment in which this NGO was functioning, had so high a cost to the "consumer" that she preferred to forego sight restoration. The second lesson is this: "Obstacles can be addressed only when the problems are owned".

REFERENCES

1. Andreasen, Alan R, "Intersector Transfer of Marketing Knowledge", Working Paper, Social Marketing Institute, Connecticut Avenue, Washington D. C., 2000.

2. Bellamy, Hilary et al, "Social Marketing Resource Manual: A Guide for State Nutrition Education Networks", Prepared for the US Department of Agriculture, Food and Consumer Service, Alexandria, VA, USA, 1997.

3. Bloom, Paul N and Novelli, William D, "Problems and Challenges in Social Marketing", Journal of Marketing, American Marketing Association, Chicago, IL, Vol. 45, No. 2, 1981.

4. Cahill, John et al, "Social Marketing – A Resource Guide", Social Marketing National Excellence Collaborative, NY Turning Point Initiative, NYS Department of Health, Albany, NY, year?.

5. Duke, Allison and Long, Charla, "Trade from the Ground Up; A Case Study of a Grassroots NGO Using Agricultural Programs to Generate Economic Viability in Developing Countries", Management Decision. London, Vol. 45, No. 8, 2007. pg. 1320.

6. Fox, Michael P, "Condom Social Marketing: Select Case Studies", Prepared for the Department of Policy, Strategy and Research, UNAIDS, Geneva, Switzerland, 2000.

7. Jha, Mithileshwar, "A Manual for Culturally Adapted Social Marketing", Editor Epstein, Scarlett T, Sage Publishers, London, 1999. pp. 31-41.

8. Kotler, Philip, "Strategies for Introducing Marketing into Non-Profit Organizations", Journal of Marketing, American Marketing Association, Chicago, Vol, 33, 1979. Pp37-44.

9. Mehta, Pavithra K and Shenoy, Suchitra, "Infinite Vision", Collins Business 2012

10. Parthasarathy, Vimala, "Social Marketing Strategies & Traits of Successful NGOs in India - A Strategic Perspective with Reference to Select NGOs in the States of Karnataka & Tamil Nadu, India", doctoral thesis for PhD, approved by Manipal University, Manipal, India, 2013

11. Smith, William, "Social Marketing An Overview", The Center for Global Health Communication and Marketing, Connecticut Ave., Washington D C, 2006.

12. Stead, Martine et al, "Research to Inform the development of a Social Marketing Strategy for Health Improvement in Scotland", Final Report for NHS Health Scotland and the Scottish Executive, University of Stirling, Institute of Social Marketing, Scotland, 2007.

13. Walsh, D. C. et al, "Social Marketing for Public Health", Health Affairs, Project Hope, Bethesda, MD, Vol. 12, No.2, 1993.

14. Weinrich, Nedra Klein, "What is Social Marketing?" Weinreich Communications, Issue of the Social Marketing Quarterly, Connecticut Ave., Washington D C.

HOW EFFECTIVE ARE SOCIO-ECONOMIC PROGRAMS OF NGOS?

Abstract

In social marketing the program corresponds to "product" in commercial marketing. As such, it is a critical function. A Ph.D. study[10] on social marketing strategies of NGOs in two states of South India identified several aspects of the program function that contribute to overall effectiveness in terms of impact on the target community. The main aspects are - stakeholder involvement in the choice of theme, design and implementation, participatory approach as indicated by the extent to which the target community is involved, adaptation to cultural needs of the target audience and use of innovative techniques to influence behavioral change. Based on the responses gathered during the survey, the article assesses how select NGOs in the two states fared in conceiving, designing and implementing social programs. A significant finding of the study was that stakeholder involvement in program theme choice, design and implementation was less than satisfactory. Level of expenditure and relationship with stakeholders were found to have a significant influence on the program component of social marketing effectiveness. The article appeared originally in Southern Economist, India (May 2012)[11] and we are grateful to the publishers of the Journal for permission to re-publish it as part of this book.

INTRODUCTION

In recent years, non-government organizations have been playing a significant role in socio-economic development, both in developed and developing countries. This is largely due to their inherent strengths such as their ability to work closely with local communities, attract funds from donors, tackle specialized issues and reach out to underprivileged sections of society. Experience across the world also shows that the application of social marketing principles in socio-economic development has led to greater success, in terms of program impact and sustainability. Some examples are – (a) the Washington-Heights Inwood Healthy Heart Program, which was successful in getting consumers to switch from whole milk to low fat milk in a low income, Latino neighborhood of New York city. The campaign's objectives and strategy were studied by Weschler and Wernick (1992) as quoted by Bellamy(1997)[4]. (b) contraceptive awareness and usage in Morocco, Dominican Republic, Peru and Turkey – implemented through the manufacturer's model, which was examined by Agha S. et al (2005). Social marketing practices helped to maintain increased use of contraceptives in these countries, even after donor support was discontinued, (c) the health intervention programs of the American Cancer Society, which successfully used geo-demographic segmentation to encourage more number of women in specific urban areas to do mammograms, as cited by Andreasen (2000)[2].

The application of social marketing principles includes the by now well-known techniques, referred to as *4 P*s of commercial marketing, with the "product", the main *P*, being the social marketing program. The program is the core function in development activities and includes many different aspects - need identification, market segmentation, program concept, design, implementation, feedback, review, refinement and ensuring sustainability. This core function and how well it is managed by NGOs was the subject of research in the study.

BACKGROUND

Developing countries, face several problems relating to poverty, health, illiteracy, child care and women's status, all requiring large monetary and human resources. The tax base in these countries is too narrow to generate adequate funds for a formidable list of several competing needs. Consequently, the governments of these countries find themselves severely limited in their capacity to meet these multifarious demands. It is in this context that NGOs have come to assume an increasingly important role in development activities.

NGOs are funded by philanthropic institutions and international agencies, many of them also extending technical assistance in the form of training in areas like communication skills and program management. Creation of impact at the community level through sound program concept, design and implementation and continuous flow of funds from benefactors are inter-dependent and mutually reinforcing. Set against this background, it is important to know how well the voluntary sector is functioning with particular reference to the effectiveness of the programs implemented by them.

INDIA SITUATION

Data available on the size, distribution of activities and funding of Indian NGOs have thrown up some interesting facts. According to the NGO database of the Planning Commission, Government of India, 2004, the majority of Indian NGOs funded by the government are small sized NGOs with annual budgets of less than ₹ 500,000 a year ($ 10,000). Out of 5146 reporting NGOs in India in 2004, as many as 3915 were small sized NGOs with annual budgets between ₹ 100,000–500,000 (Kudva 2005)[8]. According to Kudva, the majority of NGOs (40%) are engaged in rural development activities. Indian NGOs receive funding either from domestic or international sources. The Foreign Contribution Regulation Act (FCRA) governs the flow of funds from international sources. Both the number of NGOs registered under FCRA and the amount of foreign contributions have increased over the years from 1993-94 to 2002-03 – the number of NGOs registered under FCRA from 15039 to 25404 and the amount of contribution received from ₹18 billion to ₹ 50 billion ($ 360 million - 1 billion) (Source: records of the Ministry of Home Affairs, Government of India).

LITERATURE SURVEY

The importance of the program aspects for social marketing effectiveness has been emphasized in several research and scholarly articles. The Marketing Magazine, Toronto (1996) described the special features of social marketing, especially social marketing campaigns for the promotion of public health, in terms of six *P*s, with program planning being one of them - policy, proof, politics, public relations, partnership and program planning.

Program planning is the central aspect of social marketing. It refers to coordinating the efforts of all the partners, working closely with the beneficiaries of the social marketing program to develop the desired message, setting up community based organizations and ensuring implementation of the program.

The literature survey throws light on the success and failure factors in social marketing. The importance of relationships or stakeholder involvement is identified as a success factor by Raval et al (2007)[12]. The authors state that "relationship-based" social marketing programs are more successful than "transaction-based" programs in terms of achieving sustainable behavioral change. Relationship-based marketing is an important feature of socio-economic programs, compared to commercial marketing of products and services. Relationship marketing is based on building relationships with stakeholders with the objective of bringing about customer loyalty and retention. The authors provide a rationale for relationship-based *social marketing* by restating Kotler and Armstrong's (1997) dictum as: "Build mutually fruitful relationships with the recipients and stakeholders and desired behaviors will follow."

One of the main reasons advanced by these authors for a relationship-based approach to social marketing is that social marketing programs have a long-term objective and are therefore likely to be successful only if long-term relationships are built with other related organizations.

The success of any program has to pass the test of sustainability. Sustainability implies that the desired change in the target community is assimilated and maintained even after the conclusion of the program term and without the support of an outside organization. There are different facets of the concept of sustainability. O'Sullivan et al (2007)[9], in their technical report on *Moving Toward Sustainability: Transition Strategies for Social Marketing Programs*, prepared for USAID, distinguish between two dimensions of sustainability – institutional sustainability and programmatic sustainability. Institutional sustainability is "the ability of a social marketing program to continue operations with little to no outside support." This definition of sustainability refers to the financial aspects of a social marketing program. Programmatic sustainability has been defined as "using the *4 Ps* of marketing to reach maximum efficiency" to create market impact of the program.

The authors offer a comprehensive definition of sustainability – "the ability of a social marketing program over time to manage its technical, financial, institutional and market related activities to maximize efficiency, self-financing and self-governance without reliance on external support." Based on this definition, the authors have developed a "sustainability continuum", with four components of sustainability - technical, financial, institutional and market sustainability. Technical sustainability, according to the authors, is "the ability of the organization to fulfill the core mission of social marketing". Financial sustainability is defined as "the degree to which the costs of the social marketing program (including overheads) are covered, typically through revenues generated by the sale of products". Institutional sustainability is "the management skills and infrastructure required for the social marketing organization to operate efficiently over time". Market sustainability refers to "the ability of social marketing programs to adapt and innovate to respond to market changes over time".

RESEARCH METHODOLOGY

Primary research in the form of a survey among ten NGOs in the southern states of Tamil Nadu and Karnataka (the two economically progressive States of India) was done to assess the efficacy of the program aspects of NGO functioning. The sampling procedure used was "holistic probability sampling", since it took into consideration various criteria for rating and selecting NGOs and minimized room for bias. The procedure consisted of the following steps – (a) narrowing down the universe of NGOs to those engaged in social marketing (b) preparing a "multiple factor profile" for the NGOs, based on seven main criteria (c) getting experts to assign weights to the criteria (d) rating the NGOs on each of the above criteria (e) calculating the score for each NGO by applying the weights to the rating (f) calculating the coefficient of variation (CV) to assess the degree of balance in the overall effectiveness of each NGO on the various criteria (g) ranking the NGOs based on scores and CV, combining the two rank values and selecting the best NGOs. A detailed account of the methodology is in the *Preface*

HYPOTHESES

Following a comprehensive survey of available literature and research studies, hypotheses for the larger study were developed, using the Log Frame Model as a starting point. This model is used by international institutions for assessing performance of socio-economic projects and has three components – a) Input - what is put into the organization (example, resources) b) Output - what the organization puts out (example, number of self-help groups formed, number of training camps conducted) and c) Outcome - impact created by the Output (example, number of women entrepreneurs encouraged, number of persons/ groups sensitized successfully by the training). The hypotheses relevant to the program aspects are as follows:

Hypothesis 1. Input significantly influences Outcome (where input is amount of funds and outcome is social marketing effectiveness).

The underlying assumption of the above hypothesis is that social marketing effectiveness is defined in terms of individual components and is not a single, consolidated dependent variable. The different components include policy (government relations), publics (stakeholder involvement), program, promotion, service delivery, purse (funding) and partnership (networking and alliances).

Hypothesis 2: A relationship of high involvement with stakeholders creates better impact/outcome.

Outcome refers to social marketing effectiveness which is defined in terms of the individual components mentioned above, with program aspects being one of the components. High involvement with important stakeholders, particularly the local community, donors and the government would mean frequent interaction and consultation with them, regarding choice of program theme, design and implementation.

RESULTS OF TESTS OF HYPOTHESES

Statistical tests including regression, correlation, t test, F test and co-linearity were carried out to test the hypotheses stated earlier, as well as the other hypotheses that were relevant to the larger study, using the SPSS 17.0 statistical software package.

First Hypothesis

The first hypothesis may be stated in terms of null and alternate hypotheses as follows –

1. **Input** significantly influences **Outcome**

Since no reliable data with respect to the amount of funds as input was available, expenditure by each of the NGOs was taken as being indicative of the available funds. Data was also unavailable on outcome (impact), since very few attempts seem to have been made to systematically assess the ultimate impact on the target community. Where it was assessed, sharing of information was not readily forthcoming. Therefore, social marketing effectiveness in terms of seven components mentioned earlier, on which information was available, was taken as an indicator of outcome. Thus the hypothesis was interpreted with reference to *each of the components of Outcome* and *not* to *Outcome as a whole*.

Null hypothesis: There is **no relationship** between **expenditure** and **social marketing effectiveness**.

Alternate hypothesis: Level of **expenditure** significantly **influences social marketing effectiveness**.

The Significance value in the Coefficient analysis being <0.2 for Funds (0.087) indicated that Funds as an independent variable, has a non-spurious correlation with Program. F Value (4.563) being >1, the null hypothesis that there is no relationship between the independent variable and Program (dependent variable) was rejected at the 0.12 level of significance.

The other relevant statistical indicators that were taken into account to arrive at a conclusion regarding the hypotheses were as follows – (a) coefficient of multiple determination, denoted as R^2, which measures the multiple correlation or linear relationship among more than two variables, the value of "R" indicating the multiple correlation / causation between the set of independent variables and the dependent variable (b) adjusted R^2, calculated to remove the "spurious" effects of independent variables on the dependent variable, with large differences between R^2 and adjusted R^2 indicating that some independent variables have a spurious effect on the dependent variable. (c) standard error of estimate, which shows the degree of variability of effect for sample data (NGOs in this case), of the many independent variables.

Based on the above statistical values, the alternate hypothesis was accepted and may be restated as:

1. Level of expenditure significantly influences *program aspects* of social marketing effectiveness.

The program aspects of social marketing effectiveness include adaptation of program design to cultural needs, introduction of innovative features in program design, involvement of stakeholders in theme selection, program design and implementation. However, there was found to be no relationship between the level of expenditure and components of social marketing effectiveness *other than program aspects*.

Second Hypotheses

The second hypothesis may be stated in terms of null and alternate hypotheses as follows –

2. A relationship of high involvement with stakeholders creates better impact/outcome where outcome is social marketing effectiveness defined in terms of the seven components stated earlier

Null hypothesis: There is **no relationship** between **stakeholder involvement** and **social marketing effectiveness.**

Alternate hypothesis: **Stakeholder involvement** significantly **influences social marketing effectiveness**

The Significance value in the Coefficient Analysis being <0.2 only for Funds (0.087) and Relationship (0.045) indicates that apart from Funds and Relationship all the other variables have a spurious correlation with Program. F Value (4.563) being >1, the null hypothesis that there is no relationship between the independent variable and Program (dependent variable) was rejected at the 0.12 level of significance.

Based on the statistical indicators, the alternate hypothesis was accepted and may be restated as follows –

2. Stakeholder involvement significantly influences *program aspects* of social marketing effectiveness.

Thus the correlation analysis indicates that both Relationship and Funds (Expenditure) have a meaningful correlation with Program and influence the effectiveness of Programs.

FINDINGS FROM THE STUDY – INNOVATIVE PRACTICES

The detailed questionnaire designed for an in-depth understanding of the functioning of NGOs covered several critical aspects of program concept, design and implementation. The responses indicate areas for more effective use of programs for higher impact on target community and sustainability.

Out of 10 NGOs in the sample eight involved their internal management, including their field staff in the choice of theme for their major projects. Seven out of 10 NGOs involved community leaders and the general community as well.

Regarding stakeholder involvement in the design of the program, all the NGOs surveyed indicated involving their internal management, including their field staff, while half of them involved community leaders.

Similarly, in the implementation stage of the program, 9 out of 10 NGOs involved internal management, including field staff, while 7 out of 10 NGOs involved the general community.

Regarding the frequency of contact with the target community, 8 out of 10 NGOs indicated being in touch with the community at least once a month or more often.

Some of the innovative features of their programs, as perceived by them, are described here and may be of interest.

An NGO involved in the eradication of child labor used a novel method to create awareness of this issue. Known as the "public hearing method", this involved getting judges to hear out child workers directly in court, in order to verify the existence of the problem. The media was also present to witness this interaction between judges and child workers. The media coverage created public awareness and eventually led to greater program impact in terms of reduction in the number of child workers.

Another NGO, whose main activity was advocacy and the development of the *adivasis* (tribal community), a backward section in the Nilgiris hill district of Southern India, used the members of the community themselves as change agents. They selected the majority of their field team members from this community and had all problems identified and solutions implemented by them.

A third NGO involved in the formation of Self Help Groups (SHGs) came up with a unique concept to ensure sustainability at the community level without depending on any external organization. Community based organizations (CBOs) or institutions comprising of members of the local community were formed, which were not only made responsible for managing their finance, but also for taking all major decisions for the welfare of the community as a whole.

An NGO which focused on AIDS awareness and prevention invented an innovative process to increase AIDS awareness and reduce its incidence. Known as "perspective building", it encouraged communities to recognize their problems and take responsibility for finding solutions with regard to HIV issues.

An NGO whose primary activity was the promotion of the concept of Social Health Education successfully used a training technique known as "mental vaccination", which was different from the conventional lecture method. This method was found to be more effective, since it made participants analyze and logically conclude what steps had to be taken to stay healthy.

A special feature of an NGO working in the health sector was the insightful design of projects, such that it lent itself to replication at new locations. This unique feature could lead to several potential benefits – greater cost-effectiveness, shortening of the implementation cycle, saving of time, room for frequent refinement based on experience, yet retaining flexibility for required adaptation to suit local conditions. They also carried out pilot health projects which became a model for the government.

An NGO that focused on building poor people's institutions made their projects demand driven rather than supply driven. While many projects tend to be supply driven, that is, provide standard services based on a prior knowledge of ground conditions, being demand driven is unique in that it involves understanding the specific needs of the target community and is more interactive and participative.

Cultural adaptation is one of the important aspects of effective implementation. The survey showed that there is wide recognition of the need for culturally adapted social marketing (CASM)), 9 out of 10 of the NGOs rating it as "important" or "extremely important". NGOs actually practicing cultural adaptation offered their experiences which are briefly summarized in the following paragraphs.

A Karnataka based NGO, whose main activity was reduction of the incidence of AIDS, adapted its media strategy based on a study of the cultural features of its target group in two different geographical areas – Raichur and coastal Karnataka. Raichur being a more permissive society, open discussions were held with the target group on safe sex practices to prevent AIDS. In coastal Karnataka, which was more conservative but more literate, the NGO used printed material to convey the same message.

Use of the interpersonal channel itself was adapted based on the nature of the problem. For example, an NGO involved in empowerment of the working class held separate meetings for men and women in its target group to deal with gender related issues. While the meetings with women discussed issues like women's health and child marriage, the meetings with men focused only on land and property related matters.

Similarly, an NGO involved in women's empowerment conducted individual meetings with women to deal with harassment issues, but spoke to opinion leaders of a particular caste to resolve caste issues.

An NGO involved in promotion of the concept of holistic health adapted its promotion strategy for Reproductive and Child Health (RCH) to its target group comprising women in rural areas. The NGO used street theatre instead of flip charts showing explicit details and visuals, to explain the concept and to avoid offending cultural sensitivities.

An NGO that focused exclusively on the development and advocacy of the *adivasis*, a tribal community in the Nilgiris hill district of Southern India, adapted its communication strategy to the needs of this community. All their communications were in the oral medium, since the elders of the community were more comfortable with the oral, rather than the written medium. Secondly, since the *adivasis* had their own dialect, the field teams were drawn from the community, stayed in villages and spoke the dialect.

FINDINGS FROM BENCHMARK EVALUATION MATRIX

In order to judge the values and interpret them, a grading scale based on a popularly accepted model was adopted as follows – 35% or less is poor, 36-50% is moderate, 51-60% is satisfactory, 61-75% is good and above 75% is very good. A fuller explanation of the evaluation procedures is in the Preface.

The combined overall score of all NGOs in the sample for all aspects of Product (Program) Strategy was in the moderate category - 49%, which is below the satisfactory level, indicative perhaps of the nascent stage of application of social marketing principles to product aspects.

Regarding the effectiveness on the sub-traits, adaptation of program designs to cultural needs was the only aspect that registered 63% in the good category. The other sub-traits showed lower scores in the satisfactory or moderate categories. Introduction of innovative features in program design and adoption of novel strategies were in the satisfactory range. Involvement of stakeholders in theme selection and program design were in the moderate category, as it was found to be mainly with internal staff, community leaders and community. Greater involvement with government and donors seems necessary.

The coefficient of variation collectively for all NGOs for program aspects was 34%, indicating that there is wide variation among the NGOs on the level of adoption of this aspect. This, combined with a moderate score shows that not only is effectiveness low, but even within a low score, performance is not consistent among the NGOs studied. On individual sub-traits also, the CV was very high, reflecting largely varying degrees of adoption of the practices relating to social marketing product strategies.

The benchmark for this trait was in the very good category, the benchmark score being 80%. There was only one NGO out of the sample of ten setting the benchmark. Of the remaining NGOs, 1 was in the good category, 2 were satisfactory, 3 were moderate and 3 were poor. This shows that with the exception of 2 NGOs, the remaining 8 are not so strong on this trait.

SOCIAL MARKETING MODEL FOR PROGRAM ASPECTS

Based on the benchmark scores for individual sub-traits of program, a social marketing model was derived. An NGO engaged in the health sector that organizes training modules and educational materials for the promotion of Reproductive and Child Health (RCH) and prevention of RTI/STI/HIV/AIDS qualified for being the benchmark in the very good category for the program function. Its practices are listed below -

- Involves all stakeholders in program theme selection and program design – government (state, central), local bodies, community leaders, general community, donors, mother NGO, internal management including field staff
- Adapts strategies to suit cultural needs and aptitudes and decides approach after consulting community leaders, mothers, SHG leaders and youth groups on cultural sensitivities
- Believes in innovative approaches to program implementation and incorporates innovative features – training is participative and interactive, besides employing visuals, case studies, PPT, games, skits, role play and brainstorming

- Adopts overall strategy based on using cultural rather than biological factors, focusing on empowering with accountability and strengthening community involvement through formation of action groups to ensure sustainability

CONCLUSIONS

Currently, mainly the internal management, community leaders and the general community are involved in the theme selection, design and implementation of programs. The donors and the government at different levels do not seem to be given an adequate role. Since the results of the hypotheses tests highlighted the fact that relationship (stakeholder involvement) influences the program aspects of development, greater interaction with and involvement of all important stakeholders are needed to raise the level of program effectiveness. NGOs should find meaningful and institutionalized methods of mutual consultation for effective two-way involvement, rather than rely on routine, one-way reporting formats.

The high frequency of contact with the target community indicates that the NGOs in the sample are working in close consultation with them and adopting a participatory approach.

The combined overall score of all the NGOs on program aspects was only in the moderate category and was one of the lowest among all the fifteen marketing traits. This implies that there is much scope for improvement in this very critical part of NGO functioning. The scores for the sub traits, particularly stakeholder involvement and introduction of innovative features in program design and imaginative strategies are only just satisfactory and could do better. Engagement of professionally qualified managers with sound marketing background could help to infuse innovative thinking into the organization.

The results of the tests of hypotheses show that apart from stakeholder involvement, program effectiveness depends to a large extent on availability of funds. Hence NGOs need to develop persuasive fund raising strategies to ensure continuous flow of funds from diverse sources and also develop self-reliance through generation of their own funds.

REFERENCES

1. Agha S et al, "When Donor Support Ends: The Fate of Social Marketing", Global Research Brief, US AID, PSP-One, Bethesda, USA, 2005. Full text of paper

2. Andreasen, Alan R, "Intersector Transfer of Marketing Knowledge", SMI Working Paper, Social Marketing Institute, Connecticut Avenue, Washington D. C., 2000.

3. Anonymous, "The six Ps of Social Marketing: Companies can Better Society while Boosting Profits", Marketing Magazine, Toronto, Vol. 101, No. 34, September 1996. pg. 14.

4. Bellamy, Hilary et al, "Social Marketing Resource Manual: A Guide for State Nutrition Education Networks", Prepared for the US Department of Agriculture, Food and Consumer Service, Alexandria, VA, USA, 1997.

5. Cannon, Lisa, "Defining Sustainability", The Earthscan Reader on NGO Management, Edited by Michael Edwards and Alan Fowler, Earthscan India, Daryaganj, New Delhi, 2007.

6. Cousins, William, "NGOs: Advantages and Disadvantages", Abstracted from Non-Governmental Initiatives in ADB, Asian Development Bank, Manila and reproduced in the website of The Global Development Research Center (GDRC), 1991.

7. Jha, Mithileshwar, in "A Manual for Culturally Adapted Social Marketing", Editor Epstein, Scarlett T, Sage Publishers, London, 1999. pp. 31-41.

8. Kudva, Neema, "Uneasy Relations, NGOs and the State", Paper presented at the Karnataka Conference ISEC/Cornell University/The World Bank, 2005.

9. O'Sullivan, Gael et al, "Moving Towards Sustainability: Transition Strategies for Social Marketing Programs", ABT Associates and USAID, 2007.

10. Parthasarathy, Vimala, "Social Marketing Strategies & Traits of Successful NGOs in India - A Strategic Perspective with Reference to Select NGOs in the States of Karnataka & Tamil Nadu, India", doctoral thesis for PhD, approved by Manipal University, Manipal, India, 2013

11. Parthasarathy, Vimala, "How Effective are Socio-Economic Programs of NGOs?", Southern Economist, Vol. 51 No. 1, May 2012

12. Raval, Dinker et al, "Application of the Relationship Paradigm to Social Marketing", Competition Forum, Indiana, Vol. 5, No. 1, 2007. pp. 1-8.

13. Veeramatha, C, "Role of NGOs in the Prevention of HIV/Aids – A Study in Karnataka", Institute for Social and Economic Change, Bangalore, Project 2001.

14. Walsh, D. C. et al, "Social Marketing for Public Health", Project Hope, Health Affairs, Bethesda, MD, Vol. 12, No. 2, 1993.

PERFORMANCE MEASUREMENT IN DEVELOPMENT PROGRAMS – PROBLEMS AND POSSIBLE SOLUTIONS

Abstract

Although Performance Measurement is an important need and function of an NGO it is one of the neglected components in the management process, especially those at the grassroots level which are our focus. The objectives of social development projects being often intangible and not immediately visible, the task of measurement becomes difficult. The article places performance measurement in the context of the NGO's vision and mission, substantiating it with an example. The importance of evaluating the overall sustainability of the organization as an integrated entity comprising financial, technical, institutional and marketing sustainability are illustrated. Performance measurement is not an end in itself but the means to identify weaknesses that may develop either in program strategy or in the organization's capacity to handle projects effectively. Possible approaches to measurement of output and outcome are indicated. The latter being more difficult, the use of socio-economic indicators has been suggested. The need for creating a bottom-line, as in commercial marketing, has been proposed to motivate NGOs and improve their self-reliance.

BACKGROUND

That measurement of progress of any purposeful activity during its occurrence and on its completion is needed for improved performance of that activity, seems like a statement of the obvious. Yet this is one of the neglected components in the management process of NGOs, especially those of the grassroots type which are our focus. Inherent characteristics of social marketing as opposed to commercial marketing make the task of measurement difficult. Performance measurement being an indispensable necessity for relationships and alliances to be initiated, established and continued for a sustainable voluntary sector, there is need for a better understanding of its meaning and implications The possible hurdles, how they are being overcome in different situations and what type of measurement innovations are possible, form the subject of this article.

PERFORMANCE IN A LARGER PERSPECTIVE

Performance measurement in its narrowest sense is to find out whether the job has been done at all, partially, or fully. It can be viewed as a routine exercise of numbers if the results are measureable in quantitative terms, or descriptively if the results are not amenable to quantitative measurement. Often, the qualitative evaluation is graded and converted to numbers to afford a ready quantitative comparison with another result or with the goal. In a larger sense, however, performance and its measurement is an exercise to assess the extent to which objectives for a given period and for a given activity have been achieved, the objectives themselves, over a period of time, contributing to the vision of the organization through means envisaged in its mission statement.

VISION, MISSION AND OBJECTIVES

Development organizations need to have a clear vision to provide a sense of direction to the organization. Vision refers to where the organization would like to be, as opposed to where it is now. Organizational mission refers to the means the organization wishes to employ to progress towards its vision. For example, Aravind Eye Care System[8], started in Madurai, South India in 1976, has become the largest provider of eye care for the poor in the world. Its vision was that there should be no treatable blindness remaining untreated in its surroundings. The mission was to extend eye care and sight-restoring surgeries free of cost to the poor who cannot afford to pay for treatment. Eye camps to the doorsteps of the poorest of the poor in remote villages and free sight-restoring surgery to the poor, post-care medical support, providing nutrition in convalescence and unique system of assembly line surgeries to increase the surgeon's productivity for coping with the large numbers needing attention, became the organizational strategies for accomplishing its mission. These strategies are translated into quantitative objectives like number of camps, number of cases identified for surgery, number of cases undergone surgery, number of surgeries per doctor, number of sight-restorations and so on. Performance in terms of the actual numbers are periodically assessed to compare with the quantitative objective or goal.

PERFORMANCE MEASUREMENT AS PART OF MARKETING EVALUATION

Adapting the types of evaluation identified by Domegan (2007)[3] the following evaluation system for social marketing is proposed.

Formative evaluation – This is conducted even before developing the social marketing strategy and designing the program. It includes researching the target audience to understand their behavior, pre-testing messages, delivery methods and new products. It often involves in-depth primary research using both qualitative and quantitative techniques. Formative evaluation is the foundation for the social marketing program and the subsequent measurement of its impact.

Output evaluation – The measurement of the marketing efforts made in accordance with the marketing plan is the output evaluation. This measurement is made periodically, say, quarterly. Examples are: numbers of eye camps, training programs, group meetings held. These are compared with planned numbers. These outputs are the means to create a desired impact or outcome.

Outcome evaluation – This is the marketing performance evaluation for outcome (impact) from output (efforts). This is carried out after the program has been implemented and also at periodic intervals thereafter, say, half-yearly. Measurement in numbers may not always be as easy as in counting the number of persons agreeing to undergo surgery. For example, in health related issues the impact of the program in terms of, say, new health habits adopted and sustained may be more difficult to measure. The purpose is to assess to what extent there has been a change / improvement in the audience's habit or knowledge.

Process evaluation – This type of evaluation is useful immediately after implementation of the program. Bellamy et al (1997)[1], suggest that tracking performance should be done from time to time with the following checkpoints.

- Is the intervention meeting goals?
- Is the intervention reaching the target audience?
- Which interventions are more effective?
- What are the costs of different activities per unit of target hit?
- Has the intervention on schedule?
- Which are the areas requiring additional effort?

PERFORMANCE MEASUREMENT AS PART OF SUSTAINABILITY EVALUATION

Organizational performance should strengthen sustainability. Achievement of marketing objectives according to plan (goals) and cost-effectively is the marketing aspect of sustainability referred to also as programmatic sustainability. Beneficiary or community impact is a part of the marketing sustainability covered in the earlier paragraph under Outcome evaluation. Financial, technical and institutional sustainability are the remaining aspects. The overall sustainability of the organization as an integrated entity is represented by the white box in the following diagram. All the six dimensions are illustrated in the diagram. Measurement of progress towards financial, technical, institutional and overall NGO sustainability are as important for an NGO as successful completion of the year's marketing program.

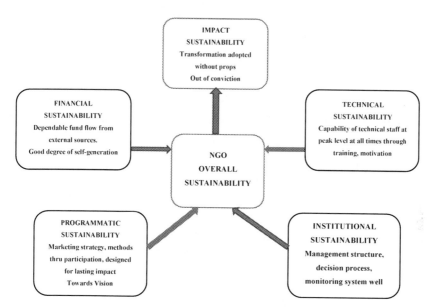

While the parameters for measurement may vary from program to program and from NGO to NGO those for evaluation of financial, technical and institutional sustainability could do with a commonalty of approach with finer changes to suit individual situations. The following Table is a suggestive list of sustainability indicators.

While some of these indicators are quantifiable, several are assessed only judgmentally preferably by an objective outsider. Periodic evaluation of these aspects would be necessary for the NGO's organizational fitness and sustainability.

GOAL SETTING

It is by now clear that performance measurement does not by itself mean anything unless it is compared with objectives which are transformed into quantitative goals set for each critical activity and staff. These goals can also be referred to as Key Result Indicators (KRI). The discussion in the previous paragraphs might have suggested some idea of how such goals are to be expressed numerically. Some goals are defined in terms of events – like "no interruption, of a duration exceeding one week, in fund flow during year" – which are easily recognizable. Goal setting should be such that the goal is not too easy as not to call for any serious effort, or so unrealistic that the person concerned gives up even before he or she has started. It should be attainable with effort and contain an element of challenge.

Bellamy et al (1997)[1], emphasize the importance of establishing clear and measurable objectives right at the beginning of the program. Setting targets requires insight and imagination to ensure their measurability and reliability as indicators of objectives.

Type of Sustainability	Indicator
Financial	Adequacy of funds for current objectives No interruption in fund flow during the period of review Introduction of new scheme/s / expansion during the period Funds for revenue as well as capital expenditure covered – latter for capacity building Fixed costs has not exceed 20% of total project expenditure. Has self-generated fund increased in absolute terms compared to previous year?
Technical	Knowledge of product/services, communication abilities of staff, periodically updated knowledge and skills Ability to retain good staff – number – continuity thru period without turnover Has access to technical resources Are the staff motivated and if so, how? Number of training for staff either in-house or external
Institutional	Durability – number of years since establishment Growth is scope, size and related diversification over preceding 3 years Is the management structure flat (not multi-layered)? Is there sufficient delegation of powers for quick decisions? Have goals been set and are staff aware of their role and objectives? External expertise in consultancy, training or on the Board of Management Is the Promoter or CEO professionally equipped? Has there been any interruption in leadership thru the last 3 years?

HOW PERFORMANCE MEASUREMENT RESULT IS USED

Performance measurement is not an end in itself but the means to identify weaknesses that may develop either in program strategy or in the organization's capacity to handle projects effectively. The following are some of its uses.

- An important use is for reporting to the Board of Trustees, funding agencies, alliance partners and the government. The first two would be interested in financial and marketing related performances. Alliance partners would be interested in knowing how the NGO has been fulfilling its share of responsibility in the strategic partnership, the definition of this share varying from case to case depending on the nature of the partnership. The government would want to know how monies funded by it have been used to complete its projects successfully and that there has been no diversion of funds. Donors would be keen to assess the institutional and technical sustainability of the NGO to review the vulnerability of the funds provided by them to the NGO's organizational vicissitudes. There are several ways performance measurement can be used:

- The NGO management can track progress, identify weak areas, weak performers among the staff, defective strategies, ineffective communication messages/media.

- Management can take corrective action, before it is too late, addressing specific weaknesses to ensure that the objectives are attained.

- Donors are not only interested in results but in their cost-effectiveness and, therefore, performance assessment should be designed to monitor cost effectiveness.

- Performance data over a period of time can be used for future projections and planning.

- If comparable data are available from NGOs engaged in similar programs and known for effectiveness, it can facilitate an honest self-appraisal to identify where improvements are possible.

DIFFICULTIES IN MEASUREMENT

As far as program effectiveness is concerned, two parameters need measuring – the effort made and the impact produced. The first covers advertising, promotional and distribution strategies employed to sell the product. These costs and quantities can be measured both in commercial marketing and in development marketing. Edwards and Hulme (2007)[5] are of the view that the nature of the work done by NGOs makes measuring their effectiveness difficult.

The second parameter – impact – in commercial marketing is measured easily in terms of volume/value sold, market share, profit. Impact in social marketing is quite often the adoption of new habits or behavior as means to, for example, better health or avoidance of disease. Measurement of this intangible is difficult as it does not register automatically in the cash register. Compounding this difficulty is the need to ascertain whether the change has occurred individually from a large number of individuals. The larger the number, the more difficult is the task of measurement. The number of the target audience is most often large. Impact, in these circumstances is measured only through sample surveys which require expertise that is unavailable in-house with NGOs.

Another performance test is for the organization as a whole which in a commercial entity is indicated by the net profit (referred to as the "bottom line" because it appears in the last line of the Profit & Loss Statement after charging all costs including interest charges and provision for depreciation). The net profit shows the return on the shareholders' risk capital. For an NGO there is no net profit or bottom line. How do we judge the NGO without knowing what non-monetary or satisfaction return it gives to stakeholders? Drucker (1990)[4] explains that while commercial organizations have a financial bottom line, with profits being a measure of performance, there is no such "bottom line" in non-profits (NGOs). Fowler's (2007)[7] view on the absence of a clear and straightforward measure of performance in non-profit organizations is similar to that of Drucker. Fowler explains that the "bottom line" for non-profit organizations cannot be defined in terms of financial returns, for the simple reason that NGOs are primarily service providers, serving a segment that cannot afford to meet the entire cost of what they receive. Therefore, they cannot be equated with consumers of a commercial organization who are willing to pay a premium for quality products.

There is a dearth of sufficiently reliable information regarding the performance effectiveness of NGOs. Even the few studies that have been carried out in this area are not representative, since they are based on small samples, or cover only NGOs working in a particular sector or context. As with all attempts to link cause and effect, there is always a problem of attribution – that is, is the impact the result of actions taken by a NGO project or some other broader factors such as macroeconomic factors.

Drucker suggests that non-profit organizations should start with a definition of the mission – the methods they would adopt to serve the cause of their vision. Performance planning needs to involve all the different constituencies or stakeholders of a non-profit organization – beneficiaries, employees, government, funding sources and the local communities. The performance *plan* is the touchstone by which *actual* performance that is measured from time to time will be tested.

POSSIBLE APPROACHES

Fowler cites organizational analyst Rosbeth Moss Kanter (1979), who suggests that non-profit organizations need to identify multiple criteria, rather than use a universal measure of performance effectiveness. Edwards and Hulme (2007)[5] suggest that some of the criteria that could be used for measuring the impact of NGOs are reduction of poverty, delivery of services in a cost effective manner as compared to the government, sustainability, use of participatory methods, flexibility and innovativeness of approach.

Edwards (2007)[6] identifies cost effectiveness as one of the most important aspects of NGO performance, considering that they are totally dependent on grants and philanthropy that require purposeful spending. He also suggests a broad method for determining NGO cost effectiveness, based on a study conducted among two NGOs in India and two projects in Bangladesh (1996). The cost effectiveness of each NGO/project selected for the study was determined in the following manner.

- The target population for each NGO/project was defined (e.g. tribal communities in 9 districts of Orissa)
- Both the direct and indirect beneficiaries of the NGO/project were determined. For example, the population of villages with fully active people's organizations were considered to be the direct beneficiaries of the NGO, while the population of villages that were partially organized by people's organizations were defined as the indirect beneficiaries.
- The total costs incurred by each NGO/project were determined, by calculating the sum of the program costs and the administration costs.
- The cost per beneficiary for each NGO/project was then determined by dividing the total costs by the number of direct plus indirect beneficiaries. This was considered to be a measure of the cost effectiveness of each NGO/project.

The two projects in Bangladesh were found to be less cost effective than the two Indian NGOs, since they were found to have higher costs per beneficiary and higher cost to benefit ratios. The reason for this was identified as higher overheads, such as large number of staff and buildings at various offices. The author suggests that NGOs should focus on reducing their overheads or fixed costs so as to improve their cost effectiveness and to concentrate their resources on actual program activities targeted at their beneficiaries.

The case study divides all costs – variable and fixed – by the target population size to calculate the cost per beneficiary. This is useful information on the cost effectiveness of the output but it does not address the problem of measuring the outcome (impact).

Thus, for output measurement a combination of the following two steps would yield a reliable indication of the efficiency of program implementation – how much of the planned program activities have been achieved (%) and at what level of cost effectiveness (₹ per head), both comparable from year to year for the same NGO and comparable with other NGOs who follow the same method. That is for output measurement.

MEASURING THE "IMMEASURABLE"

Drucker aptly describes non-profit organizations as "human change agents" whose results are measured in terms of a change, either in people's behavior, circumstances, vision, health, hopes, competence or capacity. It was concluded earlier that measurement of impact is possible mostly through sample surveys for which NGOs do not have the expertise. In the absence of an automatic self-generating indicator like the number of product pieces sold as in commercial marketing, the impact in social marketing, if measured by the NGO, may be subject to bias. Unlike output measurement which could and should be carried out periodically, say, every six months, impact does not occur so instantaneously and can be measured only at longer time intervals. One of the NGOs in the Study[9] with many years of experience said that it takes sometimes up to five years to create impact. The impact (outcome) is the cumulative effect of program efforts (output) sustained over that long a duration. Therefore, it is necessary that the donor should discuss and agree with the NGO and define the impact desired, quantify it, agree upon on the time interval for measurement and provide for the cost of an outside agency to assess impact. Involving the NGO field staff in the measurement methods (excluding aspects in which their involvement introduces bias) would help to improve their skill in measurement and survey techniques.

SOCIAL INDICATORS AS MEASURE OF IMPACT

Rajasekhar (2004)[10] suggests that performance measurement of NGOs engaged in social marketing can be facilitated by setting specific performance indicators. This is based on a study conducted to examine the economic and social benefits of the programs of two NGOs in the states of Karnataka and

Andhra Pradesh, India (2003). The economic benefits created by the programs were assessed in terms of improvement in livelihoods and access to resources. The table below explains each of these indicators.

Performance Indicators of Social Benefits – A Model

Areas	What to look for?	Specific variables
Livelihoods	Ranging from improvement to impoverishment	Occupational diversification Income levels Food security (seasonal) Ownership of assets
Resources	Ranging from access to exclusion	Access to productive assets, credit & savings facilities Affordability of school fees Affordability of health care
Knowledge	Ranging from expansion to reduction	Children's school attendance Girl education Knowledge on political institutions
Rights	Ranging from participation to alienation	Greater participation in local organizations Were the poor better organized or more assertive in their access or entitlement to rights? Reproductive rights

Source: Micro Finance, Poverty Alleviation & Empowerment of Women: A Study of Two NGOs from Andhra Pradesh and Karnataka – D. Rajasekhar, Institute for Social & Economic Change, Bangalore, 2004

In measuring impact it is important to agree upon and define, in advance, the specific variables to be measured to set measurable quantitative indicators. Depending on the nature of the project and its expected benefits to the target population, such socio-economic indicators as are likely to reflect that benefit can be selected. Normally such indicators are available in government's published statistics. Keeping track of these indicators for the area of operation of the project would become a reasonably reliable indicator of the outcome (impact) of the project.

INDICATORS OF PARTICIPATORY EFFECTIVENESS

Closely linked to performance indicators are indicators of participatory effectiveness. The basic strength of NGOs, as opposed to bureaucratic institutions, is their capacity to use participatory methods by which they encourage the participation of beneficiaries and local communities in designing and implementing programs. Carroll et al (1996)[2]quoting from the World Bank Participation Sourcebook, suggests the following as indicators of participatory effectiveness of an NGO.

- A flat management structure with decentralized authority
- Organizational structures at the community level to which funding and/or other decisions are delegated
- Use of iterative planning, involving consultation with local communities
- Contributions of cash, labor, raw materials, or local facilities by community members
- Staff recruitment criteria, incentives, and training that support participation
- Strong field presence with high proportion of staff of local origin
- Community members have a positive perception of the NGO
- Turnover of client groups as they "graduate" over time and intensive field attention transferred to new groups.

That is to say, impact of programs, once created, should be capable of continuing by itself without continued support. This enables program resources to be shifted to another area or segment.

The significance of using tests of participatory methods lies in the assumption, borne by experience, that if there is participation in the design and implementation of the program, the outcome is most likely to be satisfactory. Observance of participatory methods is used as a proxy for success in creating impact. The symptoms of participatory management listed above are verifiable without undue difficulty.

IS IT POSSIBLE TO CREATE A BOTTOM LINE?

It was mentioned earlier in this paper that the bottom line – the net profit representing the return on the stakeholders' risk capital in the organization and the consequent increase in the value of net worth – is an indicator of the standing of the concerned corporate and its growth over a period. It was also pointed out that there is no equivalent bottom line for NGOs because they are not in the business of making profit. A NGO's sustainability requires it to build its own earnings and savings to plough into enhancing its capacity to implement social development projects. Such a status places it on better bargaining terms with the donor and commands higher esteem. The term "non-profits" is, therefore, not to be interpreted to mean that making surplus to plough back into development programs is prohibited for NGOs. Making profits implies making it for the benefit of the investors. Making surplus going back into development and building financial stability is not the equivalent of making "profit". If this is accepted, there is a case for donors to consider re-structuring the compensation system for NGOs by following what may be called a "bottom line" approach.

In commercial marketing, the consumer's cost becomes the seller's monetary benefit. That monetary benefit helps the seller to reinvest, grow, increase self-reliance and sustain. The NGO marketing the program does not get any monetary return if it successfully completes the program, as commercial organization does, but only a sense of fulfilment, winning donor confidence and community's esteem. The question is: does it motivate the NGO to achieve goals, year after year, program after program and help them to increase their self-reliance?

NGOs have costs that are fixed and incurred regardless of the number of projects (FC), variable costs that are directly related to specific programs and incurred only when there are programs (VC). VC has to be fully reimbursed to the implementing NGO by the donor for the specific program. The donor also has to reimburse an appropriate share of the FC (also called overheads or management costs) - not all of the FC because other programs share the FC – to recognize the cost of management time the NGO employs to supervise implementation. When the program results are achieved the NGO gets *only* its costs – all of the VC and a share of the FC. There is no compensation for fulfilling targets of output and outcome – which it can put by to accumulate its own funds over a period of time or which it can use to strengthen the technical capacity or improve management systems. Such an element in the compensation structure, separately earmarked, seems necessary to motivate successful NGOs and help them to raise their level of sustainability. Without such a provision the good, the bad and the ugly are treated alike. A cardinal principle of marketing is that one pays according to the quality of product or service. If marketing principles are applicable to social development, the provider of a service should be no exception and receive compensation for good performance instead of getting only reimbursement of costs.

If, for example, a NGO receives from a donor all of its VC plus 15% of its FC, plus an incentive of 5% calculated on project cost (the latter payable only upon achievement), the incentive earned will be capitalized and be accumulated in the books of the NGO. This capitalized sum in the Balance Sheet is the "bottom line" indicating how the NGO has been doing over the years.

Extending the marketing practice a step further, NGOs should consider including into the staff compensation package an incentive payable every quarter based upon achieving targets agreed upon for each field staff according to his/her job responsibility. The targets would be such that they would be compatible with achievement of the project milestones and objectives. Payment of incentives to staff is a powerful motivator and may appear to increase establishment cost but, in actual fact, would increase effectiveness and reduce the cost per beneficiary. Imaginatively designed incentives are not cost but "cost-effectivizers"

EXAMPLES FROM THE STUDY[9]

Following are two examples of NGOs that have systems of evaluating their performance and impact on the community.

The NGO based in Bangalore whose mission is on making change happen in respect of responses to the HIV epidemic and sustaining the behavior change and supporting it with norm change in communities, has its objectives converted to measurable terms as follows.

- The number of persons that have been able to access services in a given project area
- Reduction of spread of HIV in the project community
- Reduction of impact on those already affected in the project community

Quality measurement, achievement of quantitative results with reference to expectations, and assessment of sustainability are undertaken. The organization's program achievements have been quantified and listed in their brochure – 10,000 women in sex work over 5 districts regularly interacting, over 14000 affected by HIV registered, of them 7000 accessing services, work spread over 1100 village communities, RSH services reached out to 21,000 women in urban areas and 18,000 in rural areas

Another NGO in the hill district of Nilgiris in South India was started with the sole objective of empowerment and development of the exploited *adivasi* community (tribal community in the hills). A program that helped to increase the productivity of land was taken over by the *adivasis* and it generates extra income from tea plantation. The NGO set up its own tea nursery, and trained *adivasi* youth and *sangam* members on tea cultivation and management of the nursery. The NGO measures its impact by the number of *adivasi* farmers that are able to acquire an extra source of income and security of land holding.

PERFORMANCE CRITERIA FOR SECTORAL REPLICATION

Having discussed various issues and possible solutions for performance assessment for individual NGOs it may be fruitful to take a broader perspective and see whether it is possible to assess critical features of successful projects and test their suitability as a model for replication. Valadez and Bamberger (1994)[11]suggest that performance monitoring and evaluation of NGOs and projects should be done on a sector wise basis, since it would help to understand the successes and failures in specific sectors of the economy, such as health or education. The authors formulate the following tests for determining "replicability":

- Which of the available methods of service delivery are the most cost effective?
- What impact would implementation of the project on a larger scale have on cost effectiveness?
- What are the conditions which make the different methods of service delivery most effective and least effective?
- What implications would replicating the project on a large scale have?
- If the project is replicated on a larger scale, which population groups are likely to benefit most and least?

Since projects are generally expected to contribute to broad sectoral objectives and improve the living conditions of people on a large scale, identifying the "potential replicability" of a project is an important criterion for performance evaluation. For example, a successful primary education project in a particular geographical area may serve as a model and lend itself to replication over a larger geographical area. The absence a unique legal identity for development NGOs is a handicap in establishing a central data base into which cost effectiveness data from various NGOs operating in a sector can be fed.

In conclusion, it must be mentioned that some of the systems and approaches for performance measurement may seem too sophisticated but in reality they are not. Whether the NGO is big or small most of the principles are relevant and applicable. There is, however, considerable room for simplification and adaptation to match the limitations and needs of smaller NGOs and it is here that apex NGOs offering services can play a role to tailor suitable measurement methodologies to answer the needs of grassroots NGOs.

REFERENCES

1. Bellamy, Hilary et al, "Social Marketing Resource Manual: A Guide for State Nutrition Education Networks", Prepared for the US Department of Agriculture, Food and Consumer Service, Alexandria, VA, USA, 1997.
2. Carroll, Thomas et al, "Participation and Intermediary NGOs", Abstract from Book by authors, World Bank Participation Source Book, Abstract reproduced in the website of The Global Development Research Center (GDRC), 1996.
3. Domegan, Christine, "The Use of Social Marketing for Science Outreach Activities in Ireland", Irish Journal of Management. Dublin, Vol. 28, No. 1, 2007. pp. 103 - 125.
4. Drucker, Peter, "Managing the Non-Profit Organization", Harper Collins Publishers, 1990.
5. Edwards, Michael and Hulme, David, "NGO Performance and Accountability: Introduction and Overview", The Earthscan Reader on NGO Management, Edited by Michael Edwards and Alan
6. Edwards, Michael, "Organizational Learning in Non-governmental Organizations: What Have We Learned?", The Earthscan Reader on NGO Management, Edited by Michael Edwards and Alan Fowler, Earthscan India, Daryaganj, New Delhi, 2007.
7. Fowler, Alan, "NGO Performance: What Breeds Success? New Evidence from South Asia", The Earthscan Reader on NGO Management, Edited by Michael Edwards and Alan Fowler, Earthscan India, Daryaganj, New Delhi, 2007.

8. Mehta, Pavithra K and Shenoy, Suchitra, "Infinite Vision", Collins Business 2012

9. Parthasarathy, Vimala, "Social Marketing Strategies & Traits of Successful NGOs in India - A Strategic Perspective with Reference to Select NGOs in the States of Karnataka & Tamil Nadu, India", doctoral thesis for PhD, approved by Manipal University, Manipal, India, 2013

10. Rajasekhar, D, "Micro-Finance, Poverty Alleviation and Empowerment of Women: A Study of two NGOs from Andhra Pradesh and Karnataka, Social and Economic Change Monographs", Institute for Social and Economic Change, Bangalore, 2004.

11. Valadez, Joseph and Bamberger, Michael, "Monitoring and Evaluating Social Programs in Developing Countries", Economic Development Institute of the World Bank, EDI Development Series, 1994.

SUCCESS AND FAILURE FACTORS OF NGOs AND CASE STUDIES

Abstract

From extensive literature survey and deriving from the study of ten NGOs of two states of South India, this article summarizes success and failure practices of the NGO sector. Several cases and models of successful NGOs are presented in the expectation that they may provide useful practical lessons for those engaged in NGO management and for organizations that provide managerial services to NGOs operating at the community and district levels.

BACKGROUND

The rapid growth of the voluntary sector in recent years and its increasingly important role in the improvement of the health and livelihoods of the poor, has attracted scholarly attention of management experts to study this new genus of the organizational species that has earned the sobriquet as the Third Sector. The emergence of this sector has had significant impact on the advancement of rural societies in developing and least developed countries. NGOs have not had a smooth ride to fame. It took considerable time for governments of these countries to accept the NGO sector, grudgingly, as a partner in development. For many years they were under suspicion – even now so in many African countries – for subversion of the ruling party or as agents of foreign funding agencies. Although some suspicions were deserved, much of it was borne of jealousy of the esteem that NGOs were able to command over the local population by virtue of their ability to deliver services. NGOs are led by local volunteers with commitment but not necessarily money or managerial talent. How are they able to tackle problems of raising resources on a sustained basis and to manage the task of bringing about transformation? How are the

206

NGOs able to establish strong relationships with alliance partners and network members without formal training in human skills? How do they set up systems and controls at the micro level without being able to engage graduates in management? What makes them grow in response to rising demand for their participation? What makes them fly or fall in the attempt to survive and grow? Although social marketing and the emergence of the voluntary sector are of relatively recent origin, the already established principles of management have produced a large amount of literature on this recent entrant. These publications may have eloquent and scientific answers – drawn from experience of trial and error. But more convincing to ordinary practitioners are examples of the rise and fall of individual NGOs that provide genuine lessons from experience. The paper will trace the views of scholars on the inherent strengths and weaknesses of this sector and examine various cases of success and failure in an attempt, wherever enough information is available, to identify the critical element that shaped their destiny.

POSITIVE ASPECTS

Empowerment and development NGOs undertake activities based on studies to determine who the poorer sections are, the reasons for their poverty and the strategies most suited to alleviate their conditions. Based on these studies, they help the poor to articulate their concerns and address their problems. Compared to the governmental agencies they are more flexible in terms of their functioning, since they are small in size and are in close touch with local communities. A few surveys among Karnataka-based (India) NGOs revealed that a majority of them covered only one or two taluks (sub-districts) in a district (Rajasekhar 2000)[13]. This makes it easier for them to implement and monitor their programs, respond quickly to local needs and change their working styles according to the needs of each community. The small staff strength also enables better coordination. Interestingly, smallness, which is considered a weakness by some international agencies, turns out to be a source of strength as close contacts with communities is essential for cultural adaptation of programs.

Empowerment and development NGOs use innovative and participatory approaches, whereby they involve the local communities with which they work. A good example is that of the Grameen Bank in Bangladesh, whose innovative credit program is implemented by both developed and developing countries. Another example worthy of mention is the Credit Management Program of MYRADA (Mysore Resettlement and Development Agency), one of the NGOs in the Study[10]), whose innovative approach inspired other NGOs to introduce similar programs.

MYRADA and the Centre for Appropriate Technology (CAT), based in Tamil Nadu, have adopted innovative approaches to watershed and dry land development. Several NGOs have successfully adapted participatory methods such as Participatory Rural Appraisal and Participatory Learning and Action and used them to derive much benefit. As a result of people's participation, they have been able to make watershed and dry land development more cost effective. Development and empowerment NGOs enjoy greater autonomy than other NGOs, since many of them have independent governing boards. People's participation in their programs also makes the development and implementation of their programs independent of the local power structures.

Rajasekhar diagnoses that NGOs are more motivated and committed than most government agencies. His view is based on a comparative study of programs implemented by the government and an NGO to benefit small farmers in Mangalore district in Karnataka, India. The NGO program scored over the government program in terms of problem definition, design, implementation and evaluation, training given to farmers, coordination and follow up activities. Other similar comparative studies in Karnataka have also led to the same conclusion.

NEGATIVE ASPECTS - OVERVIEW
The World Bank has had the experience of NGOs not having been able to contribute their full potential to support Bank operations due to the following weaknesses (World Bank Manual[16]).

- Activities of NGOs are too localized to be replicated on a regional or national scale.
- In trying to widen the scope of their activities with support from the public sector, NGOs may lose their autonomy, innovativeness and become non participatory.
- Many NGO programs are not designed to bring about sustained behavioral change.
- Even the professionally staffed NGOs have inadequate managerial resources, poor accounting systems and limited infrastructure.
- Coordination has been recognized as a constraint affecting the NGO community itself.
- Some NGOs combine development concerns with political or religious objectives that limit the extent to which the Bank can work with them while safe-guarding its primary relationship with its member governments.

Localized NGOs have a different function to perform. The larger NGOs operating at the apex level as service providers or as "wholesalers", utilize the services of local NGOs as "retailers" for program implementation at the community level. And that function is not only necessary but best performed by small NGOs that remain close to communities. They can be replicated at the community level and, naturally, not extrapolated to a larger. Their smallness cannot be dubbed as a weakness.

Criticism (e) above emphasizes the importance of an overall strategy within which individual projects should be implemented in a coordinated manner. This is not a weakness of individual NGOs but of the overall policy.

NEGATIVE ASPECTS - FINDINGS ON INDIAN NGOs

The following are some of the weaknesses of NGOs cited by Rajasekhar. Besides poor governance and lack of transparency as they grow, NGOs tend to become more hierarchical and dominated by its leadership. Decision making is confined to top levels of management, while the opinions of lower level staff are often ignored. Most NGOs also have no transparency regarding their expenditures and how the money is spent.

Inappropriate targeting of services and failure to provide services to the needy sections of society have been cited as some of the shortfalls. Inability to reach out to the poorest sections has been cited, based on a study of nine NGO savings and credit programs all over India (1996 and 2000). Rajasekhar says that factors such as the importance given to savings linked to credit, collateral requirements and short-run credit prevented the poorest from availing of credit facilities. Short-run credit offers a repayment term that is too short compared farmers' seasonal situation for sowing and harvesting and the crop duration.

Hostile attitude toward the government is another negative factor cited. This is particularly said to be true of development and charity NGOs, which sometimes try to replace the government as a provider of services and development programs which may have the effect of weakening people's trust in the government.

NGOs have shown their inability to impact government policies at various levels. One reason for this is the fact that NGOs tend to compete, rather than collaborate on various issues. As a consequence, they have not emerged as a collective force to represent the interests of their members.

Based on a study of 16 NGOs in Karnataka, India (1998), he suggests that the activities of NGOs are dictated by the donor's or the government's policies, rather than by the needs of the people.

NEGATIVE ASPECTS – FINDINGS ON BANGLADESH NGOs

Transparency International-Bangladesh[14] (TI-Bangladesh), published a study in October 2007 highlighting problems in the NGO sector. The study was motivated by reports and complaints that some of the country's NGOs had moved away from the values of volunteerism and self-less service to the poor and needy. TI-Bangladesh also noted that there have been allegations that while NGO intervention had significantly facilitated the uplift of the poor, a substantial portion of the resources is reported to have not actually reached the target group. Among the weaknesses confronting NGOs cited in the study are the following.

- lack of financial sustainability
- shortage of efficient employees and high employee attrition
- inadequate infrastructure
- lack of information and relevant research

FAILURE FACTORS

A review of the existing literature also throws light on factors that lead to failure of NGOs. Zaidi (1999)[18] analyzes some of the reasons for the failure of NGOs to bring about social development, especially in underdeveloped countries and argues in favor of the extreme step of bringing back the State. In his view NGOs, which were perceived to be better equipped, more cost effective, community oriented and participatory in their approach to delivering services than the government, have failed to live up to the high expectations. Therefore, he sees the only solution to be reforming and bringing back the government.

Zaidi considers the primary reason for the failure of NGOs to be over dependence on foreign funds. He cites Alan Fowler (1991), who also attributes the extraordinary growth in the number of NGOs to the increased flow of official aid from international agencies such as the UN and the World Bank. As an example, in 1993, one third of all approved World Bank projects involved NGOs in one way or another and by 1994 this percentage had risen to almost half. As a consequence of increasing foreign aid, the author believes that the agenda of NGOs is dictated by international donors. He quotes Adil Najam (1996): "finance provided by the donor can be a means of ensuring that the donor's policy agenda is adopted by the NGO and of holding the NGO accountable to the agenda..." This has led to a "patron-client" relationship between donors and NGOs, lack of freedom to function for the NGO and sometimes even 'fudging' of results to please donors. The author suggests that NGOs need to reduce their dependence on foreign funding, have more downward accountability (to beneficiaries), focus more on long-term results in order to be successful.

The extremist view that NGOs have failed and that the state should be brought back is similar to the stand taken by the government in Ethiopia. In any case, in countries like India there is no question of bringing back the government as the government never withdrew from development activities through its own agencies and the local governments. NGOs in Ethiopia were looked upon as a faulty mechanism for stimulating growth. "NGOs are foreign-backed and are not member-oriented. An NGO would bring all things, so that the community remained like beggars, with no role in development." Programs often collapsed when NGOs departed, and some NGOs spend up to 75 percent of their budgets on administrative costs, according to critics. Cooperatives are viewed as an improvement because Ethiopia's chronic problems are better tackled by the long-term capacity-building that cooperatives promote. Cooperatives, according to critics of NGOs, had ownership and commitment (Source: Globalissues) [15]

Rajasekhar (2000)[13] takes a different view from that of Akbar Zaidi, regarding the role of the NGOs and the government in delivering services to the poor. While Zaidi argues in favor of bringing back the government as an answer to the failure of NGOs, Rajasekhar suggests that NGOs should play an active role in facilitating the delivery of services by the government. Rajasekhar proposes that NGOs should play the role of facilitators and persuade the government to deliver services efficiently, by adopting the following strategies.

- NGOs could help to form people's organizations at different levels, train the poor and encourage leadership among them. This way they would be better equipped to become independent and be able to plan and monitor development activities.

- The people's organizations should be trained to exercise their rights and access resources from the government.
- NGOs should form networks among themselves to be in a better position to influence government policies through advocacy and lobbying.

Thus there are extreme views about the utility of the NGOs' role in development projects but judging by the experience of the growing importance in development activities in various developing countries, it seems safe to reject the extreme view of replacing NGOs with the government agencies.

SUCCESS FACTORS

Capacity building is identified by the World Bank as one of the factors contributing to the success of NGOs. Capacity of an organization refers to not only to its physical equipment and buildings, but more basically to the skills and capabilities of its working force at all levels, their empowerment to take decisions and their innovative abilities, all reinforced and strengthened by periodic exposure and training.

Ebrahim (2008)[4] argues that capacity building has typically concentrated on providing buildings, vehicles and hardware, ignoring the need to build people's skills and abilities. The author is of the view that the onus for capacity building lies with donors rather than with the NGO. Donors need to help organizations to identify their capacity needs. In addition, training programs should be designed at the local level, in order to suit the needs of the field staff.

Regarding capacity building, the authors recommend the use of the Oxfam model, which was based on training local governments in participatory methodologies. This involved working closely with villagers to identify, analyze and find solutions to community related problems. Each ministry of the local government developed a separate work plan, which was then integrated into one, after consultation with the different departments and communities and Oxfam. A single plan was then jointly implemented by Oxfam and the local government. The reason why this model was highly successful, according to the authors, was that all the parties concerned were involved in the process of identifying needs and generating solutions.

The concept of Culturally Adapted Social Marketing (CASM) suggests that social marketing strategies should be adapted to the cultural context in which they are developed, since cultural barriers are one of the biggest obstacles to social behavioral change. CASM is recommended for a better understanding of client groups. The impact of culture on behavioral change is often overlooked by social marketers. Social marketing organizations should consider hiring social scientists to help them understand the prevailing cultural norms, apart from hiring the services of technical experts in areas such as health, nutrition or education.

Powell et al (2007)[11] examined the application of social marketing to reduce alcohol consumption among population groups with low socio-economic status in Great Britain. Based on the findings, the authors suggest the use of geo-demographic analysis, or segmentation of the population based on both geographic and demographic variables, for successfully bringing about change through social marketing. The advantage of more precise targeting is that scarce resources can be allocated to those areas which need them most. Such an analysis would also help to tailor social marketing interventions to different segments of the population at the country, city or town levels, according to their respective peculiarities.

SUCCESS FACTORS – CASE STUDIES

One area where there is much scope for the application of social marketing is in promoting better water management. ("Appropriate Technology" Hemel Hempstead, UK)[6] cites the experience in South Asian countries, including India and Nepal, that shows that water management could create greater water availability, thereby helping small farmers to achieve food security through increased crop yields. There is the case study of a local Indian NGO, Seva Mandir, in Udaipur, which successfully involved the local community in water management practices. The report identifies the primary reason for the success of the program as the integration of various practices, including rainwater harvesting, afforestation, rejuvenation of grazing lands and watershed treatment.

Duke and Long (2007)[3] examine the factors that led to the successful use of a model of agricultural development by Healing Hands International, a grassroots NGO, to reduce hunger and establish economic viability in developing countries. HHI has been acclaimed globally for achieving economic viability in developing countries through its four-step approach to agricultural development. The authors identify two factors – training and establishing trust through social networks - that led to the successful implementation of their program. Since there are about 40,000 such NGOs involved in bringing about sustained economic viability in developing countries, they are also of the view that these success factors could serve as a benchmark for the programs developed by these NGOs.

Building trust and social networks was achieved by distributing medical aid, food and educational resources. They cultivated relationships with important local contacts. This helped them to build relationships with residents of the community and build the trust of social networks required to gain access to resources.

Working closely with local communities and a needs-based approach to social marketing has been identified as a success factor by Ebrahim (2001)[4], based on the lessons drawn from case studies of two well established NGOs in Gujarat, India. The author is of the view that NGOs that are closer to the field are in a better position to understand and speak about specific local issues, than those that are far removed from the community. For example, one of the NGOs, Sadguru, which was in direct contact with village communities, had developed a better understanding of rural needs and this was reflected in their successful introduction of lift irrigation as an intervention. The NGO had conducted a survey of villages in one of the districts of Gujarat, in order to gain insight into local conditions and demands. Since there was a strong local demand for irrigation, Sadguru introduced lift irrigation on an experimental basis in some districts of eastern Gujarat. Soon irrigation projects became their main activity and the NGO was able to successfully raise funds from both the government and corporates for its work.

Fox (2000)[5] draws lessons regarding the success of social marketing from selected case studies of condom social marketing in Haiti and Mozambique. An innovative approach to marketing of condoms used in these countries was Community Based Distribution. In this model, non-professional sales agents were recruited from the general population, trained in sales of condoms and rewarded through small margins on their sales. The author identifies both the obstacles and lessons to be learnt from these case studies. The CBD approach was quite successful in opening up new sales areas and outlets and in educating people about AIDS. The program was also cost effective, since the benefits of using community-based distributors exceeded the costs incurred in appointing and rewarding them. Even small margins were sufficient to motivate the community-based distributors. The lesson to be drawn from this experience is that use of low cost, innovative methods can lead to success of social marketing, in spite of cultural and other barriers.

A study of the effectiveness of the NGOs involved in promoting non-formal environmental education in Bangalore Urban District was undertaken by Yeshodhara (2004)[17]. Some of the common problems and limitations faced by the NGOs that stood in the way of effective performance were inadequacy and delays in fund flow, especially from the government and lack of information regarding fund raising procedures.

Holcombe et al (2004)[7] point out the lessons to be learnt from three case studies of NGOs in Senegal, Malawi and Pakistan, on various aspects such as accountability, trust and capacity building and partnerships with local governments. One of the case studies in Malawi was an attempt to form a partnership between an international NGO, the local government and a

Community Based Organization (CBO), with the objective of providing local solutions and community based care to AIDS orphans in Malawi. This was based on the Oxfam model of successfully using partnership to build local capacity. However, in reality, it was found that there was more competition than collaboration between the CBOs and the local government. The CBOs did not establish links with local governments as expected of them and often competed with local governments by hiring their staff. The authors suggest that smooth partnerships based on equal sharing of risks and benefits, a shared vision of common goals, trust and transparency are key factors that lead to success in social marketing. Mutual understanding of the respective roles would also be a key factor for success, through complementarity rather than competition. Preferably different functional roles could be considered in partnerships to avoid overlap and friction.

CASE STUDIES - INDIA

Although social marketing still was yet to establish itself in India, there are several success stories and models available for replication. A review of some of these gathered from the literature on the subject and websites is presented in the following paragraphs.

Akshaya Patra, Karnataka state, India is essentially a school meal program for underprivileged children. It is a pioneering effort in designing and setting up engineered kitchens that have the capacity to prepare 100,000 meals in less than six hours under hygienic conditions. The organization has a presence in 14 locations, spread across six states, covering 4500 schools and 852,000 children. The problems of procurement, manpower, hygiene, quality and nourishment involved in feeding on a large scale are addressed by this institution. Akshaya Patra's vision is to end children's hunger, empower underprivileged children with education tools and make them globally competent. It has entered into partnership with the government and gets support from corporates. A study conducted by A C Nielson showed a rise in school enrolment and reduction in drop-outs. This NGO has received several recognitions and has been used as a case study in the Harvard Business School. Use of technology and professionally designed management processes and a sound delivery system, working infallibly day after day has been the key to success. A similar approach may not be applicable in all cases.

There are a number of support groups based in Bangalore that help rural development oriented NGOs in evaluating their programs, capacity building for their personnel, creating newsletters and pamphlets. One such support group that serves the southern region and is based in Bangalore, is SEARCH. SEARCH was established in 1975 by an ex Oxfam Director and trains people in rural development. They offer a one-year course in rural development that includes a practical component. They later diversified into other areas of training such as gender sensitization and organizing women in villages through a Field Service, which they set up in Tamil Nadu. Today SEARCH offers various training programs for all levels of NGO staff. They also trained women for participation in Panchayati Raj in a program sponsored by the Department of Women and Child Welfare, Govt. of Karnataka. They have their own large training center outside Bangalore.

In addition to support groups, Karnataka also has a number of strong, formal networks of NGOs involved both in rural and urban development. The best known among these networks is the State Level Federation of Voluntary Organizations for Rural Development in Karnataka (FEVORD–K). Networks offer the advantage of being a platform for NGOs to share their problems and experiences. They also assist NGOs in interacting with the government, securing funds and preparing grant proposals. FEVORD–K was established in 1982 with the objective of promoting cooperation and understanding among its member NGOs, without direct interference in NGO affairs. Its role is merely to act as a liaison between the member NGOs and the government and donors, as well as to strengthen the NGOs through appropriate training. FEVORD–K has more than 150 member organizations that range from large organizations to small social action groups.

The majority of NGOs in Tamil Nadu, India, work in rural development, followed by health and women's and children's issues. SHARE, for example, is an NGO working with poor women from landless households in villages in a drought prone area of Tamil Nadu. It was established in 1992 and its "intervention strategy" is to set up craft centers and income generation activities for poor women and to market these products in national and international markets. These activities have helped to make the poor women, most of whom are from the backward and Muslim communities, more secure. SHARE also provides training, education and support services such as child care, safe drinking water and evening study centers for women and their children.

The Centre for Rural Education and Development is a NGO, set up in 1987, in Madurai, Tamil Nadu, India, and pioneered the concept of micro credit for the empowerment of rural women in Madurai. It also introduced the concept of Self Help Groups (SHG) among women. Selected SHG's attend training sessions on gender awareness, health, human and child rights and then promote the concepts in their target areas. Initially, the WSHG concept had to face cultural barriers in a male dominated society, but is said to have overcome these hurdles. As a result, rural women have developed an entrepreneurial mind set, financial skills, communication abilities and an organized way of solving problems. They have also gained self-esteem and greater visibility.

Y.R. Gaitonde is a company-linked NGO established in 1993 and is involved in four core areas of AIDS awareness and prevention – education, care and support, research and training. Its main sources of funding are the Ford Foundation and USAID. It claims to be one of the few organizations offering the entire range of services from prevention to care in this area. Its vision is to enable people with AIDS to live in dignity. The activities of the organization include providing support materials for information on AIDS, organizing workshops and developing a network of HIV infected people. Its marketing communication strategy involves the use of art forms such as street plays and folk music to spread awareness. Its programs have been highly successful and are reported to have won international acclaim from the UNICEF, WHO and the Red Cross.

MYRADA CASE STUDY

NABARD (National Bank for Agriculture and Rural Development, Government of India owned Bank) a donor agency for NGOs engaged in rural development, was involved in the success of an NGO project – that of MYRADA's pilot project on Self Help Groups in Mysore (1989-91). MYRADA pioneered the concept of SHGs, SHG-bank linkage and community-managed resource centers. NABARD played a significant role in the success of this project, since they were the supporting organization, and launched the SHG-bank linkage program. The basic concept was similar to that of the Grameen Bank model in Bangladesh. The project was a huge success since it was the first of its kind in socio-economic development and was replicated in other areas. Five hundred SHGs were formed, went through incubation and were rated for their thrift habits.

The innovative feature of their programs is that they are demand driven and not supply side driven. This means actually asking recipients what they want and telling donors, often, that the recipients are not interested. They provide the entire range of services to their member NGOs, including training their field staff, training their supervisors/managers, extending assistance in fund raising, extending assistance in preparation of plans and proposals, supplying promotional material and extending financial assistance for infrastructure/equipment. The methods used in designing and delivering their programs include studying the needs of the community before designing the program, informing target groups about the program features, developing a plan of action for a given period and assessing the effect of the program on the target group. In selecting their target audience, management either uses the existing database or creates its own database, depending on each project. Some innovative aspects of MYRADA's control system can be gleaned from their Annual Report for the year 2008-2009. The Compliance Audit is a novel feature. It focuses on the administration's compliance with stipulated systems and procedures.

The Sustainability Budget is another novel feature, the objective of which is to work towards sustainability in the core organization sector as well as to make all the project officers and staff review their approach to finance management. Over seven years ago there were indications that foreign donors will move away to other areas, therefore MYRADA needed to take defensive action by raising funds from local sources and building a corpus to sustain core staff. This meant that the project officers also had a role to play since the district level governments had resources which could be mobilized. In 2010-11 the project and staff drew up the annual budget covering expenditure *as well as income under each sector*, so that there is a framework to manage their budgets.

SUCCESSFUL MODELS IN INDIA

The JICA Partnership Program (JPP) (JICA Website[8] and Jose and Kannan (2004)[9]) is an initiative which supports collaborative projects with Indian NGOs working at the grassroots level. Two successful ongoing projects are briefly described below.

Bellary Project (Karnataka), India - Ecologically Sustainable Rural Development through Community Participation with a Focus on Women's Empowerment: This project is a collaborative effort between Live with Friends on the Earth (LIFE), Tokyo, Japan and Mysore Resettlement and Development Agency (MYRADA), Bangalore, Karnataka, India. The project covers 26 villages in the south-west area of Hospet Taluk, Bellary district, where farmers cannot cultivate land area due to droughts, and poor and inefficient distribution of water. The aim of the project is to bring about integrated watershed management by villagers and to increase cultivable land area and land productivity in order to enhance their economic livelihood base. Villagers are encouraged to form Watershed Development Associations (WDAs) and given appropriate training with a special emphasis on women's empowerment.

Kerala Model: A case study of the fishing community in the state of Kerala shows success in setting priorities in terms of establishing objectives and in targeting marginalized groups for social development. South Indian Federation of Fishing Communities (SIFFS) has taken the initiative of trying to enhance the welfare of the marginalized fishing folk in Kerala. A study conducted to assess the contribution of SIFFS to the fishing community used a four-pronged approach to measure its effectiveness. SIFFS contributed significantly in four ways:

- Demonstrating that marketing co-operative societies at the coastal villages are viable and sustainable and by influencing the state government to establish fisherman's co-operatives.
- Developing and designing a variety of fleets, which serve as an alternative to mechanized boats and have improved the economic conditions of the fisher folk.
- Helping to create democratic leadership among the fishing community at the village level.
- Facilitating the emergence of other organizations in the fishing sector and by networking and assisting these organizations.

Micro-insurance: The concept of micro insurance was pioneered in India by the Life Insurance Corporation (LIC) of India and is essentially life insurance coverage offered to the poorer sections of society. NGOs have been playing an active role in promoting this concept. LIC's micro insurance scheme, "Jeevan Madur", was launched in 2006 and promoted by the Confederation of NGOs of Rural India (CNRI), along with micro finance and micro entrepreneurship. The CNRI is LIC's sole authorized agent for this scheme in India. It started with an initial network of over 800 NGOs that covered the States of Tamil Nadu, Andhra, Maharashtra, Gujarat, UP and Kerala. This has been gradually scaled up over the last few years. Thanks to the efforts of CNRI, the scheme has been successful in providing insurance coverage of ₹ 110 crores ($ 22 million) to over 80,000 under-privileged people. The scheme offers benefits not only to the poor in the form of social security and life insurance coverage, but also creates employment in rural areas. CNRI gets 10% commission every time a policy is sold, out of which 1% is retained and the rest is passed on to its member NGOs. This is a good source of revenue for the NGOs, which do not have to depend on funding from the government or foreign donors. CNRI provides training to its member NGOs on how to provide this service and create awareness of the need for insurance. The member NGOs use computerized facilities and local social workers to collect a small premium on a weekly or daily basis, to make it easier for their customers. Given that a majority of the Indian population has no life insurance, the concept of micro insurance has huge potential for growth.

Women's Self-Help Groups: The Center for Youth & Social Development is an Orissa based NGO, which successfully introduced the concept of Women's Self Help Groups (SHGs) in the late 1990s to reach out to Koraput - one of the poorest regions in Orissa. The concept of SHGs is based on contributions from all members of the group to a common fund. Once this fund builds up, members can borrow from it for emergency purposes. All loan decisions, such as the contribution amount, the rate of interest and the repayment schedule are made by the members themselves. Around 15 to 20 such SHGs have been started in Koraput village of Orissa. The loans have been used by the women for purposes like meeting emergencies, starting income generating activities, strengthening the husband's income and building household assets. The SHGs have helped in creating employment opportunities and raising the standard of living of the villagers in Koraput. They have also improved the confidence level of women in the village, who have developed the capability to stand on their own. In addition, the women are now in a position to collectively voice their opinions and exert influence on the local administration and public delivery system to improve their functioning. The biggest benefit of the SHG however, is that it has freed the villagers from the clutches of the village lender who charged exorbitant interest rates on loans. Since the villagers previously had no access to formal or semi-formal financial services, they had no option but to approach the village lender on these terms.

Wasteland Regeneration: Social marketing has been used to promote an innovative new concept – wasteland regeneration. *Ananta Paryavarana Parirakshana Samiti* (APPS), an Andhra based NGO, has successfully regenerated the degraded revenue forest lands in Anantapur district of

Andhra Pradesh, India, by creating awareness and educating people about the need to conserve land, water and vegetation. Its efforts are reported to have resulted in increased forest cover and commercial crops being cultivated in the wastelands, creating a source of income for the villagers. APPS set up village level committees to promote the concept of wasteland regeneration and adopted low cost methods such as protecting the existing resources. It also involved women, and Tribes in its efforts to prevent forest fires and illicit cutting of trees. Eco-clubs were set up at the village level involving school children and encouraging them to spread the word about protecting trees and keeping the environment clean. Its efforts were spread over 50,000 acres and 125 villages. These were expected to have a multiplier effect on the economy, leading to improved water harvesting methods, crop productivity and pest control. APPS was supported by Oxfam (India) in its efforts.

Water Harvesting: The National Water Harvester's Network was formed in 1998, during the Centre for Science and Environment's conference on "Potential of Water Harvesting." Its objective is to encourage policies that incorporate "decentralized, participatory and locale-specific water harvesting systems, which use rain water and sub-surface water." Its mission is to revive the ancient practice of water harvesting, by incorporating modern inputs from scientific knowledge. The specific goals of the organization include promoting "water literacy", bringing about policy changes, and working with panchayat institutions to promote water harvesting at the local government level. The organization is involved in various activities such as interacting with government and policy makers, organizing conferences, workshops and exhibitions and promoting the concept of water harvesting. It also establishes links with people involved in water harvesting in other countries.

Professional training: Azim Premji University is an innovative approach to promoting socio economic development through training high caliber professionals for the voluntary sector. It was established under Government of Karnataka's Azim Premji University Act, 2010 and became operational from mid - 2011. Following are extracts of information from their website on their mission and activities that are relevant to the subject of this study. Two key focus areas of the University are to: (a) prepare a large number of committed education and *development professionals* who can significantly contribute to meeting the needs of the country; (b) build new knowledge in the areas of education and *development* through establishing strong links between theory and practice. For almost a decade, the Azim Premji Foundation has been active in supporting the primary education sector. It has partnered with state governments across India to pilot initiatives that have the potential for systemic reform to enhance the quality of elementary education within government-run school systems. The Foundation's Programs outreach has been to over 20,000 schools, through its work in partnership with the Governments of thirteen Indian States.

Microfinance: NABARD, referred to earlier with reference to the MYRADA model, has been playing a key role in the NGO sector through financing and otherwise supporting their activities. The objective of its Micro Finance Development and Equity Fund (MFDEF) is to facilitate and support the orderly growth of the micro-finance sector through diverse modalities for enlarging the flow of financial services to the poor, particularly for women and vulnerable sections of society consistent with sustainability. The Fund is utilized to support interventions by eligible institutions and stakeholders. The components of assistance include the following purposes: (a) training of SHGs and other groups for livelihood, skill up-gradation and micro enterprise development; (b) capacity building of staff of institutions involved in micro finance promotion such as Banks, NGOs, government departments; (c) capacity building of micro finance institutions (MFIs); (d) commissioning studies, consultancies, action research, evaluation studies relating to the sector; (e) promoting seminars, conferences and other mechanisms for discussion and dissemination; (f) granting support for research; and (g) documentation and publication and dissemination of micro finance literature.

ANECDOTES CITED BY EXPERTS INTERVIEWED[10]

While considering success factors, it is relevant to look at actual incidences of successes and failures among NGOs. In the course of the in-depth interview, experts were asked to recall and describe such examples in which they had personal involvement.

Among the negative events mentioned, one of them was based on collapse of the project of an NGO. This was described by a medical doctor working in the area of AIDS. The doctor recollects his experiences when he was part of a team set up to evaluate 40 NGOs engaged in HIV work in Tamil Nadu. While one of these NGOs was found to be excellent work-wise, investigations revealed that they had misappropriated funds, while hosting a major experience sharing event. They were blacklisted immediately and did not get any HIV projects after that.

The two other negative events mentioned were based on collapse of the NGO and throw some light on the reasons for collapse. The first of these was cited by the director of a Bangalore-based NGO offering counselling services, who was associated with an NGO for battered women. She describes how the NGO collapsed due to absence of leadership and lack of funds. The original founder of this NGO, an able leader, left to join a funding agency and the organization was then taken over by a new person who lacked leadership skills. The existing staff, though lacking formal education, were highly committed to their work, but were asked to leave and were replaced by staff with formal qualifications in social work. The funding received by the NGO also dried up in the meanwhile. Although the NGO had a good service and assets in the form of land, it collapsed after 25 years of existence. Incidentally, the original founder of the NGO returned, but had to build up the NGO virtually from scratch.

Another example given was that of an NGO which had to close down because of mismanagement of funds. This NGO was found to be involved with entities involved in security sensitive types of activities. As a consequence, they were blacklisted and their FCRA registration was cancelled, implying that they were not eligible to receive further funding from overseas. It was pointed out that this was only one of many such cases of mismanagement of funds. Interpersonal relationships were cited as another major reason for collapse of Indian NGOs.

A Program Director interviewed by the researcher mentions as a positive event, an NGO that started and built itself up entirely with its own funding, without dependence on outside sources. The NGO, according to her, has been highly focused and is involved in the area of health care.

Another positive event was cited by the Regional Director of a large, international NGO working in several areas, including HIV care and prevention. He describes the reasons for the resounding success of one of their projects, "Operation Lighthouse", which was funded by USAID. The purpose of the project was to promote safe sexual practices among males 18 – 44, working in ports, by designing interventions with port workers. The desired outcome of the project was to improve their knowledge of HIV, increase their usage of condoms and reduce the number of sex partners. The Project was highly successful in bringing about significant increases in condom use and in changing the sexual behavior of those exposed to the intervention. According to the Director, the primary reasons for the success of the project were marketing techniques and the media used to promote awareness of HIV and safe sexual practices. Apart from the mass media, innovative media such as counseling centers were used to achieve the desired outcome.

LESSONS TO LEARN

From an examination of the several cases and anecdotes thrown up by the literature survey and the Study[10] the success and failure ingredients have been identified and summarized.

The survey of NGOs throws up many aspects of functioning of the NGO sector that make references to strengths and weaknesses and in other contexts to successes and failures. Therefore, there is a need to sift these expressions for clear understanding. For the purpose of this presentation and the summary in the foregoing paragraphs, the terms strengths and weaknesses are taken as referring to those qualities that are inherent in the nature of the NGO as an institution, considered collectively or individually. Success factors and failure factors are considered as referring to specific attitudes, policies and practices that impact the success or failure of NGO/NGOs. In a way strengths-weaknesses are involuntary while success-failure factors are voluntary. The first requires structural changes and the latter a change of policies/practices most often within the control of the management.

Practice Related Success Factors

1. In partnerships, mutual understanding of respective roles is essential; roles should be complementary rather than competitive to avoid overlap and friction. Involve government and donor at each stage of project, say experts interviewed.

   Ref: three case studies of NGOs in Senegal, Malawi and Pakistan on partnerships with local governments. Holcombe et al (2004)[7]

2. Use of technology, professionally designed management processes and a sound delivery system ensure success. An NGO engaged in giving nutritious mid-day meal to thousands of children – has cut school drop-outs, and improved health.

   Ref: Akshaya Patra, NGO, Bangalore, India.

3. Project objectives should meet dire, immediate need – such as income generation for the poor. An NGO working with poor women from landless households in villages in a drought-prone area to set up income generation activities for poor women and to market these products. Experts interviewed say: Have clear objectives. Extend service that is credible, not a token.

   Ref: SHARE, Tamil Nadu, India.

4. Addressing a dire need enthuses participation and as far as possible using already known practices makes adoption easy. An NGO in Tamil Nadu, India to incorporate "decentralized, participatory and local-specific water harvesting systems, revived the ancient practice of water harvesting, incorporating modern inputs, and promoting "water literacy".
    Ref: Water Harvesting: National Water Harvester's Network.

5. Addressing a dire need ensures ownership and sustainability. The Ecologically Sustainable Rural Development through Community Participation project with focus on women's empowerment covers 26 villages where farmers cannot cultivate land due to drought. The project seeks to bring about integrated watershed management by villagers, to increase cultivable land area and land productivity to enhance the economic livelihood base.
    Ref: Bellary Project (Karnataka), India.

6. Integrated approach rather than piece meal approach enhances effectiveness and carries conviction – demonstrating that marketing co-operative societies at the coastal villages are viable, re-designing fleets by which productivity increased through more modern methods, creating democratic leadership among fishing community at the village level.
    Ref: South Indian Federation of Fishing Communities (SIFFS).

7. Innovative approaches and empowerment of staff work well - ensuring that programs are demand driven and not supply side driven. This means actually asking recipients what they want and telling donors often that the recipients are not interested in the donor's suggestion. Studying the needs of the community before designing the program, informing target groups about the program features, developing a plan of action for a given period and assessing the effect of the program on the target group. Experts interviewed say: Select service based on

target's needs and not fund availability. Adopt a "bottom-up" vs. a "top-down" approach

Ref: MYRADA, Bangalore, India.

8. System discipline, transparency and focus on sustainability. By Adoption of Compliance Audit and Sustainability Budgeting, staff draw up the annual budget covering expenditure *as well as income under each sector*, so that there is a framework to manage their budgets.
    Ref: MYRADA's (Bangalore, India).

9. Self-generation of funds gives more freedom in project selection to suit community needs. Do not become dependent on donors, say experts interviewed.
    Ref: an expert's anecdote during interview.

Practice Related Failure Factors

1. Lack of know-how on fund raising procedures.
    Ref: A study in Bangalore Urban District Yeshodhara K (2004)[17].

2. Excellent work cannot compensate for lack of integrity.
    Ref: investigations revealed misappropriation of funds by an otherwise good NGO while hosting a major event. An expert's anecdote during interview. Experts interviewed warned: appreciate that financial integrity is non-negotiable. Remain always accountable.

3. Lack of leadership and convulsive changes in organization by new leadership. An NGO collapsed due to absence of leadership and lack of funds. The original founder of this NGO, an able leader, left to join a funding agency and the organization was taken over by a new person who lacked leadership skills. The existing staff, though lacking formal education, was highly committed to their work, but were asked to leave and replaced by staff with formal qualifications in social work.
    Ref: an expert's anecdote during interview.

4. Involvement in security-sensitive types of activities.
    Ref: an expert's anecdote during interview.

5. Poor interpersonal relationships were cited as another major reason for collapse of Indian NGOs.
    Ref: an expert's anecdote during interview.

Structure Related Suggestions for the Sector's Strength

1. More apex level NGOs are needed for capacity building of frontline NGOs at the community level. The NGO provides its member NGOs a range of services like training for field staff and supervisors/ managers, assistance in fundraising, guidance in preparation of plans and proposals, and financial assistance for infrastructure/equipment.
    Ref: MYRADA, Bangalore, India.

2. Strong, formal networks of NGOs would give them a platform to share problems / experiences and ability to influence policy.
    Ref: State Level Federation of Voluntary Organizations for Rural Development in Karnataka, India (FEVORD–K).

3. New models and structures should be innovated according to circumstances. A company-linked NGO established in 1993 is successfully involved in four core areas of AIDS awareness and prevention – education, care and support, research and training. Also another example is Ethiopia preferring cooperatives at the grassroots level, because of their ownership and commitment, operating under apex NGOs extending funding and training supports.
    Ref: Y.R. Gaitonde and Ethiopia experience

REFERENCES

1. Andreasen, Alan R, "Intersector Transfer of Marketing Knowledge", Working Paper, Social Marketing Institute, Connecticut Avenue, Washington D. C., 2000.

2. Drucker, Peter, "Managing the Non-Profit Organization", Harper Collins Publishers, 1990.

3. Duke, Allison and Long, Charla, "Trade from the Ground Up; A Case Study of a Grassroots NGO Using Agricultural Programs to Generate Economic Viability in Developing Countries", Management Decision. London, Vol. 45, No. 8, 2007. pg. 1320.

4. Ebrahim, Alnoor, "NGO Behavior and Development Discourse: Cases From Western India", Voluntas, Manchester, Vol. 12, No. 2, June 2001. pg. 79.

5. Fox, Michael P, "Condom Social Marketing: Select Case Studies", Prepared for the Department of Policy, Strategy and Research, UNAIDS, Geneva, Switzerland, 2000.

6. "Appropriate Technology", (Vol. 30, no.3, September 2003), Research Information Ltd, 222, Maylands Avenue, Hemel Hempstead, herts. HP2 7TD, UK

7. Holcombe, Susan H et al, "Managing Development: NGO Perspectives", International Public Management Journal, Stamford, Vol. 7, No.2, 2004. pp. 187-205.

8. Japanese NGOs in India, NGO-JICA Desk India, website: jicaindiaoofice. org

9. Jose, Sunny and Kannan K P, "NGOs and the Welfare of Marginalized Social Groups: a Case Study of Fishing Community in Kerala, India", Paper at International Society for Third-Sector Research, Sixth International Conference, Toronto Canada, July 11-14, 2004.

10. Parthasarathy, Vimala, "Social Marketing Strategies & Traits of Successful NGOs in India - A Strategic Perspective with Reference to Select NGOs in the States of Karnataka & Tamil Nadu, India", doctoral thesis for PhD, approved by Manipal University, Manipal, India, 2013

11. Powell, Jane et al, "Social Marketing in Action – geo-demographics, alcoholic liver disease and heavy episodic drinking in Great Britain", International Journal of Non-Profit and Voluntary Sector Marketing, London, Vol. 12, No. 3, August 2007. pp. 177-187.

12. Rajasekhar D, "Micro Finance and Poverty Alleviation Issues Relating to NGO Programs in South India", Institute for Social and Economic Change, Bangalore, Working Paper No.146, 2004.

13. Rajasekhar, D, "Non-Governmental Organizations in India: Opportunities and Challenges", Institute for Social and Economic Change, Bangalore, Working Paper No. 66, 2000.

14. Transparency International (TI)-Bangladesh. Problems in Good Governance in the NGO Sector: The Way Out. October 2007 (www. ti-bangladesh.org/research/execsumngo-english.pdf)

15. Website:http://www.globalissues.org/article/25/non-governmental-organizations-on-development-issues

16. World Bank, "Working with NGOs: A Practical Guide to Operational Collaboration between the World Bank and Non-Government al Organizations", Operations Policy Department, World Bank, reproduced in the website of The Global Development Research Center (GDRC), 1995. pp 7-9.

17. Yeshodara K, "Role of NGOs in Promoting Non-Formal Environment Education: A Case Study in Bangalore District", Project Report, Institute for Social and Economic Change, Bangalore, 2004.

18. Zaidi, S Akbar, "NGO Failure and the Need to Bring Back the State", Journal of International Development, Chichester, Vol. 11, No. 2, March/April 1999. pg. 259.

A STRATEGIC OVERVIEW OF THE STRUCTURE AND FUNCTIONING OF COMMUNITY BASED NGOS

Abstract

This article is an assessment of the reforms needed in the NGO sector based on the author's[7] research material and articles. The tendency to refer to NGOs in an omnibus manner, clubbing NGOs of different sizes and operating at different levels as if they are alike, should be corrected. The article recommends that a special view must be taken of small NGOs operating at or near the communities as their stature, capacity and problems are entirely different from those functioning at the apex level, state or inter-state levels with relatively larger resources and sophisticated infrastructure. Modelling the sectoral structure according to the sensitivities of each country in the developing world, taking a fresh look at the compensation approach and creating a central registering and data collection center are considered necessary for strengthening the sector.

FOCUS ON SMALL NGOS

In the absence of reliable data on NGOs operating in the development sector, one has to rely on sample surveys. According to a sample survey[4] it is estimated that there are 1.2 million NGOs (referred to by the study team as 'non-profits') in India. It is significant that more than half the NGOs are based in rural areas. Although several NGOs based in urban areas also serve rural communities, the proximity and directness of the smaller NGOs in the interior areas away from urban centers make them a critical link in the social marketing chain. They have the feel and touch of the local population, have a first-hand idea of their priorities and are in a position to induce community leaders to take up ownership of programs. The ultimate test of success for an NGO is to make an impact on the target audience sustainable and, even more, make that impact community-wide. These can be achieved only through viable, continuously functioning community based NGOs. The role of larger NGOs operating at multi-district or state or even at time multi-state levels, is to extend funding, capacity building and management services to the frontline NGOs at the villages operating at the final point of "sale" and delivery. Larger NGOs specialize in parceling out the program to the small NGOs for implementation. The former act as wholesalers and the latter as retailers. The small NGOs have special knowledge of the community's aspirations and priorities and its cultural profile which are important inputs for project identification and design.

A large number of the small NGOs do not have adequate training, equipment and infrastructure to be able to play a crucial role. The poorer a country, the more acute the problem of inadequacy is likely to be. Taking Tanzania as an example, the Special Paper (2007)[9] on Poverty Alleviation throws light on the perceptions of Tanzanian NGOs on the problems they have to grapple with. Tanzanian NGOs were critical that only limited resources are made available for NGOs' core operating costs, personnel and infrastructure. Participants in the survey strongly argued that project funding is unsustainable in the long-term as it does not assist NGOs to maintain and improve upon their technical skills and infrastructure. When this funding is withdrawn, activities often cease abruptly and prematurely. Participants wanted funding to cover NGOs' core operating costs, infrastructure, personnel and equipment to sustain activities and achieve desired outcomes beyond the terms of current projects. They wanted to be freed from complicated bureaucratic requirements for funding applications. They wanted more technical assistance. Increased funding for transport and infrastructure to expand the presence of NGOs in more remote, rural areas was also recommended.

The predicament of the grassroots NGOs in many developing countries is similar to the Tanzanian situation to a larger or smaller degree. The success of the sector lies in keeping village-based NGOs, constituting the base of the structural pyramid, strong through training, technical assistance, equipment and financial sustainability. The focus of reform and capacity building of the voluntary sector must be the rural NGOs. This should be accompanied by a campaign for selecting, motivating and training locally influential members of the community to take up leadership responsibility and ownership of development schemes.

SMALL NGOS NEED ORGANISATIONAL CONSULTANCY

Employing a marketing approach enhances the chances of achieving objectives of development programs provided they are appropriately adapted to suit project-specific situations. Even at present, marketing practices are in vogue though not in a systematic manner and without the practitioners having formal awareness or knowledge of this approach. The informal practice is confined to apex level NGOs and at the grass-roots level the awareness and practice is at a very low level, practically non-existent. There is much need for training and consultancy to bring about systematic use of the tools which would go a long way in making NGOs more result-oriented and cost-effective. For the community level, small NGOs marketing tools should be simplified and tailored to their local needs, understanding and capabilities. There seems to be much scope for more 'mother' NGOs offering services to take up consultancy and training in social marketing.

REMOVE DISTRUST OF NGOs

Large fund inflows directly to the NGO sector and the increasing hold of foreign-managed large NGOs on small NGOs at the field level and, through them, over the rural population, has had an unsettling effect on the political system in some less developed economies. The Ethiopia experience (Globalissues) [11] is an example of the distrust in some countries of Asia and Africa. The criticism of the NGOs boils down to two issues. First, it is that they are foreign funded and managed, which clout they use to undermine the legitimacy and standing of the government in the eyes of the rural communities. Second, it is that NGOs at the villages set up by the funding sources cannot have the same degree of ownership and commitment as the cooperatives are capable of. As a result NGO efforts degenerate into being a provider of hand-outs, which is an assault on the beneficiaries' self-esteem and, consequently, often the impact is not sustained. These shortcomings of the NGO as an institutional instrument for development, as alleged by the critics, cannot be easily dismissed as being technically invalid. Of course, it can be argued that this need not be the situation across all or most countries. The poorer the country the more likely it is that the balance is tilted more in favor of the foreign funding agencies and, consequently, the more realistic the two criticisms are likely to be. The critics, however, seem to overlook certain unique merits of NGOs. They have capacity, technical expertise and ability to mobilize resources. Therefore, it should not become a choice of either the cooperatives or the NGOs. The answer perhaps lies in a synergistic combination of the two systems and re-routing of funding to lessen the visibility of the foreign tag. As the country becomes more democratically mature and materially better placed, a mutually reinforcing relationship and acceptance between the government and the voluntary sector is likely to evolve.

Thus, there seem to be two routes to the removal of distrust in the NGO-government relationship. The first is the evolutionary route which is explained by the India example. The second approach is by organizationally restructuring the relationship. Some of the possibilities are illustrated diagrammatically.

As regards the evolutionary process, the initiative is taken by the NGO sector to earn the trust by their dedication, performance and financial integrity. The sector should work pro-actively with the government in development programs in a way that does not take away the limelight from the government or the ruling political party. This should lead to acceptance of NGOs as partners in development. But this is a gradual process as evidenced by the step-by-step enlargement of the role for the NGO sector in a democratic and emerging country like India. The progressively increasing part for the voluntary sector can be observed from a perusal of the successive Five-year Plans[3, 5, 6, 8]. The recognition of the role of NGOs by the government dates back to the First Plan document (1975-80) which mentions their involvement in community and social development. The Sixth Plan (1980-85) visualized useful roles for NGOs. The Seventh Plan enlarged NGO role in rural development to supplement the efforts of the government and involved NGOs in development planning and implementation. The Eighth Plan focused on building community institutions through voluntary organizations. The Ninth Plan wanted to promote and develop people's participatory bodies through voluntary sector initiatives. The Tenth Plan evolved norms for involving the voluntary sector in community and welfare programs and encouraged the growth of the sector in states where they are weak or where the state machinery is found wanting. It is seen that from Plan to Plan, every five years, there has been a progressively more meaningful role assigned to the voluntary sector

In the set of diagrams that follow, the first model from the left is the conventional structure wherein the funding agency operates through NGOs at the supervisory and village implementation levels. The model in the middle envisages the routing of funds through the government and its appointed funding agency but utilizing the expertise of NGOs for supervision and village cooperatives for implementation. In the third and last model the government keeps out of funding and lets the funding agency utilize supervising NGOs but reserving the implementation to the village cooperatives.

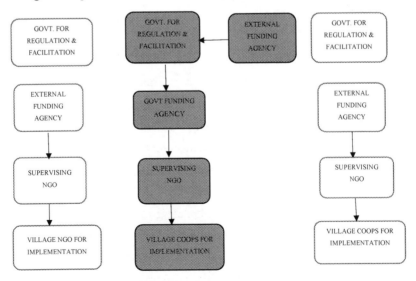

SHOULD NGOS BE TAXED?

In Bangladesh (Asian Development Bank[1]andTransparency International (TI) -Bangladesh)[10], the large flow of funds has spurred growth of the NGO sector to the point of even reducing the government to a subsidiary role in the provision of public services. The expansion has resulted in NGOs' entry into productive ventures that yield a "surplus" which enjoys tax exemption that is available to NGOs. This has met with criticism from the private sector as the latter has to face unfair competition since NGOs do not pay taxes on similar activities. NGOs argue that they do not take away the profit from ventures, but spend income earned on development works for the community. It is debatable whether NGO commercial ventures should enjoy tax relief for financing their community welfare activities. If private firms are also exempted from tax on the amount they donate to a recognized NGO engaged in community development activities, there should be no objection to the exemption being extended to NGOs. Exemption of such funds directed towards development is socially beneficial as it would gradually minimize dependence on external funding.

"BOTTOMLINE" APPROACH TO NGO'S COMPENSATION

Commercial organizations are motivated towards constant improvement by the direct financial benefits they stand to derive by improving results. If social marketing principles are applicable for successful program impact it is difficult to see how unmotivated effort could be strong and sustained enough to achieve program objectives. The commercial sector derives profits and distributes it as dividends to the owners (shareholders). Employees are incentivized at every stage to achieve their respective targets. In an NGO there are no owners in a parallel sense compared to commercial organizations but this does not mean that the organization itself should not look for a surplus to use for its own sustenance and growth. As far as employees are concerned there is no difference at all between commercial and social organizations. As such, they should have targets of performance and incentives for reaching them. There is another justification for a profit-equivalent surplus in the NGOs. Profits are a measure of the commercial organizations' standing. Presently, there is no such quick, transparent yardstick or indicator to adjudge an NGO's track record. There is need for such an indicator. For these reasons funding agencies should compensate NGOs for (i) overheads (ii) costs directly related to the project (iii) incentives for target achievement by field staff and (iv) reward to the NGO for achieving output and outcome targets. Item (iii) could be paid by the NGO out of its revenue from item (iv). The last item of revenue could be accumulated (capitalized) in the balance sheets to be drawn for improvements to infrastructure and capacity. The "bottom line" has the following advantages – (i) motivate performance by staff (ii) motivate NGO for achieving planned impact (iii) help the NGO to build its financial and technical sustainability and (iv) be a visible indicator of the NGOs standing and performance history. With this surplus going back into development it should not be taxed. There seems to be a case for donors to consider re-structuring the compensation system for NGOs by following what may be called a "bottom line" approach.

LEGAL IDENTITY IS HIGH PRIORITY

Distinguishing legal identity for NGOs engaged in development activities is necessary. In India NGOs could register themselves under a variety of laws as a result of which this important sub-sector of the NGO sector has been submerged along with a vast variety of organizations of every description and objectives. This has ramifications – funds are diverted for purposes for which they were not meant; funds that flow in ostensibly for social development are used for illegal purposes; there is no possibility of building a data base of NGOs engaged in social development activities; and there is no reliable data or information on the type of social projects, which results in overlaps and poor use of resources. There is no single national parent body or licensing authority for NGOs. There is no legal framework that binds NGOs to accountability to a central authority. One of the suggestions is that there should be some unique ID number / registration for NGOs across the states and their track records should be available for review and reference. Creation of a single identity would, according to the experts, have the following advantages: avoiding duplication and wastage of scarce funds; improving targeting; a financial and progress reporting system can be enforced, giving opportunity to private-public partnership; establishing accountability to government / district authority / funding agency; and affording scope for identifying successful models for replication or scaling up.

REFERENCES

1. Asian Development Bank, "Civil Society Briefs – Bangladesh", 2008
2. Drucker, Peter, "Managing the Non-Profit Organization", Harper Collins Publishers, 1990.
3. Eighth V Year Plan Chapter 6, NGOs and their networks, Planning Commission, Government of India.
4. Institute for Policy Studies, Johns Hopkins University, USA, 2002.
5. Minutes of the First Meeting of the Tenth Five-Year Plan (2002-07) - Steering Committee, on "Voluntary Sector", Government of India, Planning Commission, March 16, 2001.
6. National Policy on Voluntary Sector, Voluntary Action Cell, Planning Commission, Government of India, 2007.
7. Parthasarathy, Vimala, "Social Marketing Strategies & Traits of Successful NGOs in India - A Strategic Perspective with Reference to Select NGOs in the States of Karnataka & Tamil Nadu, India", doctoral thesis for PhD, approved by Manipal University, Manipal, India, 2013
8. Planning Commission, Approach Paper to the Tenth Five Year Plan (2002-2007), Planning Commission, Government of India.
9. Research on Poverty Alleviation REPOA, "Tanzanian NGO's – Their Perceptions", Special paper 07.21, 2007, website: www.repoa.or.tz
10. Transparency International (TI)-Bangladesh. *Problems in Good Governance in the NGO Sector: The Way Out.* October 2007 (www.ti-bangladesh.org/research/execsumngo-english.pdf)
11. Website: http://www.globalissues.org/article/25/non-governmental-organizations-on-development-issues

ANNEX 1 – SAMPLE NGO PROFILES

1. The Table in the following page is a summary profile of the ten sample NGOs studied.

2. The details collected prior to sample selection were either validated or updated at interviews.

3. The interviews were conducted in 2010

4. Some of the NGOs in the list operate on a much wider geographical scale than indicated in the Table as they were studied mainly in the context of their activities in the state

5. The first five NGOs are located in Karnataka State of India and the second five in Tamil Nadu State of India

6. "Districts" are administrative/revenue divisions of the state and "taluks" are sub-divisions of the district

7. FCRA is the abbreviation for *Foreign Contributions Regulation Act*

8. Indian currency ₹ one million is equal to US $ 20,000

NGO	Name of CEO or equivalent met	Geographical coverage	Annual expenditure million ₹ (₹ 50=1 USD)	Full time staff	Registered under Act	Year established	Main activity in brief
Action Aid India http://www.actionaidindia.org	Dr. Kshithij Urs	Karnataka state and parts of Kerala state	250-300	13	Societies Act and FCRA	1973	Poverty reduction
Agricultural Development and Training Society http://www.adats.com	Mr. Babu	5 taluks of Chickballapur district	380	64	Societies Act and FCRA	1977	Empowerment of working class
Mysore Resettlement and Development Agency http://www.myrada.org	Mr. Arvind Risbud	6 districts	1800	225	Societies Act	1968	Rural institution building
Samuha http://www.samuha.org	Ms. Sanghamitra Iyengar	6 districts	1600	>163	Indian Trust Act	1995	Reduction of HIV incidence
Women's Liberation and Rehabilitation Society	Ms. Jayalakshmi, Mr. D.N. Venugopal,	6 districts	15-20	48	Societies Act	1985	Women's empowerment
Action for Community Organization, Rehabilitation and Development www.adivasi.net	Mr. Manoharan	2 taluks of Nilgiri district	100	65	Societies Act	1986	*Adivasi* (tribal) development. and advocacy

NGO	Name of CEO or equivalent met	Geographical coverage	Annual expenditure million ₹ (₹ 50=1 USD)	Full time staff	Registered under Act	Year established	Main activity in brief
Deepam Educational Society for Health http://www.deshhealth.org	Ms. Saraswathi Sankaran, Mr. Navin Kumar	3 districts	64	20	Societies Act	1991	Health promotion
Development Promotion Group http://www.dpgsulo.com	Mr. R. Bhakther Solomon	10 districts	300	47	Societies Act	1986	Watershed development and Self Help Groups
Social Action Movement http://www. socialactionmovement.com	Rev. Fr. P.B. Martin	5 districts	50	20	Societies Act	1985	Eradication of child labor
Tamil Nadu Voluntary Health Association http://www.tnvha.org	Ms. J.P. Saulina Arnold	Tamil Nadu and Pondicherry	117	18	Societies Act	1971	Health promotion - training

ANNEX 2 – SOCIAL MARKETING MODEL – SUGGESTIVE CHECKLIST OF GOOD PRACTICES

ANNEX 2 - SUGGESTIVE CHECK-LIST OF GOOD PRACTICES FOR NGOs IMPLEMENTING PROJECTS

MARKETING ORIENTATION	**UNDERSTANDING THE TARGET AUDIENCE i.e. THE "MARKETING PLANNING"**
Aware of marketing concept	Conducts study to identify the audience's profile and needs
Recognizes its applicability to NGO activity	Selects homogenous segment/s of audience with similar needs and habits
Recognizes differences between Social and Commercial marketing	Profiles selected audience and tailors program design and delivery methods
	MARKETING PLANNING
	Spells out Vision, Mission and Objectives
	Develops a Marketing Plan of outputs eg No of training camps, media use etc. with time table
	Objectives are clear, consistent with Mission, practical, focused
	Objectives are measurable
	Targets and sub-targets set for operations staff
PROGRAM ASPECTS	**PROMOTION**
Recognizes need for adaptation	Tests selected design and delivery to verify its effectiveness on the ground
Recognizes need for cultural adaptation	Makes corrections as needed before implementation
Willing to apply Social Marketing practices	
Involves stakeholders in theme selection	Communication strategies, language idiom and medium to suit cultural situ...
Programs are need based, not fund-driven	Pre-tests above before launch to ensure impact
Involves stakeholders in program design	Has reasonable budget for communication
Adapts program design to suit local cultural practices	Resources being a constant constraint select most effective methods by pre-test
Innovative features built into program design	innovates special strategies/practices for better impact
	DISTRIBUTION
	Carefully design the methodology of delivery of services
	Adapts delivery methods to suit local cultural situation
	Adopts innovative distribution practices
POLICY ASPECTS	**PARTNERSHIP - STRATEGIC ALLIANCES**
Interacts pro-actively with government at appropriate levels	Has network /alliances to supplement / complement is own efforts
Ensures that all aspects of Program are in consonance with govt a...	The network aims at marketing effectiveness
Has cooperative and not competitive relations with govt.	Active cooperation with NGOs, network partners, alliances
	Uses participatory approach – works with community
	Formulates Plan iteratively with community
	Encourages community to contribute in material and/or effort
	FUNDING AND DONOR RELATIONSHIP
	Spends significant time on fund conservation and raising - it is the central part of sustainability
	Understands the concerns and reporting requirements of funding agencies
	Regular meetings and reports to donor - do not hide or gloss over problems
	Observes high standards of financial probity, transparency
	Projects image of organization and its capabilities
	In compliance with all statutory stipulations
EXTERNAL STAKEHOLDERS	**INSTITUTIONAL IMAGE**
Close touch with stakeholders, preferably institutionalised by	Is aware of the importance of institutional credibility and image
Keeping them informed of program aspects - especially of problems and possible solutions	Takes steps to project as a credible efficient institution
	Understands that there is no image to project if performance is inefficient
	institution has special features for projecting its image
	CAPACITY BUILDING, MAINTENANCE AND DEVE...
	Trains staff in marketing and technical competence
	Adequate number of trained staff at all time
	Ensures minimum turnover of trained staff with motivation - or lose trained staff to others
	Transport, spares, equipment, internet access, systems to be adequate and kept under review
MONITORING & EVALUATION	**MANAGEMENT LEADERSHIP**
Clarity on project measurability	Grasps Institution's SWOT
Evaluates Output for Performance Measurement (cost)	Has clarity and direction
Evaluates Outcome for Performance measurement (impact)	Has basic articulation and communication skills
Receives feedback from more than one source	Has marketing orientation
Assesses quality of monitoring data	Has clearly demarcated functional departments with delegated authority and responsibilities
Undertakes frequent site inspections	Controls Overheads within reasonable limits (say, 8-20%)
	Interacts regularly with staff and beneficiaries
	Transparent Reports disclosing progress, fund use, problems
	Website informative and kept up info incl financials
	Regular meetings with stakeholders
	Seeks 3rd party audit of program and cost effectiveness
	Builds Team work
	Provides creative leadership
SUSTAINABILITY	
No major difficulties in uninterrupted fund flow	
Is not dependent on one or very few donors	
Is able to generate a minimum of own funds, say at least 10-20%	
Ensures adequate infra structure (equipment space, vehicles, computers)	
Seeks expert help for improving management process, systems, controls	
Designs Programs to involve community to sustain change	

247

ANNEX 3 – NGO RATING GUIDE

The following NGO Rating Guide is aimed at evaluating an NGO's organizational fitness and sustainability expressed as a percentage score. It is meant for NGOs engaged directly or indirectly in social program implementation. The NGO may be one operating at the community level or district level spread over several community clusters. It is not applicable to other NGOs operating at the apex level or offering funding or any other management or training services.

The guide is meant to be used as a check-list for understanding the reality of the situation, as opposed to the claims of the respondent, with respect to each issue. This may involve studying related reports, results, accounts or documents and even field visits. The score is arrived at on the basis of such effort. It is not a 'quick-fire' one day exercise. For an objective assessment it may be conducted by a group of three – two independent observers and one insider - the average of the scores by the three taken as the value assigned to each issue.

The guide is divided into seven parts – marketing capacity, relationship strengths, accountability, funding sustainability, technical capacity maintenance, performance measurement and, finally, management caliber. The total score for each part is converted to percentage and the total of the percentage scores for the seven parts is divided by seven to arrive at the overall percentage score. This implies that the seven parts (functions) are considered to be of equal importance. Further sophistication requires assigning weights to the score of each part but it has not been attempted, in the interests of simplicity.

The aim of the exercise is to assess the NGO's organizational capacity and identify weak areas for improvement. Organizational capacity is the result of internal as well as external factors, the latter beyond NGO's control. For example, a given NGO may not have any say on the program theme as it is assigned to it by the funding agency or the apex NGO. In such a top-down approach there could be a mismatch between what the community needs and what it gets, thereby infecting the program with an in-built risk of failure. Therefore, a low score, for instance, need not necessarily be a reflection on the NGO management. Detailed examination of the responses to each part may help to identify reasons for poor or good performances.

A scoring method has been devised for the answers to different questions. Multiple option questions (MOQ) carry as many marks as options chosen, subject to a maximum of 4; open-ended questions (OEQ) are assigned marks judgmentally according to the findings as high, moderate or low standard/ compliance, carrying three, two and one mark respectively; and graded option questions (GOQ) are assigned marks according to a scale. In this manner, all responses are converted to numerical values. The question type codes are indicated against each item in the attached guide.

The second step is to total the numerical scores for *each* of the seven parts, divide it by the *maximum attainable for that part* and multiplying it by 100 to give a percentage score for *that* part. The total of scores of *all* questions is divided by the *maximum achievable score for all the questions* to arrive at an *overall* fitness score.

Thus, we have a percentage score of effectiveness for each of the seven functions of the NGO as also an overall score for the NGO as an entity. A grading scale based on popularly accepted model, as follows, gives the "verdict" – 35% or less is poor, 36-50% is moderate (the two combined for simplification as "below satisfactory"), 51-60% is satisfactory, 61-75% is good and over 75% is very good.

There is much scope for refining, expanding and improving the simple system, presented here, to suit individual situations and needs. It is offered in that spirit and not as a final answer to all institutional evaluation requirements.

NGO RATING GUIDE

BACKGROUND INFORMATION		
1	Name of NGO	
2	Contact Details	
3	Web-site	
4	Brief nature of Activity	
5	Geographical Coverage	
6	Approximate Annual Budget	
7	Full-time Staff	In Office: In the Field:
8	Part-time / Volunteer Staff	In Office: In the Field:
9	Under which Law Registered	
10	Year of Establishment	
11	Name/s of Evaluator/s	
12	Location and Date	

MARKETING CAPACITY

M1. Who are directly involved in the SELECTION of objective for projects?

Check as many as applicable to your situation

(a)	Government state/central	
(b)	Local body of the government	
(c)	Community leaders	
(d)	General Community	
(e)	Donors	
(f)	Mother NGO	
(g)	Your internal management, including field staff	
(h)	Any other (specify below)	

Assigning the maximum 4 marks is subject to one of c, d or g is checked

Question Type	Maximum Marks	Marks Given
MOQ	4	

M2. Who are directly involved in DESIGNING projects?

Check as many as applicable to your situation

(a)	Government state/central	
(b)	Local body of the government	
(c)	Community leaders	
(d)	General Community	
(e)	Donors	
(f)	Mother NGO	
(g)	Your internal management, including field staff	
(h)	Any other (specify below)	

Assigning the maximum 4 marks is subject to one of c, d or g is checked

Question Type	Maximum Marks	Marks Given
MOQ	4	

M3. To what extent does the management believe that marketing practices are useful in project implementation?

Check only ONE of the following

(a)	Not at all applicable	
(b)	Rarely applicable	
(c)	Occasionally applicable	
(d)	Largely applicable	
(e)	Very much applicable	

0 for a and b, 1 for c, 2 for d and 3 for e

Question Type	Maximum Marks	Marks Given
GOQ	3	

M4. Which of following methods, if any, are used?

Check as many as applicable to your situation

(a)	Studying the needs of the community before designing the Program	
(b)	Dividing the market into groups based on needs	
(c)	Developing services for specific groups	
(d)	Developing a system for delivery of services	
(e)	Informing target groups about the program features	
(f)	Developing a plan of action for a given period of say, one year	
(g)	Assessing the effect of your program on the target group	
(h)	Any other (specify below)	

Question Type	Maximum Marks	Marks Given
MOQ	4	

M5. Is any special strategy or practice adopted to ensure success? State briefly.

Answer:

Mark of 1 or 2 or 3 assigned judgmentally based on special nature of the approach and its impact potential

Question Type	Maximum Marks	Marks Given
OEQ	3	

M6. What means of communication to the target group is adopted?

Check as many as applicable to your situation

(a)	Local newspapers/magazines	
(b)	Printed leaflets	
(c)	Propaganda vans	
(d)	Group meetings	
(e)	Using opinion leaders	
(f)	Posters	
(g)	Audio visuals	

(h)	Radio	
(i)	Word of mouth	
(j)	Any Other (specify below)	

Question Type	Maximum Marks	Marks Given
MOQ	4	

M7. How important are social and cultural features of target community in affecting project success?

Check only ONE of the following

(a)	Least important	
(b)	Not very important	
(c)	Somewhat important	
(d)	Important	
(e)	Extremely important	

0 for a and b, 1 for c, 2 for d and 3 for e

Question Type	Maximum Marks	Marks Given
GOQ	3	

M8. If the answer to the above is (d) or (e), name example/s of how design or other practices had to be changed to suit the social and cultural needs of the community. If not, skip this question, giving zero mark

Answer:

Mark of 1 or 2 or 3 assigned judgmentally based on special nature of the insight

Question Type	Maximum Marks	Marks Given
OEQ	3	

M9. If the created impact is sustained in post-project phase, name key factor/s that sustained impact. If not, skip this question, giving zero mark

Answer:

Mark of 1 or 2 or 3 assigned judgmentally based on the impact potential of the factor

Question Type	Maximum Marks	Marks Given
OEQ	3	

SUMMARY – MARKETING CAPACITY		
1	Total of scores as evaluated	
2	Possible maximum total score	31
3	Effectiveness % (1/2*100)	

RELATIONSHIP STRENGTHS

R1. Indicate the frequency of touch with the government at any appropriate level

Check only ONE of the following

(a)	Once in > a year	
(b)	Once a year	
(c)	Once in 6 months	
(d)	Once in 3 months	
(e)	Once a month	

0 for a and b, 1 for c, 2 for d and 3 for e

Question Type	Maximum Marks	Marks Given
GOQ	3	

R2. What is the nature of relationship with the government?

Check only ONE of the following

(a)	Antagonistic (relationship of conflict)	
(b)	Passive (mutually non-interfering)	
(c)	Co-operative (supporting mutually)	
(d)	Facilitative (where NGO assists govt. through advice, training etc.)	

0 for a, 1 for b, 2 for c, 3 for d

Question Type	Maximum Marks	Marks Given
GOQ	3	

R3. If there is any alliance or strategic partnership indicate the strategic purpose and with whom

Answer:

Mark of 1 or 2 or 3 assigned judgmentally based on the synergy value of the partnership

Question Type	Maximum Marks	Marks Given
OEQ	3	

R4. What is the nature of your relationship with neighboring NGOs operating in the same activity/area?

Check only ONE of the following

(a)	Conflicting	
(b)	Non-interfering	
(c)	Mutual adjustment to resolve conflicts	
(d)	Active cooperation towards common goals	

0 for a, 1 for b, 2 for c, 3 for d

Question Type	Maximum Marks	Marks Given
GOQ	3	

R5. Is there community involvement in the following form?

Check as many as applicable to your situation

(a)	Effort in asset creation	
(b)	Effort in institution building	
(c)	Monetary contribution	
(d)	Payment for services	
(e)	Contribution as material	
(f)	Any other – specify	

Marks as many as the number of ticked items subject to a maximum of 4

Question Type	Maximum Marks	Marks Given
MOQ	4	

SUMMARY – RELATIONSHIP STRENGTHS		
1	Total of scores as evaluated plus values for M1 to M2*	
2	Possible maximum total score plus max values for M1 to M2*	24
3	Effectiveness % (1/2*100)	

values for M1 to M3 are relevant to assess relationship strength

ACCOUNTABILITY

A1. Who are kept informed of the organization's performance and results?

Check as many as applicable to your situation

(a)	Board of trustees/Board of Management	
(b)	Your staff	
(c)	Main funding agencies	
(d)	Government /local bodies	
(e)	Local community leaders	
(f)	Mother NGO	
(g)	Any other (specify below)	

Assigning the maximum 4 marks is subject to one of the parties is e

Question Type	Maximum Marks	Marks Given
MOQ	4	

A2. Reporting frequency, information adequacy, quantification, comparison with targets, transparency
Answer:

Mark of 1 or 2 or 3 assigned judgmentally based on compliance with criteria in the question

Question Type	Maximum Marks	Marks Given
OEQ	3	

A3. Are targets set, reviewed and accounted for?
Answer:

Mark of 1 or 2 or 3 assigned judgmentally based on compliance with criteria in the question

Question Type	Maximum Marks	Marks Given
OEQ	3	

A4. Is there a website – updated, informative and transparent?
Answer:

Mark zero for no website and 1 or 2 or 3 judgmentally based on compliance with criteria in the question

Question Type	Maximum Marks	Marks Given
OEQ	3	

A5. Are statutory compliances up-to-date?

Mark zero for total non-compliance and 1 or 2 or 3 based on fullness of compliance

Question Type	Maximum Marks	Marks Given
OEQ	3	

SUMMARY – ACCOUNTABILITY		
1	Total of scores as evaluated	
2	Possible maximum total score	16
3	Effectiveness % (1/2*100)	

FUNDING SUSTAINABILITY

F1. Who are main funding sources?

Check as many as applicable to your situation

(a)	Domestic - Government – State and central	
(b)	Domestic – Institutions	
(c)	Domestic – General Public	
(d)	Overseas – Institutions and Individuals	
(e)	Your own generated surplus	
(f)	Any other (specify below)	

Assigning the maximum 4 marks is subject to one being e.

Question Type	Maximum Marks	Marks Given
MOQ	4	

F2. How much time is spent by management on fund raising activities?

Check only ONE of the following

(a)	Once in > a year	
(b)	Once a year	
(c)	Once in 6 months	

(d)	Once in 3 months	
(e)	Once a month	

0 for a and b, 1 for c, 2 for d and 3 for e

Question Type	Maximum Marks	Marks Given
GOQ	3	

F3. Approximately how often do you interact with your funding benefactors?
Check only ONE of the following

(a)	Once in > a year	
(b)	Once a year	
(c)	Once in 6 months	
(d)	Once in 3 months	
(e)	Once a month	

0 for a and b, 1 for c, 2 for d and 3 for e

Question Type	Maximum Marks	Marks Given
GOQ	3	

F4. Do any of the following affect fund raising capacity?
Check as many as applicable to your situation

(a)	Lack of necessary contacts	
(b)	Lack of knowledge of fund raising methods	
(c)	Want of information regarding sources	
(d)	Differences with funding agency over project feature/s	
(e)	Lack of legal status to create confidence in donors	
(f)	Any other negative factor (specify)	
(g)	None – our fund raising capacity not affected	

Checking g earns zero and others a **minus score** subject to a maximum of -4

Question Type	Maximum Marks	Marks Given
MOQ	**Minus** 4	

F5. If there are income generating sources indicate % of income/expenditure generated per year?

Answer: %

0 for no sources, 1 for < 10%, 2 for 11 to 20%, 3 for > 20%

Question Type	Maximum Marks	Marks Given
GOQ	3	

SUMMARY – FUNDING SUSTAINABILITY		
1	Total of scores as evaluated	
2	Possible maximum total score	13
3	Effectiveness % (1/2*100)	

TECHNICAL CAPACITY MAINTENANCE

T1. If outside expert is engaged for special assistance indicate purpose/s. If not, skip this question, giving zero mark

Check as many as applicable to your situation

(a)	Training field staff	
(b)	Training supervisors/managers	
(c)	Assistance in fund raising	
(d)	Preparation of their plans, proposals	
(e)	Marketing training	
(f)	Progress monitoring	
(g)	Designing Reporting systems	
(h)	Management audit	
(i)	Participatory methods	

(j)	Leadership training	
(k)	Any Other (specify below)	

Question Type	Maximum Marks	Marks Given
MOQ	4	

T2. How are field staff enabled to handle their responsibilities?

Check as many as applicable to your situation

(a)	They have learnt by experience	
(b)	They are periodically trained internally	
(c)	They are periodically trained by external agencies	
(d)	A few of them have marketing diplomas/degrees	
(e)	Many of them have marketing diplomas/degrees	
(f)	Any other (specify below)	

Assigning the maximum 4 marks is subject to one being c.

Question Type	Maximum Marks	Marks Given
MOQ	4	

T3. Indicate adequacy of field staff strength to handle responsibilities effectively?

Check only ONE of the following

(a)	Over-staffed as there not enough projects	
(b)	Enough staff but not adequately trained	
(c)	Under-staffed – managing as they are trained	
(d)	Enough staff well trained	

0 for a, 1 for b, 2 for c, 2 for d and 3 for e

Question Type	Maximum Marks	Marks Given
GOQ	3	

T4. What is the staff turnover in year?

Check only ONE of the following

(a)	< 10% leave every year	
(b)	>10 and < 20% leave every year	
(c)	> 20 % and < 30 % leave every year	
(d)	> 30% leave every year	

3 for a, 2 for b, 1 for c, 0 for d

Question Type	Maximum Marks	Marks Given
GOQ	3	

T5. Are equipment, vehicles, space etc. adequate?

Check only ONE of the following

(a)	Need badly and urgently	
(b)	Not enough but can manage	
(c)	Adequate	

1 for a, 2 for b, 3 for c

Question Type	Maximum Marks	Marks Given
GOQ	3	

SUMMARY – TECHNICAL CAPACITY MAINTENANCE		
1	Total of scores as evaluated	
2	Possible maximum total score	17
3	Effectiveness % (1/2*100)	

PERFORMANCE MEASUREMENT

P1. If there are measurable targets of different types of activities to achieve the impact name 2. If not, skip this question, giving zero mark

Answer:

Mark of 1 or 2 or 3 assigned judgmentally based on clarity, measurability and relevance

Question Type	Maximum Marks	Marks Given
OEQ	3	

P2. If there is formal statement of mission and objectives assess clarity and practicality. If not, skip this question, giving zero mark

Mark of 1 or 2 or 3 assigned judgmentally based on criteria in the question

Question Type	Maximum Marks	Marks Given
OEQ	3	

P3. If the impact of the project on beneficiaries is assessed periodically, is it done internally or by an independent individual or agency? If not, skip this question, giving zero mark

Internally / by outside expert / both

1 for internal, 2 for external and 3 for both

Question Type	Maximum Marks	Marks Given
GOQ	3	

P4. Give actual figures as example/s of impact on target beneficiaries

Answer:

Mark of 1 or 2 or 3 assigned judgmentally based on whether it is guestimate or evaluated and quantified

Question Type	Maximum Marks	Marks Given
OEQ	3	

P5. Are targets set for staff, reviewed with them periodically (minimum once a month) and corrective action taken to achieve results?

Mark of 1 or 2 or 3 assigned judgmentally based on criteria in the question

Question Type	Maximum Marks	Marks Given
OEQ	3	

SUMMARY – PERFORMANCE MEASUREMENT		
1	Total of scores as evaluated	
2	Possible maximum total score	15
3	Effectiveness % (1/2*100)	

MANAGEMENT CALIBER

L1. Length of uninterrupted experience of the NGO in the present field of activity

Check only ONE of the following

(a)	< 3 years	
(b)	> 3and < 6 years	
(c)	> 6 years	

1 for a, 2 for b, 3 for c

Question Type	Maximum Marks	Marks Given
GOQ	3	

L2. From whom is the feedback sought on project?

Check as many as applicable to your situation

(a)	Actual beneficiaries at community level	
(b)	Community leaders	
(c)	Your field staff	
(d)	Any other (specify below)	

Question Type	Maximum Marks	Marks Given
MOQ	4	

L3. What is annual administration expense as % of total expenditure? (i.e. expenses on staff and office facilities which are incurred irrespective of activity volume)

Check only ONE of the following

(a)	10-20%	
(b)	21-30%	
(c)	31-40%	
(d)	51-60%	
(e)	Over 60%	

3 for a, 2 for b, 1 for c and 0 for d, e.

Question Type	Maximum Marks	Marks Given
GOQ	3	

L4. Over the last 3 years, what is the trend of administration expenses as value – without any diminishment of activity?

Check only ONE of the following

(a)	Increasing	
(b)	About constant	
(c)	Decreasing	

1 for a, 2 for b and 3 for c

Question Type	Maximum Marks	Marks Given
GOQ	3	

L5. If there any measures to further increase program volume / effectiveness briefly indicate plans. If not, skip this question, giving zero mark
Answer:

Mark of 1 or 2 or 3 assigned judgmentally based on whether it reflects growth in volume/efficiency and thought out strategically

Question Type	Maximum Marks	Marks Given
OEQ	3	

L6. What importance does the management give to maintain and project the organization's image?
Check only ONE of the following

(a)	Least important	
(b)	Not very important	
(c)	Somewhat important	
(d)	Important	
(e)	Extremely important	

0 for a and b, 1 for c, 2 for d and 3 for e

Question Type	Maximum Marks	Marks Given
GOQ	3	

L7. If answer is (d) or (e), is there specific method/s to project the image to stakeholders?
Check only ONE of the following

(a)	Yes, we do vigorously	
(b)	Yes, but not much	
(c)	Not at present	

3 for a, 2 for b and 1 for c

Question Type	Maximum Marks	Marks Given
GOQ	3	

L8. If answer is (a), how is it projected?

Answer:

Mark of 1 or 2 or 3 assigned judgmentally based whether it is substantiated

Question Type	Maximum Marks	Marks Given
OEQ	3	

L9. Name an outstanding features of the organization, if any, of which the management is proud

Answer:

Mark of 1 or 2 or 3 assigned judgmentally based on uniqueness

Question Type	Maximum Marks	Marks Given
OEQ	3	

L10. How are functions in the organization assigned?

Answer:

Mark of 1 or 2 or 3 assigned judgmentally based clarity of roles and appropriate delegation of authority

Question Type	Maximum Marks	Marks Given
OEQ	3	

L11. Name one most important factor against each of the following as relevant to your organization?

Respond to all 4

		Name one against each
(a)	Organization's strength	
(b)	Organization's weakness	
(c)	Major opportunity for expansion	
(d)	Any threat for growth / survival	

Mark of 1 or 2 or 3 assigned judgmentally based on quality of perception

Question Type	Maximum Marks	Marks Given
OEQ	3	

SUMMARY – MANAGEMENT CALIBER		
1	Total of scores as evaluated	
2	Possible maximum total score	34
3	Effectiveness % (1/2*100)	

GRAND SUMMARY - %		
1	Marketing Capacity	
2	Relationship Strengths	
3	Accountability	
4	Funding Sustainability	
5	Technical capacity Maintenance	
6	Performance Measurement	
7	Management Caliber	
Overall NGO Effectiveness = Total of scores for all questions divided by 150 (total achievable maximum) * 100		

Note:

50% or less is below satisfactory, 51-60% is satisfactory, 61-75% is good and over 75% is very good.